OFF THE BEATEN PAT

Northern California

FIFTH EDITION

Mark R. Williams

GUILFORD, CONNECTICUT

Text design by Laura Augustine
Maps created by Equator Graphics © The Globe Pequot Press
Illustrations by Carole Drong

ISSN: 1536-6286
ISBN: 0-7627-2746-2

Manufactured in the United States of America
Fifth Edition/First Printing

To my parents, who took me
on that very first trip

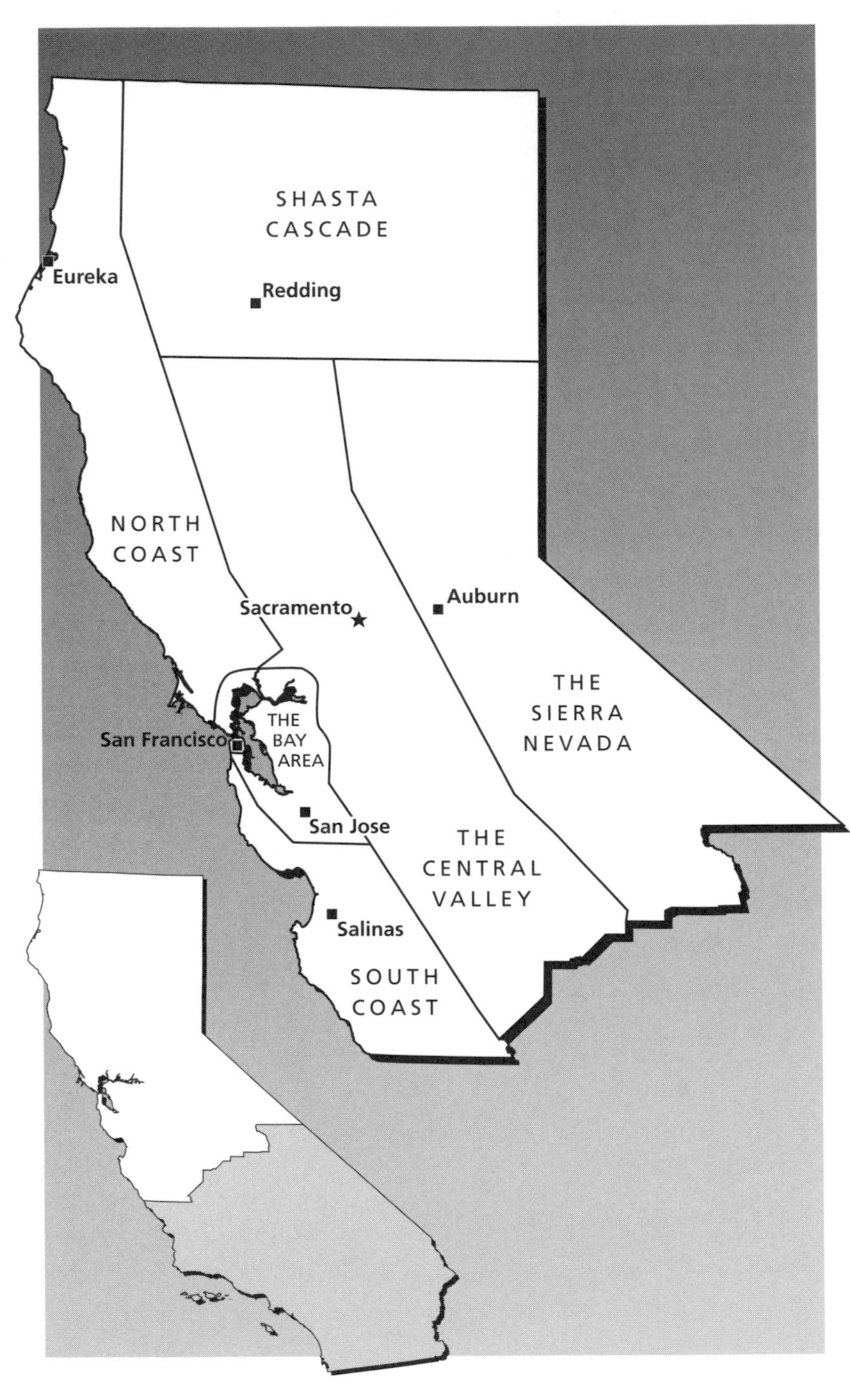

SHASTA CASCADE
Eureka
Redding
NORTH COAST
Sacramento
Auburn
THE SIERRA NEVADA
THE BAY AREA
San Francisco
San Jose
THE CENTRAL VALLEY
Salinas
SOUTH COAST

Contents

Victorian house on Bush Street, San Francisco

Introduction

> "California, more than any other part of the Union, is a country by itself, and San Francisco a capital."
>
> —James Bryce, *The American Commonwealth,* 1901

How can anyone get "off the beaten path" in Northern California, you ask? This is the larger half of the country's most-populous and most-visited state, whose sights and attractions have become household names. Part of the answer lies in the sheer size of California and the astounding variety of natural and man-made wonders found here.

Another part derives from the nature of this book. It is *not* a guide to Fisherman's Wharf, Alcatraz, Yosemite, Lake Tahoe, Carmel, Sausalito, or any other well-trodden destination. We have deliberately chosen to ignore such people magnets as Napa Valley wineries, the Santa Cruz Boardwalk, Great America and other amusement parks, the state capitol, and a fistful of gold-country tourist traps. That's where most people go.

The nice flip side, however, is that with everyone visiting *those* places, the rest of Northern California is surprisingly crowd-free most of the time. (Try to heed the experienced traveler's motto: "Never on Sunday.")

Nor is this book a guide to the rural "back roads" of Northern California, at least not by definition. You will indeed be sampling several country roads, but there are as many little-known, seldom-visited places in urban San Francisco as in the sticks.

With this guide you'll be able to explore the dank streets of Chinatown or sip espresso with an aging Beat poet in North Beach. You'll go to an island that was off-limits until recently or follow the bloodstained trail of Sam Spade and other characters from *The Maltese Falcon.*

San Francisco is only the beginning, just one of seven geographical areas covered by this book. More than one hundred different attractions are highlighted in detail, a kind of personal "best of" Northern California based on years of experience. Although this may seem a bit arbitrary, a *selective* guidebook allowed us to go beyond the "once over lightly" approach to an endless number of places. It was also a lot more fun to research and write.

This book will help you discover that California means Chinese Joss houses and a Russian fort as much as Spanish missions, and that Hollywood was really just an upstart when it came to making movies.

The first film capital was right here at Niles. Everyone knows about the gold rush, but what about the great "California Coal Rush"? You can visit the mines of black gold and a cemetery with gravestones inscribed in Welsh. And if that doesn't excite you, choose instead to stroll around the ornate mansion that the Reagans refused to live in.

You will visit museums on everything from Egyptian history to cartoon art, surfboards to pickup trucks. The book will show you a slew of superlatives: the world's smallest mountain range and tallest tree, matched by a pygmy forest of the shortest full-grown trees on earth, some less than a foot tall. You'll take a behind-the-scenes look at the world's only cable-car system and find out about beer and sake making, and orchid and grape growing. Enjoy a belt-stretching meal at the last lumberjack-style cookhouse in the West. And for visitors with adventuresome palates, we describe a restaurant that specializes in artichokes cooked two dozen different ways.

If you equate California with sandy beaches and warm Pacific waves, you may want to take a sharp left when you get to Fresno (if coming from the east, that is) and head for Southern California. The north, on the other hand, offers spectacular seacoast drives past Big Sur and Mendocino, the hissing volcanic terrain of Lassen and Lava Beds parks, wild river canyons, and a snow-shrouded peak with its own mystical powers. And if California means freeways to you, get ready for a visit to the state's "Empty Quarter," where you will see more buzzards than cars.

Man-made marvels are also included in the bargain, from landmark lighthouses to ultramodern cathedrals and temples. And, yes, we take you along some of those scenic shortcuts and elusive back roads to places called Volcano and Fiddletown and to a region whose name speaks for itself: the Lost Coast.

For their generous assistance in the preparation of this book, we would like to offer our sincere appreciation to the following: California Office of Tourism; San Francisco Convention & Visitors Bureau; Monterey Peninsula Chamber of Commerce; Redwood Empire Association; Mariposa Chamber of Commerce; Amador County Chamber of Commerce; Sacramento Convention and Visitors Bureau; Chico Visitor & Information Bureau; Shasta-Cascade Wonderland Association; Golden Gate National Recreation Area; Recreation and Park Department, City and County of San Francisco; Carmel Valley Chamber of Commerce; Pacific Grove Chamber of Commerce; Department of Fish and Game, State of California; California Artichoke Advisory Board; National Steinbeck

Center, Salinas; San Juan Bautista Chamber of Commerce; Humboldt County Convention & Visitors Bureau; Lake County Marketing Program; Point Reyes National Seashore; Fort Bragg-Mendocino Coast Chamber of Commerce; and Mono Lake Tufa State Reserve.

California Welcome Centers (Northern Area)

Anderson, 1699 Hwy. 273, (530) 365–1180, (800) 4–SHASTA

Arcata, 1635 Heindon Rd. (707) 822–3619

Auburn, 13411 Lincoln Way, (530) 887–2111

Merced, 710 W. Sixteenth St., Ste. S, (209) 384–2791

San Francisco, Pier 39 at Beach & Embarcadero Sts., Building P, Marina Plaza, 2nd Level, (415) 956–3493

Helpful Phone Numbers and Web Sites

California Division of Tourism: (800) 462–2543; www.visitcalifornia.com

California State Coastal Conservancy: www.coastalconservancy.ca.gov

California Travel Parks Association: www.camp-california.com

Department of Transportation Road Conditions: (800) 427–ROAD

National Parks: (415) 556–0560; www.nps.gov

Sierra Club: www.sierraclub.org

Ski Reports: (415) 543–7036; www.californiasnow.com

State Fish and Game: www.dfg.ca.gov

State Parks Camping Reservations: (800) 444–7275

State Parks Information: (916) 653–6995; www.parks.ca.gov

Major Newspapers

San Francisco Chronicle

San Jose Mercury-News

Oakland Tribune

Marin Independent Journal

Contra Costa Times

Monterey County Herald

Sacramento Bee

Santa Rosa Press Democrat

Fresno Bee

Redding Record Searchlight

Transportation

Air: Major airports with regularly scheduled out-of-state flights include San Francisco, Oakland, San Jose, Sacramento, Fresno, Monterey, Arcata, and Reno, Nevada (for Lake Tahoe area).

Train: Amtrak provides passenger travel between all major cities; the *Coast Starlight* runs from Los Angeles along the coast to the Bay Area (Emeryville), then inland and north to Redding, Mt. Shasta, and Oregon. (800) USA–RAIL; www.amtrakwest.com; www.coaststarlight.com; www.pacificsurfliner.com.

Bus: Greyhound is the major carrier with service to most towns; (800) 229–9424; www.greyhound.com.

Climate

Northern California's climate is characterized by general sun and warmth with rain mainly in winter. It does vary greatly based on distance from the ocean and elevation, however. There are five main climatic zones in the area: *coastal* (mild temperatures and moderate rainfall); *desert* (great variations in temperature with very little rainfall); *mountain* (sunny summers and cold winters, heavy snowfall); *valley* (high temperature/low humidity in summer, low temperature/high humidity in winter); *foothill* (1,000 to 3,000 feet in elevation, similar to valley but with more rain and less fog).

Famous Northern Californians

Ansel Adams (photographer); Lloyd Bridges, Clint Eastwood, Tom Hanks (actors); Dave Brubeck (musician); Joe DiMaggio, Tom Seaver, and Billy Martin (baseball players); Peggy Fleming and Kristi Yamaguchi (figure skaters); Ernest and Julio Gallo (wine makers); Jack London, William Saroyan, Irving Stone (writers); George Lucas (film maker); Mark Spitz (swimmer).

Recommended Reading

Guidebooks, Travel, and Ecology:

California State Parks Guide, various authors (Olympus Press, 1994)

Sierra Club Guide to the National Parks of California, Joseph E. Brown, ed. (Sierra Club Books, 1996)

California's Gold Rush Country, Barbara Braasch (Johnson & Assoc. International, 1996)

San Francisco Almanac, Gladys Hansen (Chronicle Books, 1995)

This Is San Francisco: A Classic Portrait of the City, Robert O'Brien (Chronicle Books, 1994)

Craft of Northern California, Victor D. Hanson (Alcove Books, 2003)

Steinbeck Country, David Laws (Windy Hill Press, 2002)

A Wheelchair Rider's Guide to San Francisco and Nearby Shorelines (California State Coastal Conservancy, 1998)

Atlas of California, Michael Donley (Academic Book Center, 1979)

An Island Called California: An Ecological Introduction to Its Natural Communities, Elna Bakker (University of California Press, 1985)

Not Man Apart: Photographs of the Big Sur Coast, David R. Brower and Robinson Jeffers (Sierra Club Books, 1965)

The Monterey Bay Shoreline Guide, Jerry Emory (University of California Press, 1999)

History and Literature:

Assembling California, John A. McPhee (Noonday Press, 1994)

California: A History, Andrew F. Rolle (Harlan Davidson, 1998)

Americans and the California Dream (five volumes), Kevin Starr (Oxford University Press, 1973–1997)

Unknown California, Jonathan Eisen and David Fine, eds. (Collier, 1985)

Landmarks of San Francisco, Patrick McGrew (Harry Abrams, 1998)

Historic San Francisco, Rand Richards (Heritage House, 2001)

Days of Gold, Malcolm J. Rohrbough (University of California Press, 1997)

Panning Out: 150 Years of Gold Rush Writing, Michael Kowalewski (Heyday Books, 1997)

The Celebrated Jumping Frog of Calaveras County and *Roughing It,* Samuel L. Clemens (Mark Twain), various editions

The Nature Writings of John Muir, John Muir (Library of America, 1997)

City by the Bay, A History of Modern San Francisco, Charles A. Fracchia (Heritage Media, 1998)

The Other California: The Great Central Valley in Life and Letters, Gerald W. Haslam (Capra Press, 1990)

Fast Facts

- *Time:* California is in the Pacific Time Zone and observes Daylight Savings Time.
- *Taxes:* The state sales tax is 7.25 percent; local taxes may be as much as 1.25 percent.
- The region's *most-visited amusement/theme parks* are (in order): Santa Cruz Beach/Boardwalk; Paramount's Great America (Santa Clara); Monterey Bay Aquarium; Six Flags Marine World (Vallejo).
- Northern California's *professional sports teams* include the Oakland A's and San Francisco Giants (baseball), Oakland Raiders and San Francisco 49ers (football), Golden State Warriors and Sacramento Kings (basketball), San Jose Sharks (hockey), San Jose Earthquakes (soccer), and San Jose Sabrecats (arena football).
- Among U.S. states, California has the largest number of senior citizens living within its borders. More than four million residents are over sixty years of age.
- California produces more than one trillion dollars worth of goods and services each year, which is 13 percent of the U.S. Gross National Product. California has the world's sixth largest economy.
- The Bear Flag Revolt in 1846 achieved California's independence from Mexico, and the banner used became the state's official flag.

The prices and rates listed in this guidebook were confirmed at press time. We recommend, however, that you call establishments before traveling to obtain current information.

Help Us Keep This Guide Up to Date

Every effort has been made by the author and editors to make this guide as accurate and useful as possible. However, many things can change after a guide is published—establishments close, phone numbers change, and facilities come under new management.

We would love to hear from you concerning your experiences with this guide and how you feel it could be improved and be kept up to date. While we may not be able to respond to all comments and suggestions, we'll take them to heart and we'll also make certain to share them with the author. Please send your comments and suggestions to the following address:

The Globe Pequot Press
Reader Response/Editorial Department
P.O. Box 480
Guilford, CT 06437

Or you may e-mail us at:
editorial@GlobePequot.com

Thanks for your input, and happy travels!

San Francisco

Someone once wrote: "Every man should be allowed to love two cities—his own and San Francisco." As visitors know, there *is* something special about the place, an extra dollop of character that sets it apart from other cities. How else could the same place be known as America's most European *and* its most Asian city? To most Northern Californians, it's merely "The City," as if none other exists or matters.

Mention just about any place, and a postcard vista or someone else's video show snaps into view. Images carried like baggage by first-time visitors to San Francisco include all the famous sights (and sites) on everyone's "must see" list: Coit Tower, Fisherman's Wharf, Chinatown, Union Square, Golden Gate Bridge, Alcatraz, and, of course, the cable cars.

San Francisco Don'ts

There's plenty to do, but here are a few tips for what not to do, with help from the San Francisco Convention & Visitors Bureau.

- *Don't pack a tropical wardrobe for sunny California. It's often cool to downright cold, even in summer.*
- *Don't stand directly behind a cable-car gripman unless you want the wind knocked out of you when he brakes.*
- *Don't board a bus or cable car without coins; drivers don't make change.*
- *Don't park on a hill without curbing your wheels or you may end up chasing a runaway car.*
- *Don't wear shorts and T-shirts to the opera or symphony; these are formal affairs.*
- *Don't try swimming in San Francisco Bay without a wet suit, unless you're part polar bear.*
- *Don't expect Golden Gate Bridge to be golden; it's red-orange in color.*
- *Don't ask for Rice-A-Roni in any restaurant; it's virtually unknown despite decades of ads to the contrary.*
- *Above all, when visiting "The City," please don't call it "Frisco," especially if you're from L.A.*

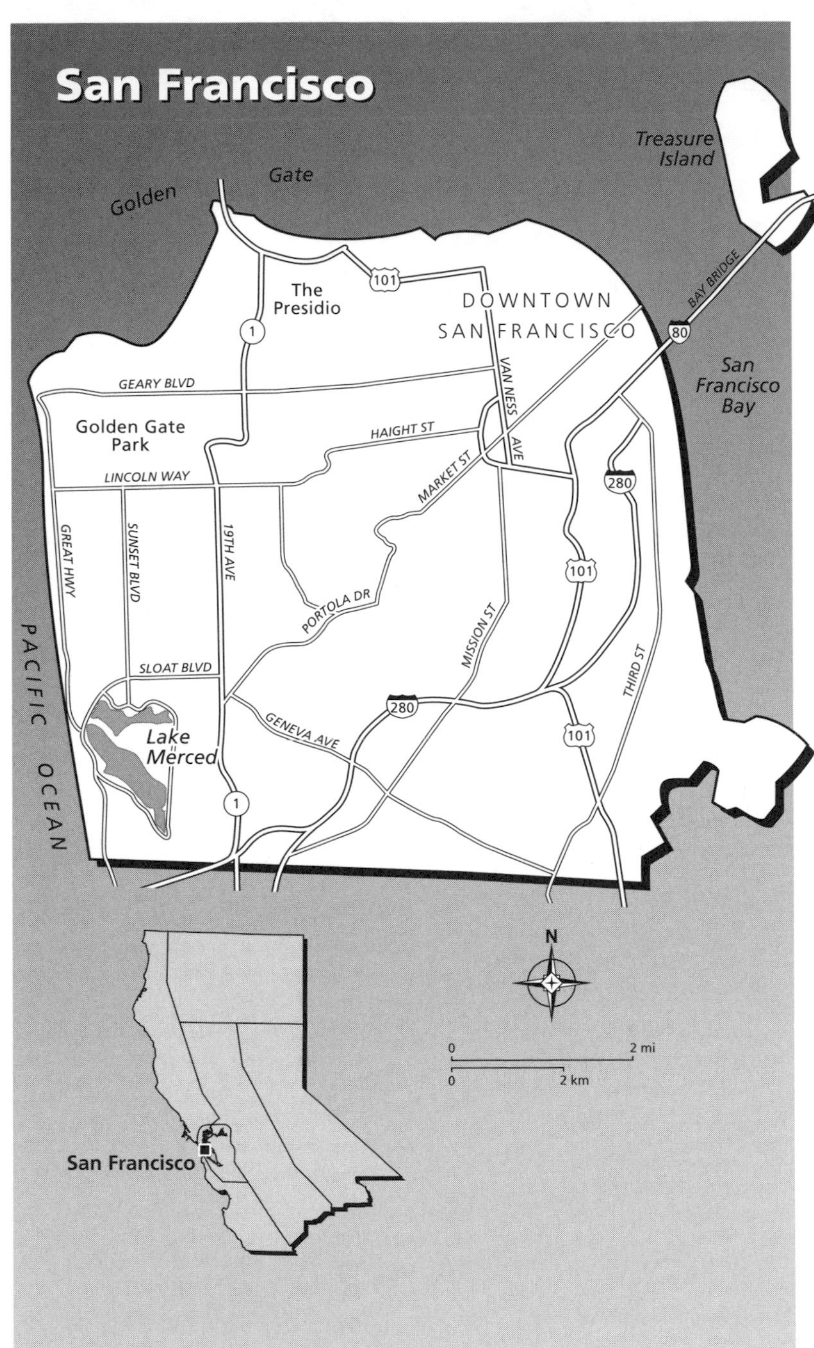

San Francisco
Golden
Gate
Treasure Island
The Presidio
DOWNTOWN SAN FRANCISCO
BAY BRIDGE
San Francisco Bay
GEARY BLVD
Golden Gate Park
HAIGHT ST
VAN NESS AVE
MARKET ST
LINCOLN WAY
GREAT HWY
SUNSET BLVD
19TH AVE
PORTOLA DR
MISSION ST
THIRD ST
SLOAT BLVD
GENEVA AVE
Lake Merced
PACIFIC OCEAN
101
1
80
280
N
0
2 mi
0
2 km
San Francisco

But beyond these The City packs a dazzling assortment of attractions into its compact site, just 47 square miles at the tip of a narrow peninsula between the Pacific and San Francisco Bay. Dig a little deeper, and the landscape will yield still more nuggets, from a stupendous, soaring cathedral and the delightfully cramped shops of North Beach to the haunts of fictional detective Sam Spade.

San Francisco is one of the world's most scenic cities, and it's also one of the easiest to explore. If you can't walk to your destination, you can reach it via an extensive public transportation system that includes the cable car—a national landmark in motion. So let us take you "off the beaten path" through a San Francisco most visitors never see.

Author's Top Ten for San Francisco

Hidden Chinatown

Italian North Beach

Museum of Russian Culture

Treasure/Yerba Buena Islands

SS **Jeremiah O'Brien**

Fort Point

Victorian Homes Tour

Cathedral of St. Mary of the Assumption

Golden Gate Park

Anchor Brewing Company

Hidden Chinatown

During the gold rush many Chinese who didn't make it as far as the mines sought their fortunes on the streets of *Gum San Dai Fow,* "Big City of the Golden Hill." Their laundries and cafes formed the nucleus of Chinatown, presently the largest Chinese settlement outside Asia, comprising about 20 blocks where tens of thousands live and do business.

Chinatown is a top attraction, but it's also a real community, with its own schools, industries, banks, shops, social clubs (called family or benevolent associations), and chamber of commerce. Grant Avenue overflows with tourist shops and restaurants, including a McDonald's, but just 1 block over lies Stockton Street, where Chinatown's real business is carried on (especially between Jackson and Broadway Streets).

On any normal day Stockton throbs with shoppers buying exotic produce such as fuzzy melon and bok choy, dried fish and roast duck, incense, and an assortment of strange ointments and pills. In the fish markets old women in quilted jackets poke at the gills and prod the crabs amid wicker baskets filled with wizened fish skin and salted yellow croaker. Herbal shops offer a peek into another form of medicine, in which ailments are treated with roots, bark, and berries. ***Hop Hing Company*** (1027 Stockton) sells ginseng in its many forms, including candy, and such medicinal oddities as dried sea horse and starfish. There are scores of similar shops, including the Great China Herb Company at 857 Washington Street and Tung Shing Trading Company at 734 Jackson.

Between Grant and Stockton a series of dank alleys and cramped streets seem to shelter the secret business of Chinatown. These narrow corridors at one time provided havens for prostitution, gambling, and opium dens, and many cellars still connect through a maze of tunnels.

In 1879, Waverly Place (between Sacramento and Washington Streets) witnessed the first Tong War, fought over the affections—and ownership—of a Chinese slave girl named Kum Ho. Now it's noted for ornate balconies, herbalists, and oriental places of worship. The ***Tin Hou Temple*** at 125 Waverly Place honors the "Taoist Queen of Heaven," the protectress of travelers, sailors, and ladies of the night. Open to respectful visitors (daily 9:00 A.M. to 4:00 P.M.), Tin Hou occupies the top floor of a ramshackle building. You must climb four flights of wooden stairs and ring a

San Francisco Facts

Colors	*Black and gold*
Elevation	*Highest Point: Mount Davidson (938 feet)*
	Lowest Point: Sea level
Flower	*Dahlia*
Founded	*September 17, 1776, by Spanish army*
Hills	*Forty-three in all, including Twin Peaks, Nob, Russian, and Telegraph*
Islands	*Fourteen in San Francisco Bay, twelve within city limits*
Patron Saint	*St. Francis*
Population	*About 800,000*
Song	*(Two) "San Francisco" and "I Left My Heart in San Francisco"*
Streets	*Steepest: Filbert between Leavenworth and Hyde (31.5 percent grade)*
	Longest: Mission (7.29 miles)
	Widest: Sloat Boulevard (135 feet)
	Narrowest: De Forest Way (4.5 feet)

buzzer to enter the sumptuous interior, done up in gold and lots of red, the color of good luck. Amid bowls of fruit, porcelain statues, and tasseled lamps, clouds of incense rise from a three-legged bronze pot as old women kneeling on cushions quietly fold offerings to be burned at the main shrine. Stay a while and soak up the mystical energy. If closed, go to the Norras Temple at 109 Waverly Place (irregular hours).

Spofford Lane (between Clay and Washington Streets) is a corridor of painted doorways and brick facades that hums with the strains of peculiarly Chinese melodies, like the click of mah jong tiles and animated talk behind the floral curtains at number 50. Crossing Washington, Spofford becomes Old Chinatown Lane, formerly famous for its brothels and gambling dens.

Among the hundreds of Chinatown restaurants, ***Sam Wo's*** (813 Washington Street) has become a landmark of sorts. To enter you pass right through a frenetic kitchen crammed with shouting cooks juggling exotic dishes between the hot iron stoves. Unflustered diners proceed upstairs via a rickety staircase to a cramped but colorful dining room. The restaurant is open for lunch and dinner; closed Sunday.

Nearby Ross Alley claims the ***Golden Gate Fortune Cookie Factory*** at number 56; the owner often leaves the door open, and you can find out how they get those little messages inside. In the days when Ross boasted twenty-two fan-tan parlors, it earned the nickname "the street of gamblers." The dens were heavily fortified with doors of boilerplate iron to stave off police raids.

At 27 Ross Alley, there's a factory filled with Chinese women sewing busily, and you'll find an exceptional selection of porcelain statues, candles, and incense at number 51, Sam Bo Trading Company. There's also an old-fashioned barbershop and one of Chinatown's original dry cleaners.

Another hidden corner worth exploring is Commercial Street east of Grant, an interesting stretch of old brick buildings and claustrophobic

Top Annual Events in San Francisco

Chinese New Year Celebration, *Chinatown (February)*

St. Patrick's Day Parade, *along Market Street to the Civic Center*

Cherry Blossom Festival, *Japantown (April)*

San Francisco International Film Festival, *various venues (April–May)*

Bay to Breakers Footrace, *The Embarcadero to The Great Highway (mid-May)*

Cinco de Mayo, *Mission District (May)*

North Beach Festival, *Grant Avenue and Green Street (mid-June)*

Cable Car Bell–Ringing Celebration, *Fisherman's Wharf (mid July)*

San Francisco Blues Festival, *Fort Mason (mid-September)*

Columbus Day/Fleet Week, *North Beach/Fisherman's Wharf (mid-October)*

San Francisco Jazz Festival, *various venues (late October)*

shops, noodle factories, and sewing factories. It's also home to the local Chinese radio station.

Another equally seedy street off Commercial is Beckett, home to ***Red's Place*** (corner of Jackson), a genuine hole-in-the-wall hangout for locals. A couple of blocks away, at 916 Grant Avenue, the ***Li Po Bar*** looks and feels like an opium den, complete with cavelike design and surly bartender.

Before the earthquake and fire of 1906, Grant Avenue was called Dupont Street and was infamous as a red-light district in the heart of gang-controlled Chinatown. One island of faith in a sea of sin was ***Old St. Mary's Church*** (corner of Grant and California). It was built back in 1853 with bricks shipped all the way from Boston around Cape Horn, and it survived the '06 disaster largely unscathed while all the brothels perished. The church is open to visitors daily from 8:00 A.M. to 6:00 P.M.

History buffs should also visit the ***Chinese Historical Society Museum,*** which highlights Chinese contributions in areas such as agriculture, mining, and railroad construction during their 150 years in California. Among dozens of artifacts on display are a braided queue, opium pipes, a Buddhist altar, a three-pronged fishing spear, and a water-cannon used during the gold rush. The museum has moved to 965 Clay Street, a historic red-brick building designed by Julia Morgan. Expanded exhibits include the Ching Collection of negative stereotypes of Chinese found in advertising and news media. Call (415) 391–1188 for current hours and admission fees or go to www.chsa.org.

Most visitors to San Francisco ride one of those little cable cars "that climb halfway to the stars." But does it really dawn on them that the cars have no motor and are actually *towed* along the tracks by a moving cable? That's why they are called *cable* cars, and it is like no other system in the world. Just 2 blocks up from Chinatown, the ***Cable Car Barn*** provides a fascinating behind-the-scenes look at this unique form of public transportation.

Built in 1907, this three-level brick building was enlarged and completely renovated with the rest of the 4.4-mile-long system during the eighties. Both the Powell-Mason and Powell-Hyde lines run past the barn, and you can watch the ten-ton cars coming and going. Inside, on the mezzanine level, you look down on twelve winding sheaves that look like giant wagon wheels. This is the guts of the system: machinery that winds four separate cables, each in a closed loop, for the four lines traversing 69 blocks at a steady 9.5 miles per hour. That's 56,600 feet, or

10.7 miles, of 1¼-inch-diameter steel cable moving up and down some of the city's steepest terrain.

Most of the system's thirty-nine cars were built between 1887 and 1914. A museum here features several of the oldest cars and scale models of others. According to legend, kindhearted Andrew S. Hallidie dreamt up the ingenious system after he watched a team of horses pulling a wagon falter and tumble backward down a steep hill. Although there may be some truth to this yarn, it is an interesting coincidence that Hallidie also owned the California Wire Works, a company that manufactured steel cable. The very first cable car operated for a disbelieving crowd on August 2, 1873. Car no. 8 on display here was among the first group made.

The Cable Car Barn is the powerhouse and repair shop that keeps the simple yet delicate system in working order. In addition to design flaws that crept in during renovation, there is the problem of the cable itself, which has a limited life. New wire must be spliced in when the old wears out, and there's a strand on display. As a finale, you can descend to the underground sheave-viewing room and watch the cable being neatly and methodically wound into figure-eight patterns 365 days a year.

The Cable Car Barn and Museum, 1201 Mason Street (at Washington), is open daily from 10:00 A.M. to 5:00 P.M. (to 6:00 P.M. April through September); no admission charged. For information call (415) 474–1887.

Italian North Beach

North Beach, a flat sliver of land between Telegraph Hill and Chinatown, means different things to different people. Many visitors see only the raucous street scene and lewd revues along Broadway. Others can recall the beatniks of the fifties, the poets and painters whose legacy still lives on at City Lights Bookstore and the Tosca Cafe. Yet long before, North Beach was called "Little Italy," and quite a few traces of the old Italian neighborhood still survive.

But where's the beach? The name goes back to the 1850s, when a narrow finger of the bay extended inland. As generations came and went, the bay was slowly filled in. Italian immigrants had arrived in force, and they fished from what is now called Fisherman's Wharf and lived in North Beach. Their story, from Bank of America founder A. P. Giannini to poet Lawrence Ferlinghetti, is told at the ***North Beach Museum*** at 1435 Stockton Street. Open Monday through Friday from 9:00 A.M. to 5:00 P.M.; no admission charged. Call (415) 626–7070 for more information.

Although North Beach is slowly becoming an extension of Chinatown, you can still see a glimmer of the city's "most European" neighborhood. A cynosure of the Italian community is the fairy tale ***Church of Saints Peter and Paul*** on Washington Square. Built in 1924, it is a dim and quiet retreat filled with incense and flickering candles. Stained-glass windows and bronze fixtures lead to an elaborate altar where daily Mass is offered. And residents still come for baptisms, confirmations, weddings, and funerals, not to mention weekly bingo.

Outside, Washington Square (with a statue of Benjamin Franklin, not Washington!) is a pleasant park lined with shops, restaurants, and stubborn holdouts such as the ***San Francisco Italian Athletic Club*** for members only (1630 Stockton). On the east side of the square, the venerable ***Fior d'Italia*** (601 Union Street) claims to be America's oldest Italian restaurant (1886) and is a place that honors tradition. According to local lore, the owners donated barrels of wine to help douse the great fire of 1906, and there's a room dedicated to Tony Bennett, the great Italian crooner who left his heart here a long time ago. Call (415) 986–1886.

At the ***Bohemian Cigar Store*** (566 Columbus), you can sip a cappuccino at a table overlooking the square. Nearby are a few cafes and bars where elderly Italians enjoy red wine and discuss the day's affairs. ***Gino and Carlo's,*** for example, sits at 548 Green Street, right across from the old Buon Gusto sausage factory.

North Beach remains a self-contained enclave. The Italian imprint lingers in the old-style family businesses, although high rents are slowly driving them out. There are bakeries and pastry shops, delicatessens and butcher shops, sausage and pasta factories, and little neighborhood markets with fruits and vegetables so fresh they glow.

Pastry shops feature rum *babas,* marzipan, *cannolis* filled with sweetened ricotta cheese, and *cialdi* cookies. Each bakery boasts a specialty in addition to long loaves of sourdough bread and *panettone,* a round, sweet loaf filled with raisins and candied fruit. Specialty shops sell noodle machines and cheese graters, ravioli rolling sticks and baking irons for *pizzelle,* and you can find *carpetto, prosciutto,* and *provolone* at any corner deli.

Wander around and savor the sounds, smells, and tastes of old North Beach while you still can. Here are some traditional Italian businesses still going strong.

Florence Italian Delicatessen and Ravioli Factory (1412 Stockton) makes fresh pasta daily and offers a wide selection of meats and sausages.

Victoria Pastry (1362 Stockton) offers *zuccotto,* a frozen dessert soaked in liqueur, and has specialized in towering wedding cakes since 1914.

Liguria Bakery (1700 Stockton) makes only one thing, a pizzalike bread called *focaccia* that is covered with different toppings.

The Italian French Baking Company (1501 Grant) specializes in thick, handmade bread sticks (*grissini*) and tubular *cialdi* cookies.

Danilo Baking (516 Green) specializes in *casareccio* bread and sells *tiramisu* dessert cake by the slice.

Caffè Trieste (609 Vallejo) sells *espresso* machines and a variety of roasted coffees, including the "North Beach Blend," next door to the West Coast's first coffeehouse, started back in 1956.

A. Cavalli & Company (1441 Stockton), which has been around since 1880, features Italian books and magazines, records and tapes, as well as travel posters, opera prints, and other curiosities.

Biordi Art Import (412 Columbus) has worked directly with artists to bring high-quality, handcrafted ceramic pieces to San Francisco for more than fifty years. The store is like a gallery, filled with exquisite and whimsical dishware, vases, and lamps.

Another North Beach institution is ***City Lights Bookstore*** at Broadway and Columbus, owned by poet Lawrence Ferlinghetti since 1953. It started as the nation's first bookstore featuring paperbacks only, then rocketed to literary fame for selling Allen Ginsberg's now-classic poem *Howl,* once judged obscene, but then acquitted on the grounds that it held redeeming social importance. City Lights still boasts an unusual stock of books, ignoring best-sellers for politics (mostly leftish), Eastern religions, avant-garde fiction, and poetry. A regular clientele includes many writers, some from the Beat Generation, who drop in to pick up their mail, and Ferlinghetti himself still maintains an office on an open balcony overlooking the main floor.

Next door, across Jack Kerouac Alley, sits the classic North Beach bar and coffeehouse ***Vesuvio,*** which has been serving the community, literary and otherwise, since 1948.

Minimuseums

Museums come in all shapes and sizes, especially in a city as diverse as San Francisco. At some of the larger museums, you might have to purchase advance tickets for well-publicized shows. But at the lesser-known repositories, you may find yourself sharing the premises with the caretaker. Here are some of the city's best small museums.

The ***San Francisco Fire Department Pioneer Memorial Museum*** holds an outstanding collection of historical photos, memorabilia, and fire-fighting equipment going back to the first volunteer brigade in 1849. It sits right next to a modern station, and you may have to ring the bell to gain entrance.

The very first engine—a hand-pulled, hand-pumped beauty—is there, piled high with trophies won by modern-day firefighters at various pumping competitions. The department had its biggest challenge during the three-day blaze following the 1906 earthquake, remembered in a wealth of photos and documents.

A glass-enclosed display tells the story of Lillie Hitchcock Coit, an eccentric millionaire who used to follow the brigade to fires and became an honorary member. To pay homage to the city's firemen, she financed the building of Coit Tower on Telegraph Hill, which bears an uncanny resemblance to the nozzle of a fire hose.

Several fire engines in mint condition show how far techniques have come since pioneer days, when the bucket brigade would put out blazes using water-filled buckets made from buffalo hide. Other curiosities include brass "speaker trumpets," a kind of early megaphone for issuing orders at the scene of a fire, and the city's first fire hydrant, formerly used by pioneer dogs.

The museum, at 655 Presidio Avenue, is open free of charge Thursday through Sunday from 1:00 to 4:00 P.M. For information call (415) 563–4630.

The ***Museum of Russian Culture*** is a treasure chest devoted to Russia's troubled history before the fateful 1917 Revolution. Now fifty years old, the museum sits at the top of a dark staircase in the gracefully aging Russian Center. This monument to Old Russia displays an eclectic collection gathered mostly from the mementos brought here by refugees from the Communist regime. One of these old-timers is usually on hand to greet visitors and provide personal details that help bring the collection to life.

Among hundreds of items on display are fading photographs of Czar Nicholas II with his family, all of whom (including Anastasia, despite Hollywood mythology) were murdered by the Bolsheviks. Historical novelties include a captured German flag from World War I and a model of Fort Ross on the Northern California coast, a little-known Russian outpost 150 years ago. There are even tributes to famous inventions by Russian Americans, the helicopter and cathode ray tube (forerunner of television) to name just two.

Yet Russia's history stretches back many centuries, and the emphasis here is on this lengthy tradition. There's a suit of chain-mail armor made with thousands of individual rings, and the small collection of paintings contains a rendering of the Tartar invasion back in 1237. But the emphasis is on the Romanov dynasty that ruled Russia for three centuries: a silver tea service, military medals, imperial currency, as well as correspondence and photographs of the ill-fated royal family and other nobles. A picture of the teenage heir, Crown Prince Alexei, taken just months before his murder, is especially touching. But one word of advice: Don't ask to see photos of Lenin, Trotsky, Stalin, or anyone else responsible for bringing down the old regime. Your guide will shout "*Nyet*!"

The Museum of Russian Culture, located at 2450 Sutter Street, is open for free Wednesday and Saturday only from 10:30 A.M. to 2:30 P.M. There's also a library with 14,000 books in Russian and hundreds of original manuscripts, not to mention a rare photograph of Leo Tolstoy. Call (415) 921–4082 for further information.

Anyone interested in Russian culture should also visit one of San Francisco's eight Orthodox churches. The golden-domed ***Holy Virgin Cathedral*** in the Richmond district is the largest and most beautiful Russian Orthodox church in the West. Located on Geary Boulevard at 26th Avenue, it's open during services only: 8:00 to 9:00 A.M. weekdays and 8:00 A.M. to noon on Sunday. Another noteworthy church sits at the corner of Green and Van Ness Streets.

Everyone should see the spectacular San Francisco Museum of Modern Art and adjacent Yerba Buena Gardens. But just a block away is a lesser-known gem, the ***Cartoon Art Museum,*** with a collection of 11,000 items: from a 1760 engraving to Walt Disney's pre–Mickey Mouse sketches of Oswald the Rabbit to original pasteup boards of *Peanuts.*

Everyone has a favorite cartoon, the first thing they reach for in the Sunday paper: *Nancy and Sluggo, Green Lantern, L'il Abner, The Wizard of Id, Superman* or *Dick Tracy, Fritz the Cat.* Here, too, are western cartoons such as *Blueberry* in other languages, and you learn that although "Bam!" is universal, "Pow!" becomes "Paw!" when translated into French.

Cartoons are not always a laughing matter, and the museum does not ignore "the darker side" of the art form: old Marvel boards so realistic that the weapons seem to literally drip with blood, and underground and avant-garde drawings that are violent or obscene. And then there are the political cartoons and caricatures of celebrities, from Ross Perot to Wayne Newton.

The collection is rotated constantly, and there are frequent special exhibitions. For instance, one recent show spotlighted *The Simpsons* television series, whose classic characters, such as Homer and Bart, have become true icons of American pop culture. The *Simpsons* director was on hand to trace the show's evolution over 300 hilarious episodes. Located at 655 Mission Street, the museum is open daily except Monday; admission charged. Call (415) 227–8666 or go to www.cartoonart.org for hours and information on current exhibitions.

Two excellent museums in the heart of the financial district focus on the history of California and the West. After the discovery of gold in 1848, banks played a lively role in that story, and Wells Fargo & Company got its start in 1852 by supplying banking and express delivery service.

Billions in Sierra Nevada gold and Comstock silver thundered into San Francisco on the two-man, six-horse Concord stagecoaches that formed the backbone of the company's transport network. A perfectly restored specimen of these coaches forms the centerpiece of the ***Wells Fargo History Museum.*** These 2,500-pound vehicles were as much a fixture in the Old West as the six-gun and tin star. Wells Fargo used them to transport passengers (up to nine fit snugly inside) and freight, especially gold. Upstairs is an exhibit that details the skills involved in the forgotten craft of building these fine coaches. There's also a collection of framed letters using Wells Fargo's own stamps, 1848–1865, before the U.S. Postal Service took over.

Also upstairs are artifacts related to Charles E. Bolton, alias Black Bart, a man who never cowered before a company shotgun. In a period from 1875 to 1883, Bart ambushed twenty-seven coaches, and he often left comical verses at the scene of the crime in which he claimed to be a Wild West version of Robin Hood. Bart was finally tripped up by Wells Fargo's top detective, who traced the bandit through a laundry mark on his handkerchief.

Naturally, the gold rush receives most of the attention, with well-presented exhibits of strongboxes, photos from those raffish days, stock certificates, and, of course, the glorious, glistening gold itself. One outstanding display shows how the yellow stuff actually looked, and it was rarely yellow. Only the experts could tell sometimes, because gold came in such a wide variety of color and textures. But oh my, how nice it looked when refined and made into jewelry or shiny twenty-dollar gold pieces.

The Wells Fargo History Museum, at 420 Montgomery Street, is open free of charge Monday through Friday (except bank holidays) from 9:00 A.M. to 5:00 P.M. Call (415) 396–2619 for information.

The ***Museum of Money of the American West*** is just a couple of blocks away in the basement of the Bank of California. The bank is the oldest on the West Coast, and its headquarters sits entrenched in a neoclassical building that looks more like a temple than a financial institution. The museum downstairs contains a tantalizing selection of the stuff that all the fuss was over. Beckoning from behind glass cases are nuggets of gold and quartz, bullion, ingots, and shiny coins in flawless condition. Many coins on display were minted by various states, such as Utah (known as Deseret at the time) and Colorado, and even by banks. These were produced to cope with a shortage of coins at the time but were phased out once the U.S. Mint was established in San Francisco. (Look for one privately minted coin with the imprint "In Gold We Trust.")

The Museum of Money of the American West, at 400 California Street, is open Monday through Friday 9:00 A.M. to 4:30 P.M. Call (415) 765–2701 for information.

Along the Bay

The "City by the Bay" does in fact sit perched on a narrow peninsula between San Francisco Bay and the Pacific Ocean. And, naturally enough, the north shore is fringed with quite a few docks and piers, known collectively as the ***Embarcadero.*** (One stretch has been renamed Herb Caen Way, in honor of the city's beloved columnist.)

From the gold rush through World War II, great ships came and went, bringing passengers and cargo from distant places. The cavernous pier sheds overflowed with the exotic and the mundane, from oriental spices to Kansas wheat. But times changed, and most waterborne trade moved across the bay to the more modern port at Oakland. Subtract the hustle and bustle, the dirt and grime, and what's left is the Embarcadero. The city has demolished an ugly freeway here and has replaced it with palm trees and other landscaping to create a showcase of urban renewal, including beautiful PacBell Park, home of the Giants. In addition, the stretch south of Pier 35 is home to several smart cafes such as Fog City Diner. Public transportation (Muni) runs from China Basin at the Embarcadero's south end to Market Street. From here the "F" line continues north as far as Fisherman's Wharf using historic trams and streetcars such as Presidential Conference Cars, nicknamed "green torpedoes."

The Embarcadero's centerpiece remains the ***Ferry Building*** at the foot of Market Street, at one time the tallest structure along the waterfront and former symbol of a city now dwarfed by modern highrises. From the Ferry Building radiate the city's old piers, odd numbered to the north, even numbered to the south. Before the two great bridges were built during the 1930s, this terminal was the hub of traffic to and from Marin County and the East Bay. During its peak period eight ferries made 170 trips daily, moving as many as 100,000 passengers at 10 cents a ride. Although this number has declined dramatically, ferries still commute several times a day to Larkspur and Sausalito in Marin.

Designed in the beaux arts style by architect Arthur Paige Brown, the Ferry Building was constructed over a seven-year period starting in 1896. Brown modeled its 235-foot tower on the Giralda Tower in Seville, Spain. At 5:12 A.M. on April 18, 1906, the hands on the tower's clock

Movie Magic: The Streets of San Francisco

More than a hundred feature films, not to mention countless television episodes, have added to the city's aura. Here's a select list of a few to watch out for:

(1930s)
Fog over Frisco: *Bette Davis stars in a silly whodunnit praised for its cinematic style.*

San Francisco: *Classic Clark Gable melodrama about the 1906 earthquake contains the rousing song of the same name.*

(1940s)
Dark Passage: *Bogie breaks out of San Quentin, and Bacall drives him over the Golden Gate Bridge to safety in S.F.*

The Lady from Shanghai: *Written and directed by Orson Welles and best remembered for its Hall of Mirrors finale.*

The Maltese Falcon: *Fancy detective work by Sam Spade/Bogart brings Dashiell Hammett's classic to life.*

(1950s)
Pal Joey: *Sinatra tries to open a nightclub (the old Spreckels Mansion), but a "dame" steps in.*

Vertigo: *Hitchcock's classic if confused mystery features a bevy of beautiful vistas, including site of faux suicide near Fort Mason.*

(continued)

stopped; exactly a year later they were set in motion again. Yet the building survived undamaged by the great earthquake, and the beautiful clock still chimes out the hour. The Ferry Building underwent restoration and reopened in May 2003. Ferries, of course, continue to run.

Immediately behind the Ferry Building is the modern terminal and a wide plaza with an oddly out-of-place statue of Gandhi. Just beyond this area anglers can try their luck, but for some the fishing is just an excuse to come and gape. Sinbads Restaurant nearby offers decent fish and terrific views.

The city has created a delightful walk along the shoreline south of the Ferry Building, called the ***Embarcadero Waterfront Promenade.*** It's an ideal spot for strollers, picnickers (there are benches), and anyone interested in stunning views of the bay and the Bay Bridge. When this

(1960s)
Bullitt: *Steve McQueen as a tough cop is involved in the ultimate car chase.*

The Days of Wine and Roses: *Jack Lemmon and Lee Remick battle alcohol while living the pre-yuppie high life in the Financial District.*

(1970s)
The Conversation: *Gene Hackman as a surveillance pro becomes obsessed with his work; shot in and around Union Square.*

Dirty Harry: *Eastwood as Harry Callahan strides through North Beach and into movie immortality. Others in the series include* The Enforcer, Magnum Force, *and* Sudden Impact.

The Towering Inferno: *McQueen and Newman fight the big hot one at the Bank of America headquarters downtown.*

What's Up Doc?: *Streisand's screwball comedy takes her and Ryan O'Neal up and down the city's famous hills.*

(1980s)
Escape from Alcatraz: *Clint yearns for the city by the bay, seen in panoramic glory.*

The Presidio: *Not Sean Connery's best, but there are good scenes of the former army post and environs.*

(1990s)
Mrs. Doubtfire: *The city's own star Robin Williams discovers that life is a drag.*

The Rock: *Who can resist Alcatraz and Sean in one blazing package?*

was old East Street, forerunner of the Embarcadero, the Oregon & Mexican steamship wharf lay just to the south, and offshore you can still see pilings that supported the pier.

One recent addition is a colossal metal sculpture of a cupid-style bow and arrow. Other points of interest along the promenade include the city's fireboat, berthed next to a historic firehouse; the old redbrick Hills Brothers Coffee building at the foot of Harrison Street (now Gordon Biersch Brewery), and "tidal stairs" leading into the lapping waters of the bay.

For most commuters **Yerba Buena Island** is merely considered the principal anchor of the San Francisco–Oakland Bay Bridge. Yet this densely wooded isle and adjacent ***Treasure Island,*** formerly an important naval base, offer several points of interest and the best overall view of San Francisco's skyline.

Costanoan Indians used the island as a fishing station, and archaeologists have unearthed the remains of a village and cremation pits, along with contraband from smugglers and part of a shipwrecked galleon. Spanish explorers called the island Yerba Buena because of a fragrant herb that grew there in abundance.

Things remained quiet until builders used the island as the midpoint of the Bay Bridge, completed in 1936. Then ambitious promoters decided to create an artificial island on 400 acres of shoals offshore to serve as the site for a world's fair celebrating completion of the span, as well as the Golden Gate Bridge, finished about the same time. More than a year of dredging and a seawall built with 300,000 tons of rock went into the project, and in 1939 the Golden Gate International Exposition opened on the new Treasure Island.

That same year the famous China Clippers were launched as a trans-Pacific air service for mail and passengers. In 1941, after the bombing of Pearl Harbor, the U.S. Navy took over Treasure Island in a big way, and millions of sailors during the war and after were trained here and shipped off to the Pacific. The military finally abandoned its cherished base in 1997, but it continues to retain ownership for future contingencies. Everywhere there are remnants of old barracks and sheds, rusty machinery, and oil drums.

Architecture for the 1939 fair was a whimsical art deco style, including the 400-foot-tall Tower of the Sun, and there were dozens of plazas, pyramids, fountains, and statues from this "Pageant of the Pacific." The most important survivor is the semicircular building right inside the main gate, former command post for the base commander. Sharp-eyed movie buffs will recognize it as the setting for Captain Queeg's trial in *The Caine Mutiny* and the Berlin Airport in *Indiana Jones and the Last Crusade.*

With the U.S. Navy's departure, many old hangars are being leased out to filmmakers, who have completed such movies as *What Dreams May Come* here, not to mention episodes of television's *Nash Bridges.* Many ideas for the island's future use have been tossed about—including as the site for a theme park or casino—but for now people come for the spectacular views and the chance to glimpse a film star. The gates are open weekends only from 8:00 A.M. until sunset; a shuttle to the island from Transbay Terminal (#108) operates hourly from 9:00 A.M. to 6:00 P.M. If driving, take the Treasure Island exit from the Bay Bridge and continue north.

The best spot (with parking) for photographing the city skyline, especially in the early morning and at dusk, lies just outside the entrance gate. Here seabirds frolic and ships glide past as you take in an inspiring panorama of city and bay. Entering the old base, you follow a palm-lined avenue fronting the bay. A bit north is the Perimeter Walking Path, affording more of those phenomenal views of Alcatraz, Angel Island, and the East Bay.

Trivia

The Golden Gate National Recreation Area welcomes more than 14 million visitors each year.

Yerba Buena Island itself is home to a sumptuous mansion formerly used by navy admirals (and now claimed by San Francisco's mayor) as well as several U.S. Coast Guard facilities. By calling ahead you can visit the ***Coast Guard Vessel Traffic Service,*** which monitors a huge area of water from outside the bay to the California Delta and port of Sacramento. The service was launched back in the 1970s after a serious collision right under Golden Gate Bridge, when port authorities realized that the old "rules of the road" were no longer adequate.

Marked by a tall radar tower, the center sits at the island's highest point. Inside, a staff officer will explain in detail how controllers use high-tech computer, radar, and closed-circuit TV systems to track every type and size of vessel, from tugboats to aircraft carriers. The traffic service provides information about weather and fog conditions, obstacles of every sort, and vessel movements—more than 100,000 transits per year. Happily, as a result of the service, collisions have been virtually eliminated on the bay.

The Vessel Traffic Service (VTS) center is open daily for visitors, but prior arrangements must be made by calling (415) 556–2760. It's reached by taking Macalla Road up the hill and following signs with the

Trivia

"East is East, and West is San Francisco . . . Californians are a race of people; they are not merely inhabitants of a state."

—O.Henry, 1910.

VTS logo to the bunkerlike building with the radar tower on top.

Another San Francisco pier shelters a very different kind of attraction. Liberty ships were an emergency response to a critical shortage of cargo vessels at the start of World War II, when enemy subs were sinking Allied ships faster than they could be built. In one of history's greatest mass production efforts, 2,751 Liberty ships were constructed between 1941 and 1945. Yet the ***SS* Jeremiah O'Brien,** docked at Pier 45, is the sole survivor in its original condition.

Because "Libertys" were assembled from prefabricated sections, construction time averaged only six to eight weeks. Shipyards operated twenty-four hours a day, seven days a week, and about one-third of all workers were women—the legendary Wendy the Welder and Rosie the Riveter of popular song. The *O'Brien,* named for a Revolutionary War naval hero, was built in South Portland, Maine, and was launched on June 19, 1943.

One great thing about touring the ship is that you feel carried back to those days, with the nation at war and everyone pulling together. It is kept in full working order, right down to sacks of coal sitting on pallets and fresh coffee brewing in the crew's mess. There's even piped-in big band music down in the engine room. Take a self-guided tour, or let a salty old docent guide you on a ramble fore and aft.

A full tour of the 441-foot-long gray goliath includes the officers' quarters (it paid to be an officer) and mess, cargo hold, wheelhouse, chart room, and radio shack. The engine room in the bowels of the ship is reached via a series of intricate catwalks and grated decks. This mass of pipes and valves, gears and wheels, surrounds a huge triple-expansion steam engine.

Liberty ships ferried troops and made vital cargo runs to Allied armies in Europe and the Pacific. The *O'Brien,* for instance, carried food and ammunition to Britain, served as a shuttle to the Normandy beachhead (eleven trips), and later transported supplies to the South Pacific.

The slow speed (11 knots maximum) of these ships made them easy targets for enemy subs, so it's surprising that fewer than 200 were sunk during the war. Traveling in convoys and armed with ten defensive guns, they proved to be remarkably resistant to attack. Now you can crawl right up on the artillery turrets and sit in the gunner's seat.

After the war the *O'Brien* joined the ranks of the "mothball fleet." There she rode at anchor for thirty-three years while other Libertys were sold off or scrapped. But volunteers saved the ship from oblivion, and it became a premier example of maritime preservation.

In the spring of 1994, this proud Liberty steamed all the way from San Francisco to England, manned by an all-volunteer crew that included many old-timers. The occasion was the fiftieth anniversary of the D-Day landings on June 6, 1944, and the *O'Brien* was the only original invasion ship to return to the beaches of Normandy. The 18,000-mile voyage was an incredible feat of determination and hard work.

The SS *Jeremiah O'Brien,* located at Pier 45 in Fisherman's Wharf, is open daily except major holidays from 9:00 A.M. to 4:00 P.M. Admission charged. Call (415) 441–5969 for information.

Leaving the crowded wharf area, San Francisco's waterfront opens out into the former ***Fort Mason*** complex (now part of the Golden Gate National Recreation Area). The military base serves as home to a variety of cultural activities (such as art fairs and blues festivals) as well as Green's, a renowned vegetarian restaurant in Building D. Farther on lies the fashionable Marina District, whose residents include a few older Italian families (Joe DiMaggio grew up here) and enough yuppies to fill several yachts.

Tucked away on Baker Street, a block off the bayside promenade, sits the neo-classical ***Palace of Fine Arts,*** a true gem of a building built for a world's fair back in 1915. It was designed by architect Bernard Maybeck to house a priceless art collection from around the world and features a rotunda and sweeping colonnade of wooden columns. In front is a large pond where swans glide by contentedly. This fine old structure is currently being restored to its former glory. No admission charged.

Crissy Field is located at the southeast end of the former army base called the Presidio, just west of Marina Green. A 100-acre park, blending seamlessly into the surrounding urban landscape, includes a 20-acre tidal marsh, a huge meadow, revitalized sand beaches and dunes, and thousands of restored native plants. The open space wraps delicately around the Community Environmental Center, where nature festivals and environmental workshops take place. It's hard not to feel grateful for being in San Francisco while cruising down an idyllic path, launching from the board-sailing site, or quietly musing on the meaning of life while peering into the depths of a tidal pond.

Several miles away, at the entrance to the bay, lies a very different kind of sentinel. ***Fort Point*** is a mammoth brick bastion from the Civil War

Fort Point

era, hunkered down directly beneath the Golden Gate Bridge. The fort is part of the Presidio.

Joseph Strauss, the bridge's Austrian architect, created a graceful arch over the fort to save it from demolition, and the old stronghold actually served as the operations base during construction. Then, during World War II, about one hundred soldiers stationed here manned searchlights and guns to help protect a submarine net that stretched across the entrance to the bay.

This grand old fortress was completed in 1861. Millions of bricks went to form the 5- to 12-foot-thick walls, and for a time it stood as the largest brick structure west of the Mississippi. Fort Point protected the bay, and it's true that no enemy ship ever entered, nor was there ever a single shot fired in battle. As one guide remarked, "The Civil War never made it far enough west and World War II never made it far enough east."

National Park Service guides recount the fort's quiet but colorful history. The site was originally a high promontory where, in 1776, Colonel Juan Bautista de Anza raised the Spanish flag. Spaniards erected the adobe Castillo de San Joaquin here, but in 1853 the U.S. Army blew up this fortress and the cliff on which it stood to make way for Fort Point.

At present you pass through a large wood-and-iron door and enter a chilly, dank courtyard. On display here are several types of cannons, including a stumpy mortar that could fire a 100-pound shell 1 mile, piles of black cannonballs, and a covered wagon. The fort housed 600 soldiers and could mount up to 126 cannons, which were located in arched cubicles called casemate rooms.

Spiral staircases made with granite slabs lead to the upper levels. Here you can wander through the tiers of casemates, which acted as bombproof shelters for the big guns. At the top level you will be standing directly under the concrete pillars and steel girders of Golden Gate Bridge and be able to hear the clank of cars passing above. Also topside are a lighthouse built in 1864 and emplacements for thirty-six pieces of artillery.

The museum contains a collection of old photos, a sampling of uniforms, and a special historical tribute to black soldiers. Fort Point National Historic Site is open from 10:00 A.M. to 5:00 P.M.; call (415) 561–4395 for more information. (Friday through Sunday.)

To reach the fort from inside the Presidio, take Long Road off Lincoln Boulevard, or walk down from the bridge observation area. San Francisco's waterfront begins here, and it's a fabulous spot to watch stormy Pacific waters surge through the Golden Gate and slam into the seawall. Fort Point is also the terminus of the Golden Gate Promenade.

Above It All

Everyone goes to look at the Golden Gate Bridge, but there must be hundreds of great spots to catch an eyeful in San Francisco. It's a city of forty-two hills, and dozens of skyscrapers boast spectacular viewing rooms. And what an eyeful it is!

There's nothing wrong with classic ***view points*** such as Twin Peaks and Coit Tower, except that they get very crowded at times. So here's an insider's selection (in no particular order) of great places to see San Francisco from on high.

le-known ***Tank Hill,*** south of Golden Gate Park, provides a wrap-around view of the city and East Bay in a tourist-free environment. Go to the south end of Stanyan Street and turn left onto Belgrave Street; go to the end and take the footpath to the top.

Carona Heights offers superb views but also the chance to get a good workout. Located above a maze of winding streets not far from Market and Castro Streets, the outcropping of rock is reached via a precipitous trail. Take Roosevelt Way to Museum Way.

From the top of ***Nob Hill,*** look east down California (at the Powell intersection) for a spectacular view of the bay. Office towers of the financial district and the tiled roofs of Chinatown bracket the Bay Bridge.

There's a public park on ***Potrero Hill,*** at the corner of Vermont and Twentieth Streets, with good views of the downtown skyline, Twin Peaks, and

Catching a Play

Seeing live theater can be a costly affair, but here's a checklist for getting good seats without breaking the budget.

- ***Get half-price tickets at Union Square.*** *The TIX Bay Area booth in a pavilion on Union Square sells tickets for the same day of performance and only selected shows and seats, but some bargains can be had, especially on orchestra seats. Open Tuesday through Saturday from 11:00 A.M. to 6:00 P.M. Call (415) 433–7827 for information.*
- ***Take your chances at the theater.*** *Unused house seats and cancellations often turn up at bargain prices an hour or so before show time.*
- ***Go with friends.*** *Many theaters give discount ticket prices to groups.*
- ***Watch for special offers.*** *Sale prices are offered even on hit shows during slow times of the year—January and February—and during certain holiday weekends.*
- ***Catch a preview.*** *Pre-opening performances are normally cheaper (up to half off) and sometimes more exciting.*
- ***Choose a weeknight or matinee.*** *Many theaters discount tickets on certain days and times, such as discount Tuesday nights at Theatre on the Square.*
- ***Sit in the balcony.*** *A good seat higher up is always cheaper than the orchestra and often better for seeing the show. City's best balconies are at the Orpheum Theatre, Geary Theater, and Club Fugazi ("Beach Blanket Babylon").*

Mount Davidson. Then you can drive down Vermont on a route that's just as crooked as the famous (and traffic-choked) stretch of Lombard Street.

In the little-visited Sunset District on the west side of town are two parks, Grand View and Golden Gate Heights, that provide stunning views all the way from Fort Funston and the zoo north along a 3-mile beach to Golden Gate Bridge. On exceptionally clear days the panorama stretches to Point Reyes and the Farallon Islands. The parks sit atop two small peaks reached from 10th Avenue between Noriega and Pacheco Streets south of Golden Gate Park.

At the westernmost point of the San Francisco Peninsula lies Land's End. ***Ocean Lookout,*** at the end of El Camino Del Mar off Point Lobos Avenue, offers a superb vantage point for seeing the Pacific and Golden Gate.

On ***Russian Hill*** go to the intersection of Hyde and Greenwich Streets to gaze upon Telegraph Hill and Coit Tower, then to Hyde and Chestnut for a gripping view of the Hyde Street Pier and Alcatraz Island. If you want to enjoy coffee or a snack while you gape, try the cafeteria at the San Francisco Art Institute, 800 Chestnut Street. (There's also a huge Diego Rivera mural.)

Great views abound, but there are other reasons to visit Russian Hill. Novelist Herb Gold called it "a metropolitan village," an unpretentious blend of redwood shingle houses, cobbled lanes, and towering pine trees just a few blocks from downtown. Blessed with picturesque cul-de-sacs and stunning bay views, Russian Hill possesses "patrician elegance and Bohemian charm," as one writer put it.

The name remains something of a mystery—the area was never a Russian colony, nor were there many immigrants until much later. One legend has it that some Russian seal hunters are buried here; another, that a Russian sailor fell into a well and drowned after drinking too much.

The Powell-Hyde cable-car line goes right over Russian Hill along Hyde Street, but don't get off at Lombard—that's "the crookedest street in the world" and also one of the most crowded. On the other hand, little-known Filbert Street between Hyde and Leavenworth is the steepest in town, with a 31.5 percent vertical grade that provides a heartrending descent.

The hill's rustic informality has always appealed to writers, and the sounds of clicking typewriter keys (or is that a laser printer?) can still be heard, if you listen carefully, as you stroll along byways like Russian Hill Place. At its literary zenith in the late nineteenth century, queen of the hill was Ina Coolbrith, California's first poet laureate, who edited

The Overland Monthly with colleagues Bret Harte and George Sterling. The latter described San Francisco as "the cool, gray city of love" long before the hippies arrived with flowers in their hair. Other writers who drifted through included Mark Twain, Joaquin Miller, Ambrose Bierce, Jack London, Frank Norris, Robinson Jeffers, and Helen Hunt Jackson.

Macondray Lane, where Coolbrith had a home, captures the village atmosphere that still defines Russian Hill, despite the intrusion of highrises and traffic. The lane makes for a tranquil, reflective walk, passing shingled houses with bay windows, eucalyptus trees, and lush vegetation alive with the sound of songbirds. Even though residents must struggle with their groceries down this car-free passageway, they swear by life on the lane.

The heart of Russian Hill is bordered by Hyde, Taylor, Greenwich, and Broadway Streets. Another street worth exploring is the 1000 block of Green. A delicate Italian house built in 1886 occupies 1055 Green Street, and there's an eight-sided "octagon house" at number 1067, reminder of an architectural fad that swept the city during the 1850s. The old firehouse at number 1088 once served the neighborhood as Engine 31, and the Tudor-style building has been remodeled for use as a private residence; the original fire pole stands in the doorway.

The far end of Vallejo Street has an aloof air about it. The brown shingle house with the double gable at number 1013–1019 was built by renowned architect Willis Polk for his own family, and number 1034 and number 1036 are two more homes from the original row. Branching off Vallejo are Russian Hill Place, a brick-paved lane lined with Mediterranean-style villas, and Florence Street, which boasts the oldest cottage on Russian Hill (1857), a stark contrast to the ornate Victorians.

Architectural Delights

Pacific Heights is San Francisco's finest residential area, and the western section in particular contains several blocks of grand residences. Not that the wealthy enclaves of other cities can't match the mansions here, but the stunning setting makes them unforgettable. Pacific Heights is sandwiched between the Marina and Western Addition districts, but with one important distinction—it's higher up. Property values and rent increase in direct proportion to altitude in San Francisco.

Begin the tour on Pacific Street along one stretch that's an architect's dream, the 3200 block between Presidio and Walnut. On this steep hill are clustered several of the city's finest houses, including number 3233 by renowned architect Bernard Maybeck, which features a distinctive balustrade. The deep brown, weathered shingles of several homes along the block create a wonderful architectural harmony.

The view from the corner of Pacific and Lyon looks down over neighborhoods called Cow Hollow and the Marina. Farther east along Pacific Street are a sprawling mansion at the corner of Baker, the Egyptian consulate, and an impressive row of redbrick and white-trim Georgian homes in the 2800 block. The El Drisco Hotel at number 2901 was for many years the only hotel in Pacific Heights.

Broadway is definitely one of the more schizophrenic streets in San Francisco. From an inauspicious start at the Embarcadero, it plummets straight into a sleazy strip of bawdy nightlife, skirts the edge of Chinatown, then disappears into the Broadway Tunnel. Emerging on the other side, the street traverses the lower part of Russian Hill and all of Pacific Heights before dead-ending outside the walls of the former Presidio. Here is a splendid view of the city and a flight of stairs down to Vallejo Street and more mansions.

One block east (2898 Broadway), at the Baker Street stairs, sits a stately redbrick Georgian that epitomizes the best of Pacific Heights mansions—dignified, conservative, self-assured. You can also see the former James Leary Flood mansion, now the Hamlin School, in the 2100 block. The Convent of the Sacred Heart High School, originally another of Flood's many homes, sits at 2222.

Here are a few more gems to look for from among the scores of lovely Pacific Heights homes:

- The grand Renaissance mansion at the intersection of Vallejo and Divisadero Streets has been used in several movies including *Bullitt.*
- The Adolph Spreckels Mansion at 2080 Washington Street is a French Baroque palace from 1913. (Twenty-seven rooms are open to the public.)
- A former firehouse (1893) at 3022 Washington has been converted into a private residence.

You could hardly call San Francisco a Victorian city, except when it comes to architecture. Some 14,000 "painted ladies" of seemingly endless size, shape, color, and ornamentation stand proudly throughout the town. About half of these have been restored or kept up over the years in a state befitting their stylish past.

The survival rate is astonishing when you consider that more than 500 blocks went up in smoke after the infamous 1906 earthquake. The fire raged through the town's northeast side, wiping out nearly everything between the bay and Van Ness Avenue. The most sumptuous homes lined this wide street but were dynamited by the army to form a firebreak, which finally halted the blaze. Thus the richest depository of Victoriana lies west of Van Ness in the Pacific Heights and Western Addition sections of town. (Many Victorians also reside in the Mission district.)

Why so many Victorians in San Francisco? Primarily because the City of Bay Windows sprang up during a few hectic decades of building after the gold rush. This was precisely the time when the so-called Victorian style was the rage, a style oozing with decorative details—fretwork, friezes, corbels, cartouches, plaster rosettes, fluted panels, carved medallions, and stained glass.

A driving tour of the city's finest ***Victorian Homes*** starts with a cluster of lovely ladies at the intersection of California and Gough Streets. One highlight is the stately ***Haas-Lilienthal House*** at 2007 Franklin. Built in 1886 for Mr. Haas, a wholesale grocer from Bavaria, the home harkens back to the exuberant heyday of imposing wooden Victorians. During the great fire the Haas family climbed to the roof of the three-story house and watched nervously as the flames moved toward them, only to be halted a block away at Van Ness. Their descendants occupied the home until 1972, when they donated it to an architectural foundation. (The group offers guided tours on Wednesday, Saturday, and Sunday afternoons. Call (415) 441–3004 for tour times and entrance fees.)

The ***Octagon House*** (2645 Gough) is a perfectly preserved treasure from 1861. Eight-sided homes enjoyed a vogue because some people believed they made for a healthier lifestyle. (Tours are given three days a month; call 415–441–7512 for information.) The 700 block of Steiner Street at Alamo Square flaunts a row of Victorians with a famous backdrop of downtown seen on countless postcards. Another impressive lineup stands on McAllister near Scott in the same neighborhood. Bush Street, between Fillmore and Webster, has a row of houses moved from former sites during urban renewal, then spruced up and given front gardens.

Among the unusual places you can stay are the Queen Anne Hotel (1590 Sutter), with forty-nine rooms in a building designed for Miss Mary Lake's School for Girls and the exclusive Sherman House (2160 Green), fourteen rooms in a landmark Pacific Heights mansion and carriage house built by a music company magnate. It's *the* place for millionaires and movie stars.

Walking tours of Victorian and other vintage residential neighborhoods are conducted by Heritage Walks (415–441–3004) and Victorian Home Walk Tour (415–252–9485).

San Francisco loves its Victorians, but another truly uplifting architectural thrill is a visit to the ***Cathedral of St. Mary of the Assumption,*** perched regally atop Cathedral Hill. In 1962 a major fire gutted the seventy-two-year-old redbrick church at Van Ness and Post, but before long monolithic concrete pylons began to rise 2 blocks away. By the time the dust had settled, the city could boast a remarkable, marble-covered structure that has been likened to a schooner in full sail, among other striking metaphors. But none do justice to this masterwork, designed and built by a team of world-class architects and engineers.

The ornate main entrance of St. Mary's Cathedral (as it's commonly called) opens onto a white-marble baptismal font with seventy-eight diamond-faceted sides. Then, as in the great Gothic churches, all your

Cathedral of St. Mary of the Assumption with St. Mark's Lutheran Church in foreground

attention lifts upward to the stunning 190-foot-high dome and its faceted colored-glass windows, which scale the walls like colored streamers to form a cross. The windows symbolize the classical elements: water, earth, fire, and air. The entire colossal structure rests on four giant pillars; between them are curved walls made from 1,700 pre-poured concrete coffers that form a vast, columnless nave. Windows at the four corners open out to views of San Francisco, creating a dynamic interaction of interior and exterior space.

The radiant colors of the window rising behind the main altar reflect in the free-hanging *baldachino,* a kinetic sculpture by Richard Lippold, suspended above the sanctuary. Its 7,000 aluminum rods symbolize both the ascending prayers of the faithful and the flow of divine grace from above. Natural air currents keep this shimmering pendant in perpetual motion. An enormous Ruffatti organ with 4,842 pipes rests on a contoured concrete pedestal, and exceptionally good acoustics make the cathedral an ideal setting for musical performances.

Six niches around the nave contain solid bronze sculptures of Mary that weigh several tons, and fourteen bronze-on-rosewood stations of the cross line the east wall. But ostentation has no place here; even the vestments worn by the clergy conform with the clean lines and simplicity of this ultramodern masterpiece.

Cathedral of St. Mary of the Assumption, at 1111 Gough Street (at Geary), is open daily from 8:30 A.M. to 5:00 P.M. For information about tours and free organ recitals call (415) 567–2020.

Civic Center

A very different kind of pilgrimage is devoted to a book and its author. It told the story of "the stuff dreams are made of," the black bird whose enamel hid a king's ransom in precious gems. But when Dashiell Hammett created his superb detective novel *The Maltese Falcon,* he could not have imagined the cult that would grow up around it. Of course, John Huston's film ensured the immortality of Sam Spade, the Fat Man, and the rest of Hammett's carefully etched characters.

Falcon buffs can spend a day (preferably a foggy one) poking around the fading reminders of this exciting tale on a ***Maltese Falcon tour.*** All the action of *The Maltese Falcon* took place in a 10-block area between Union Square and Civic Center. Moreover, Hammett lived in San Francisco during his formative years, roughly from 1921 to 1929, and began his writing career here.

On Eddy Street off Larkin, for example, the Hammetts paid $45 a month for a furnished apartment. A nondescript building at 891 Post Street was the first place the writer lived after separating from his wife; it also served as the address of the hero, cynical gumshoe Sam Spade. It was here that Hammett wrote the first draft of his mystery masterpiece. He also lived for a time at 20 Monroe, a short street between Bush and Pine.

The old Hunter-Dulin Building at 111 Sutter Street housed the offices of Spade and his partner, Miles Archer, and it was here that they first laid eyes on the fickle Miss O'Shaughnessy. Later, on a little alley called Burritt Street (off Bush just above the Stockton Tunnel), she bumped off Archer. A bronze plaque reads: ON APPROXIMATELY THIS SPOT, MILES ARCHER, PARTNER OF SAM SPADE, WAS DONE IN BY BRIGID O'SHAUGHNESSY.

Quite a lot of "bumping off" took place in the story. On Geary near Leavenworth, Floyd Thursby was done in by "the kid," AKA Wilmer Cook. Another identifiable locale is the Geary Theater, site of a meeting between Spade and "the oily Joel Cairo."

To wind up the tour, head for 870 Market Street and the Flood Building, a gray edifice jutting out like the prow of a battleship. At this address Hammett worked briefly as a Pinkerton detective, or so the legend goes. Walking through the neoclassical lobby, you'll come out on Ellis Street, and at number 63 sits ***John's Grill,*** a classic establishment since 1908 and one of Hammett's hangouts in the twenties. It also served as the setting for one minor scene in *The Maltese Falcon.* Before setting out on a wild goose chase after Brigid, Sam stops by the grill for a quick dinner of "chops, baked potato, and sliced tomatoes."

Done up in dark wood, leather, and glass chandeliers, the restaurant looks pretty much as it must have in Hammett's day. And the management really "hamms" it up too, serving "Sam Spade's Chops," priced at a discouraging $22.95, and the "Bloody Brigid," a potent concoction of vodka, soda, pineapple juice, lime, and grenadine. An excellent replica of the black bird rules the roost upstairs, and there are copies of Hammett's works, a letter from his longtime friend, Lillian Hellman, and lots of good stills and posters from the classic film. The restaurant also serves as headquarters for the Dashiell Hammett Society of San Francisco and offers live jazz nightly.

For many years a local character named Don Herron has given animated tours of Hammett's San Francisco, covering the 3 miles of key locations in the Tenderloin, Nob Hill, and downtown hotel district. The walks leave the main branch of the San Francisco Public Library in Civic Center Saturdays at noon, May and June only. You shouldn't have any trouble spotting Herron; he'll be the one in a trench coat and fedora hat emerging from the fog. For further information call (510) 287–9540 or visit www.donherron.com.

While at Civic Center be sure to stop by ***San Francisco City Hall,*** which has been beautifully restored to all its former glory. Designed by Arthur Brown Jr. in the beaux arts style, the soaring edifice boasts a 300-foot dome modeled on St. Peters in Rome. Like the rest of the building, the dome was completely renovated in the late 1990s and now features its original copper-gold color. It's larger than the dome of the U.S. Capitol and fifth tallest in the world. In fact, City Hall and the entire Civic Center area, including the opera house, public library, and other buildings, look like they belong in Vienna or Paris rather than California. Inside City Hall there is a sweeping marble staircase and two "light courts" bathed in natural sunlight pouring through the glass ceiling. Here reside a city museum and gift shop.

City Hall is open weekdays from 8:00 A.M. to 8:00 P.M. and weekends from noon to 4:00 P.M. Guided tours are available.

Another recommended stop at Civic Center is the ***Farmer's Market,*** 2 blocks east of the City Hall on United Nations Plaza. Colorful and cosmopolitan—with a distinct Asian influence in produce selection—it unfolds under blue awnings every Wednesday and Sunday from 7:00 A.M. to 5:00 P.M.

Here, farmers can sell only what they raise or catch themselves. Dozens of stands overflow with eggs, almonds, live chickens, and fish on ice, oysters, flowers, leeks, and mushrooms the size of dinner plates. Shoppers poke and prod and finally pick their own produce, whether mangoes or garlic or lush red cherries. Many sellers will let you sample the goodies before you buy, but don't misuse the custom to have a free lunch!

The West Side

On a nice day you can always head for the city's most famous retreat. ***Golden Gate Park,*** one of the largest man-made parks in the world, had to be wrested inch by inch from the grip of sand dunes and other worthless land. San Francisco was much smaller when the 1,017-acre site was selected in 1870, and it lay in what were known disparagingly as "the outside lands." Yet "the great sand bank" grew into a lush urban paradise largely through the efforts of William Hammond Hall and John McLaren, two farsighted landscape architects.

Naturally, such an idyllic retreat attracts loads of visitors, especially on sunny weekends. Even so, the park is so large that you can easily find solitude in a misty forest or by a tranquil pond. (Remember, after the 1906 earthquake some 40,000 refugees managed to camp here!) Generally, the park's eastern half is busier, especially around the complex of excellent museums. One nearby spot rarely grabs the attention of visitors, however.

Come ride a painted pony—and a dog, frog, or reindeer—on the vintage ***Carrousel*** at the Children's Playground. Built in 1912 and fully restored a decade ago, this rare, wood-carved Herschell-Spillman merry-go-round is housed inside a pillared rotunda. It features a pipe organ, gleaming brass poles, dazzling mirrors and glass jewelry, and pictorial panels painted with idyllic scenes of bygone times.

And, of course, the delightfully carved animals, lined up in four bobbing rows, including giraffes, ostriches, camels, cats, roosters, and horses with roses in their manes and cherubs on their saddles. Even if you don't hop on for a ride, it's worth a trip just to see the superb craftsmanship and attention to detail, such as real horsehair in the tails of those wonderful painted ponies.

Located off Bowling Green Drive at the park's eastern edge, the carousel is open daily June through Labor Day from 10:00 A.M. to 5:00 P.M., and Friday through Sunday the rest of the year from 9:00 A.M. to 4:00 P.M. A ride costs $1.00 for adults and 25 cents for kids.

If ruins are your thing, head over to tiny Lloyd Lake, just west of Cross Over Drive, to see the strangely evocative ***Portals of the Past.*** This curious landmark consists of six white marble pillars that at one time formed the entrance to the grandiose A. N. Towne residence atop Nob Hill. But they were all that remained after the 1906 disaster.

Next, take a trip to the ***Buffalo Paddock*** in the park's wide-open western spaces. The fences here are so carefully concealed by artful landscaping that the buffalo seem to be roaming free. Just when visitors think they have exhausted the park's variety, something new turns up. For example, just across from the Buffalo Paddock sits another unique attraction, the ***Flycasting Pools*** and Angler's Lodge.

There are no fish here, but fishermen find the next best thing: an enormous cement-lined pool with almost two acres of water for practicing distance casting, accuracy, and the difficult technique of fly casting. The Golden Gate Angling and Casting Club makes its headquarters at the adjacent lodge. Inside are walls paneled in knotty pine and hung with classic rods, mounted trout, and displays of hand-tied flies. For information about hours, call (415) 386–2630.

Next head west to the final stop of a crowd-free trip to the park. At the far end of John F. Kennedy Drive, just before it reaches the Great Highway, is the ***Dutch Windmill,*** another lesser-known jewel. Built in 1902, the mill was designed to pump water to the reservoir atop Strawberry Hill. It has been restored with a new copper dome and scalelike shingles and turns happily away in the breeze. In perfect complement are the Queen Wilhelmina Tulip Gardens, which erupt in a symphony of color early each spring.

A great way to get a different perspective on San Francisco's endless diversity is to visit one of the outlying neighborhoods seldom frequented by tourists but known and loved by locals. Among the more intriguing count Potrero Hill, the Mission, Haight Ashbury, the Sunset, and, perhaps most diverse of all, the Richmond District in the west corner of town north of Golden Gate Park.

Running right through the Richmond is ***Clement Street,*** a true amalgam of the ethnic influences felt in the city. For many years it was the first American home for Middle and Eastern European immigrants, who opened bakeries, tearooms, groceries, barber shops, and neighborhood bars. Newer settlers include Russians, Middle Easterners, Thais, Vietnamese, and large numbers of Chinese—so many, in fact, that Clement and its environs have been nicknamed Little Chinatown.

Clement Street comes alive during the day with the vibrant pace of grocery shoppers busily sifting through mounds of produce. Exotic food shops abound—oriental bakeries selling turnip cakes, Chinese donuts (they're not round and don't have holes), and sesame balls; open-air stands overflowing with strange fruits and vegetables with delightful shapes and colors and unpronounceable names; and fish markets chock-full of fat catfish and live lobsters, pancake-flat pressed duck, and gobs of bright red fish eggs.

The food shops and eateries along Clement between Arguello (1st Avenue) and 12th Avenue are packed in so densely that they seem to have elbowed out almost every other kind of business. It would take weeks to eat in every restaurant, where you can sample from Vietnamese, Persian, Italian, Danish, Indonesian, Japanese, Cajun, and old-fashioned American cuisines. But Chinese cooking predominates, with the aromas of fried rice, boiled fish, and Peking duck wafting from dozens of bustling kitchens.

Among the more popular Chinese establishments are the Shanghai-style Fountain Court, 354 Clement Street; the no-frills King of the Noodle House at 639; and the family-style Ocean Restaurant at 726. Quietly resonating with an almost legendary status is Minh's Garden at 208, the place to go in San Francisco for Vietnamese food. This unassuming little restaurant boasts delicious fresh spring rolls, spicy sour lemongrass soup, and tasty entrees at reasonable prices. Down the street sits a quasi-futuristic Russian banquet hall called the Russian Bear, 939 Clement, and great Burmese food with enormous portions is found at Burma Super Star (at number 309). Chapeau is a quaint little French bistro at 1408.

Then there are the bars and clubs. The Plough and the Stars at 116 Clement is what you might call a serious Irish pub, judging from its decor of Sinn Fein flags, faded photos of IRA heroes, and patrons passionately discussing the state of the world—in Gaelic. The bar features traditional folk music played with fiddles, flutes, harps, banjos, and Irish bagpipes. All that aside, the place has won awards for pouring the "perfect pint" of Guinness.

Two other rowdy watering holes with regular live entertainment are found on the 400 block, The Last Day Saloon and The Bitter End, and O'Rourke's at 540 is another Irish-American hangout.

All this and shops, too—delicatessens selling *piroshkis* and Indian pickles, pleasantly cramped second-hand and rare bookstores like Green Apple Books at 522, shops of antique furniture, gifts, and, for those whose taste in fish runs to the tropical variety, aquarium supplies. Clement Street can be reached by bus from the Union Square area and is best visited on a warm evening, when locals partake of the passing parade.

Another outstanding ethnic enclave of bustling commercial life is outer ***Irving Street,*** found in the Sunset District south of Golden Gate Park. The 8-block stretch between 19th and 26th Avenues is packed with more than one hundred businesses, including nineteen restaurants and a dozen hair salons. There is wide ethnic variety here, although the Chinese influence has earned the area a reputation as the city's "Third Chinatown."

The Final Stop

Finally, you can go south of Market Street to find out what happens when the scion of one of America's wealthiest industrial families decides to become a brewmaster. Young Fritz Maytag of the famous washing-machine empire heard that the maker of his favorite beer,

Anchor Steam, was tottering on the edge of bankruptcy. So he decided to step in and save the ***Anchor Brewing Company.*** That was back in 1965, and Fritz proved that Maytags can create more than one kind of suds!

One delightful result of Maytag's personal passion is a great tour. It begins by meeting the guide and fellow beer-lovers in the tasting room, done up nicely with antique brewing paraphernalia and serving trays from around the world. A wall of windows looks out on gleaming copper kettles used in the beer-making process, which will be explained later in detail. But wait.

First, the guide describes the origin of steam brewing, a unique process developed in the nineteenth century to get around the need for ice, then scarce in San Francisco. With the iceless technique, the unfermented beer is transferred to large, shallow pans instead of deep vats so that the bigger surface area can dissipate the heat faster. Although the origin of the term *steam beer* remains obscure, one version says that the final product emerged so heavily charged with natural carbonation that it appeared to let off steam when kegs were tapped.

The forty-five-minute tour takes visitors through the magic of steam brewing. First, the barley is malted and crushed for mashing, then blended with warm water and gradually heated in huge copper kettles. The filtration process yields wort, an unfermented liquid that will eventually become beer. But first the wort must be boiled and combined with whole hops, the magical vine flower that lends beer its aroma and slight bitterness. Next comes fermentation; yeast is introduced into the wort, which has meanwhile been transferred to shallow pans for cooling. Wait three days and—*presto*—you have beer!

Next comes the fun! The tour group—by now having worked up a tremendous thirst—marches off to the tasting room to try a series of delightful liquids. Although steam beer gets most of the attention, the brewery also makes three kinds of ale, a dark porter, and the first wheat beer produced commercially in years. Your guide doubles as barman in dispensing pitchers of each heady brew in ascending order of potency, and before long your tourmates seem like old friends.

If you take the tour between Thanksgiving and the end of January, expect an extra treat: a spicy Christmas ale brewed to the carefully prepared specifications of master brewer Fritz Maytag.

The Anchor Brewing Company, at 1705 Mariposa Street, conducts free tours and tastings by reservation only on weekdays at 1:00 P.M.; call (415) 863–8350 for information.

Places to Stay in San Francisco

Union Square/Nob Hill

Amsterdam Hotel,
749 Taylor Street;
(800) 673–3444

Andrews Hotel,
624 Post Street;
(800) 926–3739

Beresford Hotel,
635 Sutter Street;
(800) 533–6533

Cartwright Hotel,
524 Sutter Street;
(800) 227–3844

Chancellor Hotel,
433 Powell Street;
(800) 428–4748

Cornell Hotel de France,
715 Bush Street;
(800) 232–9698

Handlery Union Square Hotel,
351 Geary Street;
(800) 843–4343

Juliana Hotel,
590 Bush Street;
(800) 328–3880

Monticello Inn,
127 Ellis Street;
(800) 669–7777

Nob Hill Lambourne Hotel,
725 Pine Street;
(800) BRI–TINN

San Francisco Residence Club,
851 California Street;
(415) 421–2220

Shannon Court Hotel,
550 Geary Street;
(800) 228–8830

Hotel Triton,
342 Grant Avenue;
(800) 433–6611

York Hotel,
940 Sutter Street;
(800) 808–9675

Embarcadero/Fisherman's Wharf

Harbor Court Hotel,
165 Steuart Street;
(800) 346–0555

Tuscan Inn,
425 North Point Street;
(800) 648–4626

Wharf Inn,
2601 Mason Street;
(800) 548–9918

Van Ness/Lombard

Broadway Manor Inn,
2201 Van Ness Avenue;
(800) 727–6239

Castle Inn Motel,
1565 Broadway Street;
(800) 8–CASTLE

Comfort Inn by the Bay,
2775 Van Ness Avenue;
(800) 228–5150

Hotel Richelieu,
1050 Van Ness Avenue;
(800) 295–7424

Pacific Heights Inn,
1555 Union Street;
(800) 523–1801

Ramada Limited,
1940 Lombard Street;
(800) 2–RAMADA

Travelodge by the Bay,
1450 Lombard Street;
(800) 578–7878

Places to Eat in San Francisco

(All area codes are 415)

Union Square/Downtown

Akiko's Sushi (Japanese),
542 Mason Street;
989–8218

Anjou (French),
44 Campton Place;
392–5373

Annabelle's Bar and Bistro (American/Californian),
68 Fourth Street;
777–1200

Cafe Claude (French),
7 Claude Lane;
392–3505

Cafe de la Presse, (Continental),
352 Grant Avenue;
398–2680

David's Restaurant/ Delicatessen (Jewish),
474 Geary Street;
276–5950

Globe (American),
290 Pacific Avenue;
391–4132

Grand Cafe (Continental),
501 Geary Street;
292–0101

Jeanne d'Arc (French),
715 Bush Street;
421–3154

Johnny Foley's Irish House (pub food),
243 O'Farrell Street;
954–0777

Le Central (French),
453 Bush Street;
391–2233

Le Colonial (Vietnamese/French),
20 Cosmo Place;
931–3600

Marrakech Moroccan Restaurant (North African),
419 O'Farrell Street;
776–6717

Sam's Grill (seafood),
374 Bush Street;
421–0594

Sushi Boat Restaurant (Japanese),
389 Geary Street;
781–5111

Tadich Grill (seafood),
240 California Street;
391–1849

Tiramisu de Sera (Italian),
28 Belden Place;
421–7044

North Beach/Chinatown

Caffe Sport (Italian),
574 Green Street;
981–1251

Calzone's (Italian),
430 Columbus Avenue;
397–3600

Chung King Restaurant (Chinese),
606 Jackson Street;
986–3899

House of Nan King (Chinese),
919 Kearny Street;
421–1429

Kan's Restaurant (Chinese),
708 Grant Avenue;
362–5267

L'Osteria del Forno (Italian),
519 Columbus Avenue;
982–1124

Lotus Garden (Chinese),
532 Grant Avenue;
397–0707

North Beach Restaurant (Italian),
1512 Stockton Street;
392–1700

The Pot Sticker (Chinese),
150 Waverly Place;
397–9985

Tomasso's Restaurant (Italian),
1042 Kearny Street;
398–9696

Yank Sing (Chinese),
101 Spear Street;
957–9300

Embarcadero/Wharf

Buena Vista Cafe (American/Californian),
2765 Hyde Street;
474–5044

Castagnola's Restaurant (seafood),
286 Jefferson Street;
776–5015

Fog City Diner (American/Californian),
1300 Battery Street;
982–2000

Garydanko (French),
800 North Point;
749–2060

Lapis (Mediterranean),
Pier 33;
982–0203

Waterfront Restaurant & Cafe (American/Californian), Pier 7,
The Embarcadero;
391–2696

Van Ness/Civic Center

Green's Restaurant (vegetarian),
Fort Mason Building A;
771–7955

Harris' Restaurant (American/Californian),
2100 Van Ness Avenue;
673–1888

Hayes Street Grill (seafood),
320 Hayes Street;
863–5545

Little Joe's (Italian),
2550 Van Ness Avenue;
433–4343

Matterhorn (Swiss),
2323 Van Ness Avenue;
885–6116

Max's Opera Cafe (American/Californian),
601 Van Ness Avenue;
771–7300

The Meetinghouse (American),
1701 Octavia Street;
922–6733

Millennium (vegetarian),
246 McAllister Street;
487–9800

Suppenkuche (German),
601 Hayes Street;
252–9289

Zarzuela (Spanish),
2000 Hyde Street;
346–0800

Helpful Web Sites for San Francisco

Cable Car Coupons: www.sftravelcoupons.com

Cable Car Museum: www.cablecarmuseum.com

Cartoon Art Museum: www.cartoonart.org

City Search: www.citysearch7.com

Golden Gate Park: www.parks.sfgov.org

Map West, Inc.: www.mapwest.com

San Francisco Chronicle: www.sfgate.com

San Francisco Convention & Visitors Bureau: www.sfvisitor.org

San Francisco Guide: www.sfguide.com

San Francisco Magazine: www.sanfran.com

Jeremiah O'Brien: www.ssjeremiahobrien.com

TIX outlet: www.theatrebayarea.org

Worth Seeing/Doing in San Francisco

Alcatraz Island Tour

Bay Cruise

Cable Car Ride

Coit Tower (North Beach)

De Young and Asian Art Museums (Golden Gate Park)

Fisherman's Wharf

Golden Gate Bridge

Japantown

Legion of Honor Fine Art Museum

Museum of Modern Art/Yerba Buena Gardens

The Bay Area

Most visitors are amazed to discover that San Francisco has only about 800,000 residents, hardly big enough, it would seem, for its big-city reputation. But taken as a whole, the San Francisco Bay Area (including Marin, Alameda, Contra Costa, Solano, San Mateo, and Santa Clara Counties) is home to about five million people, making it the nation's fourth largest metropolitan area. Many people commute daily to San Francisco, while others rarely visit, preferring to live quietly in their own self-contained communities.

Geologists tell us that the famous bay was formed thousands of years ago, when rising water levels caused the Pacific to punch through the Golden Gate and fill a valley that had been carved by river runoff from the interior. The bay still receives drainage from the San Joaquin and Sacramento Rivers, as well as a number of smaller streams, and has been a major shipping avenue since the gold rush.

Although many visitors find it hard to pull themselves away from San Francisco, it's definitely worth the effort. The Bay Area is among the country's most diverse places in terms of natural beauty and visitor attractions. Using San Francisco as a base, you can reach most of the area's scenic and cultural delights within an hour or so by car or public transportation.

Marin County

Jutting down from the north, Marin County is reached via the Golden Gate Bridge or by ferry across the bay. The coastal mountains neatly divide Marin—one side fronts the bay and the other, the ocean. The east is known for its fashionably cute seaside towns like Sausalito and Tiburon, where you can shop, stroll, and watch sailboats skim the surface of the bay. A windy, often fog-draped landscape of mountains and craggy shoreline awaits you to the west. Here, San Francisco seems so close you want to reach out and grab it, yet nature remains remarkably unspoiled by modern incursions.

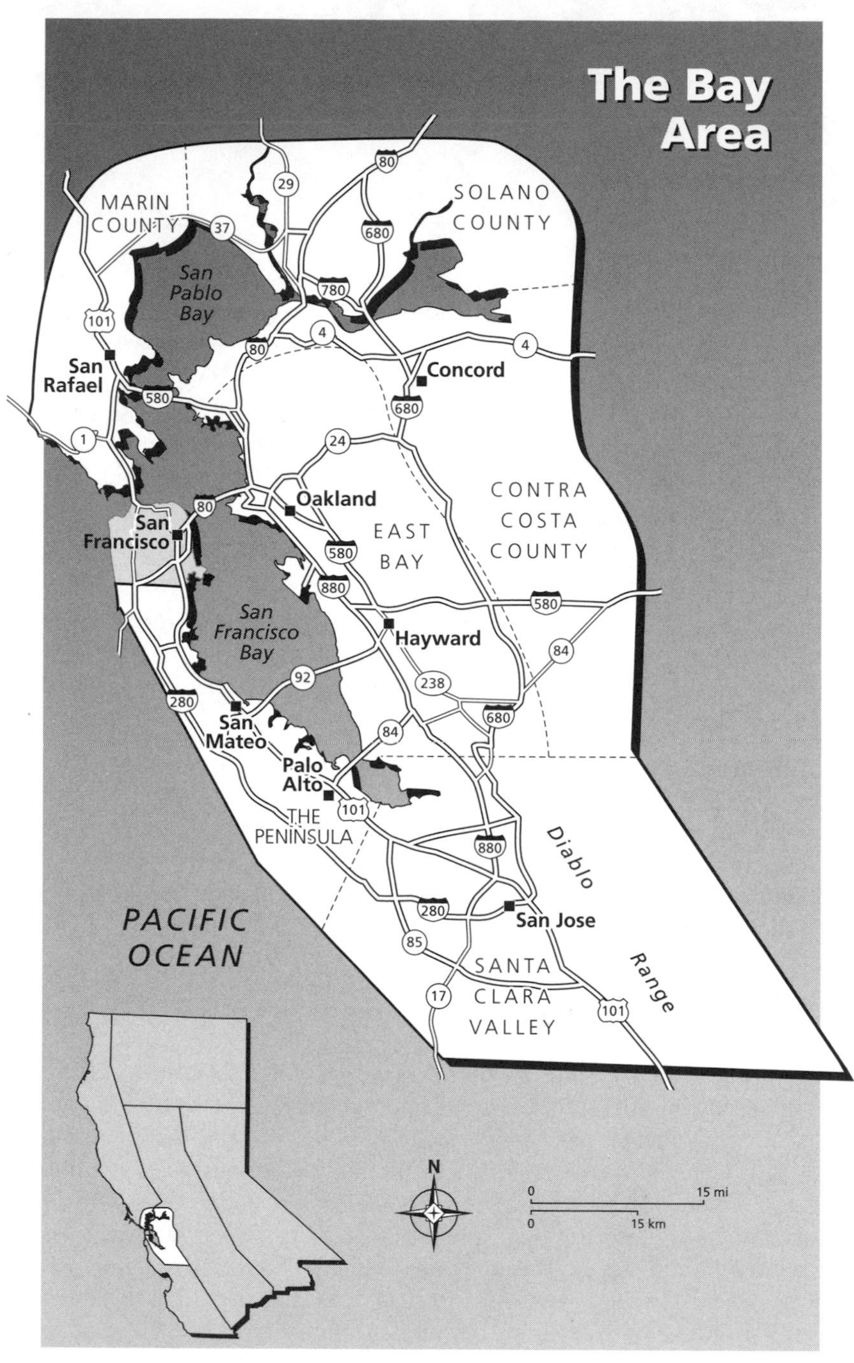

The Bay Area
MARIN COUNTY
SOLANO COUNTY
San Pablo Bay
San Rafael
Concord
Oakland
San Francisco
EAST BAY
CONTRA COSTA COUNTY
San Francisco Bay
Hayward
San Mateo
Palo Alto
THE PENINSULA
Diablo Range
San Jose
SANTA CLARA VALLEY
PACIFIC OCEAN
N
0
15 mi
0
15 km

Author's Top Ten in the Bay Area

Marin Headlands
Tiburon
Angel Island
Benicia
Paramount Theatre
Oakland Temple
Stanford University
Skyline Boulevard
Rosicrucian Egyptian Museum
Mount Hamilton

Just a mile of bridge separates hectic San Francisco from the grassy slopes and windswept ridges of the ***Marin Headlands,*** which stretch from the bridge to Muir Beach. The area encompasses jagged coastline, tranquil valleys, and isolated beaches; grassy bluffs high above the surf provide spectacular views of San Francisco and the bay. Although close to the city in distance and time, the headlands seem far removed from urban life.

One reason the area has remained so unspoiled is that from the 1870s to 1972 much of it belonged to the U.S. Army and thus escaped commercial development. (The rest of the land belonged to dairy farmers and a hunting group.) You can still sense the military's legacy everywhere, especially in three forts and numerous concrete artillery batteries that protect the entrance to the bay.

For a good overview of the Marin Headlands, take the loop drive on Conzelman and Bunker Roads. Along the way you'll spot several turnouts offering magnificent views, and at Kirby Cove you can take a 1-mile hike down to the beach to see the Golden Gate Bridge from below (a *must* for photographers). At the junction of Bunker and Field Roads sits the visitor center. (It's open daily from 9:30 A.M. to 4:30 P.M.; 415–331–1540.) Around you are the white frame structures of Fort Barry, a turn-of-the-twentieth-century seacoast artillery post. Just uphill from the visitor center is the historic Nike Missile Site, an outdoor museum of Cold War–era defenses. Now fully restored the site is open Wednesday, Thursday, Friday, and the first Sunday of each month from 12:30 to 3:30 P.M.

At the far western end of this driving route lies the unique ***Marine Mammal Center,*** run by a private organization dedicated to rescuing and rehabilitating injured and ailing ocean animals—seals, sea lions, and the occasional whale or dolphin—then releasing them. The group patrols the area between San Luis Obispo and the Oregon border and treats marine mammals brought in for anything from skin diseases to injuries from boats. The center is open daily from 10:00 A.M. to 4:00 P.M.; for information call (415) 289–7330.

Trivia

It's said that Marin County has the world's highest concentration of hot tubs and BMWs.

San Francisco Bay is the largest natural harbor and estuary on the West Coast.

Another popular place is ***Point Bonita Lighthouse,*** perched like a sentinel at the peninsula's southern tip. You can drive part way out, then follow a trail along a wind-pummeled ridge, through a tunnel, and across a 120-foot-high bridge before reaching the light. Here you see the Golden Gate as you would if coming in from sea. The station still uses the original hand-ground French lens, installed after the first system (an army sergeant firing a cannon every half hour during foggy spells) failed. The lighthouse and trail are open Saturday, Sunday, and Monday from 12:30 to 3:30 P.M. but are subject to closure due to high wind. Check at the visitor center for information about guided tours.

The Wonderful Bay

I'm sitting here beside the little ferry dock at Tiburon in Marin County, marveling at my good fortune. It's December 31, and the weather is sunny and warm, almost balmy. Sailboats glide across the water, and seagulls flutter overhead. Except for a few cottony clouds, the sky is clear and the views superb: south across the bay to San Francisco, its larger avenues visible as they climb the city's hills. I scan the skyline 10 miles distant, spotting familiar landmarks like Coit Tower and the Transamerica Pyramid.

Glistening in the morning sun, the bay is sprinkled with sailboats and catamarans, rubber dinghies, and much larger vessels. I can see Alcatraz clearly off to the left, and Angel Island sits directly across narrow Raccoon Strait like a pocket-size Isle of Capri. (It's accessible by ferry on weekends from this same dock.) The ferry from San Francisco pulls in several times a day after a stop at Sausalito, and the ride back to the city takes just fifteen minutes.

The cute, upscale village of Tiburon (which means "shark" in Spanish) sits on a 4-mile-long peninsula crowded with expensive homes and clapboard-sheathed condominiums clinging to the hills. Tiburon faces south, which means great views and lots of sunshine, and I stop to partake of both blessings and a cappuccino at Sweden House Bakery on Main Street, one of several cafes with outdoor terraces. (Other popular spots are Sam's Anchor Cafe and Guaymas Restaurant.) I'm looking out on a small marina flush with craft belonging to the exclusive Corinthian Yacht Club.

Afterward I stroll along Main Street, which old-timers say hasn't changed much in decades, though most stores are now gift shops, galleries, and even a wine-tasting room for visitors. From here a pleasant promenade skirting the shore is alive with people walking dogs, inline-skating, or just lounging on benches and enjoying the views. But it's not crowded even on this holiday weekend.

At the far end of the promenade, I decide to stop for lunch at Caprice Restaurant overlooking the bay, and my jaw drops when I see the menu—and the prices. It's expensive, but I don't worry about such things today. After all, how many people are lucky enough to visit a place like this?

The Marin Headlands are a favorite with hikers. The Coastal Trail scrambles over spectacular shoreline and can be reached at the trailhead just west of Rodeo Lagoon. The 2-mile Tennessee Valley Trail may be the best for putting some distance between you and the parking lot.

Tennessee Valley was named for a shipwreck lying just offshore, a steamer called *The Tennessee,* which went down in 1853. The beach is quiet, and the warm, sheltered valley is great for walking. Nothing bigger than a bush is indigenous to the Headlands, and any trees you see were planted by the military, mostly as camouflage for artillery. But wildlife abounds, including the highest concentration of hawks on the Pacific Coast. From September through November bird-watchers flock to Hawk Hill as thousands of birds from various species of raptors (hawks and kestrels) stop here before hopping across the bay on thermals.

To reach the Marin Headlands, northbound drivers must take the Alexander Avenue exit from Highway 101; southbound should get off at the second Sausalito exit. Follow the signs to Conzelman Road or Fort Cronkhite to join the loop.

Among Marin's many popular sights are Muir Woods and Mount Tamalpais, and they are often jammed with camera-clicking visitors. Yet the north side of the mountain, the rainiest spot in the Bay Area, offers several small lakes little known even to residents.

Part of the twenty-acre ***Mount Tamalpais Watershed,*** these lakes (Bon Tempe, Lagunitas, Alpine, and Phoenix) are actually man-made reservoirs built between 1873 and 1954. The water is clear and clean, and there is some trout fishing but no swimming or boating. There are many easy trails around the lakes (get a map at the entrance) that wind through woods of oak, madrone, Douglas fir, and redwood. One steep trail at Alpine Lake leads to beautiful Cataract Falls, and many animals

Top Annual Events in the Bay Area

Hillsborough Antique Show, *San Mateo (mid-January)*

Golden Gate Kennel Club Dog Show, *Daly City (early February)*

Santa Clara Arts Fest *(early May)*

Sonoma-Marin Fair, *Petaluma (mid-July)*

Los Altos Arts and Wine Festival *(mid-July)*

TCI San Jose Jazz Festival *(early August)*

Victorian Days in the Park, *San Mateo (mid-August)*

Camel Races, *Benicia (late August)*

Chinatown Street Fest, *Oakland (late August)*

Fiesta de Merienda, *Angel Island State Park (mid-September)*

Suisun City Harbor Days Festival *(early October)*

Day of the Dead, *Oakland (November 1)*

Mountain Man Rendezvous, *Felton (mid-November)*

Lighted Yacht Parade, *Oakland (early December)*

Las Posadas, *San Jose (early December)*

Trivia

Mount Tamalpais State Park receives about 2.2 million visitors each year.

thrive in the area: deer, jackrabbits, squirrels, raccoons, bobcats, and birds such as red-tailed hawks.

To reach the Mount Tamalpais Watershed, drive north on Highway 101 to Sir Francis Drake Boulevard, then west to Fairfax. Take Bolinas–Fairfax Road south and turn left at Sky Oaks Road, leading to the

Best Factory Tours

Hundreds of thousands of people visit Bay Area factories each year, sampling everything from beer to banana splits and seeing how things get made, not to mention learning secrets like how they get those little messages into fortune cookies. Here's a list of the best tours around:

- *Bradbury & Bradbury, 940 Tyler Street, Studio 12, Benecia; (707) 746–1900. By appointment only Tuesday through Friday from 10:00 A.M. to 4:00 P.M. See how silkscreen wallpaper is designed and produced.*
- *Dreyer's Grand Ice Cream, 1250 Whipple Road, Union City; (510) 471–6622. Weekdays at 9:15 and 11:15 A.M. and 2:00 P.M.; $2.00 per person, first grade and older; reservations needed for guided tour through the ice-cream assembly lines and the warehouse/freezer. Free taste of fresh ice cream off the assembly line, and two scoops at the end of the tour.*
- *Fortune Cookie Factory, 261 Twelfth Street, Oakland; (510) 832–5552, Monday through Friday from 10:00 A.M. to 3:00 P.M.; $1.00 per person; reservations needed for groups of ten or more. See how a fortune cookie is made.*
- *Intel Museum, 2200 Mission College Boulevard, Santa Clara; (408) 765–0503. Open weekdays from 9:00 A.M. to 6:00 P.M.; Saturday from 10:00 A.M. to 5:00 P.M. Free, reservations not needed. Self-guided exhibit on the chip-manufacturing process and the history of the microprocessor; docent-guided tours available to groups by appointment.*
- *Marin French Cheese Factory, 7500 Red Hill Road, Petaluma; (800) 292–6001. Tours daily from 10:00 A.M. to 4:00 P.M. on the hour; free, reservations for groups of ten or more. See cheese-making and packing rooms, free tasting of Brie, Camembert, and the like.*
- *Mrs. Grossman's Paper Co., 3810 Cypress Drive, Petaluma; (707) 763–1700. Open weekdays, four tours a day; free, reservations needed. See how kids' stickers are made; free stickers are handed out.*
- *New United Motor Manufacturing, 45500 Fremont Boulevard, Fremont; (510) 770–4008. Tuesday throuh Friday from 10:00 A.M. to 1:00 P.M.; free 10 years and older, reservations needed. Guided tram ride through the only car-making plant on the West Coast.*

entrance. Open sunrise to sunset daily; $5.00 per vehicle. Call (415) 945–1455 for information.

Another pleasant side trip from the affluent town of Fairfax (go north 4 miles on Nicasio Valley Road) leads to the tiny village of ***Nicasio.*** Lying at the geographical center of Marin, early settlers tried to make it the county seat. But San Rafael prevailed, and the area remains rustic and unspoiled: grazing sheep and dairy farms, golf courses, and big, beautiful homes (George Lucas's Skywalker Ranch is nearby).

The village itself is like something from a pleasant daydream, with a little red schoolhouse, the white-steepled Our Lady of Loretto church, and a Little League baseball diamond in the old town square. Across the street Rancho Nicasio Restaurant has a big western-style bar and outdoor tables for a lazy lunch "far from the madding crowd."

Most visitors see a very different side of Marin County's split personality: yacht harbors, trendy restaurants, smart boutiques, and a profusion of BMWs. Sun-splashed Sausalito is quintessentially quaint, and most visitors are happy to shop, stroll, and eyeball the high-living locals. But Sausalito boasts a most unusual attraction that few people know about: the ***San Francisco Bay and Delta Model.***

Built by the Army Corps of Engineers to simulate bay conditions, this mass of concrete, water, wires, and gauges sprawls over a two-acre site inside an old World War II warehouse. That's right—two acres, and you'll only grasp how big the model is by walking around it and seeing things from a simulated height of 12,000 feet. Who says you have to climb a mountaintop for a great view!

Upon entering the building, you proceed up a ramp to view a new eleven-minute video, "The Story of San Francisco Bay," which clearly describes how the California Delta was formed by the interaction of salt and freshwater. Proceed to an impressive overview of the sprawling model (the size of two football fields), which re-creates 343 square miles of the bay on concrete slabs ingeniously formed to mimic the real landscape. But as you stroll the pathways crisscrossing the model, keep in mind that this is not an exact re-creation of familiar landmarks. It was designed almost half a century ago to find answers to complex hydrodynamic problems by monitoring the effects of tides, currents, geology, pollution, and a host of other natural and human factors, for example, by studying the delicate dynamics of water mixing in the narrow Carquinez Strait.

All this is possible because the model was built to scale with the real world; for example, the 350-foot-deep Golden Gate Channel is 3½ feet e model. Channels were carefully molded into concrete, and ce of the bottom corresponds closely to the real thing. Along es various types of land, from marsh to heavily urbanized, are in identifying colors.

The Author's Favorite Falling Waters

Perhaps the Bay Area's greatest secret is its hidden waterfalls, often seen along the trails of some great hikes. There's nothing like the sound of rushing water to drown out the cacophony of modern life, but in this area the falls come and go like wildflowers. Try to visit in winter or spring after any significant rainfall. Here's a personal list of the best:

Berry Creek Falls, *Big Basin State Park, Boulder Creek. Reached by a 4.7-mile hike (allow about six hours round-trip), this 70-foot cascade is enclosed in a redwood canyon and lush grotto of ferns and sorrel.*

Cataract Falls, *Mount Tamalpais State Park. Hike from the Laura Dell Trailhead about 2 miles to the falls, a long and dramatic series of cascades.*

Brooks Falls, *San Pedro Valley Park, Pacifica. A stunning 175-foot silver strand in three tiers tumbles down into a canyon. Take the Montara Mountain Trail.*

Silver Falls, *Big Basin State Park, Boulder Creek. A pristine cascade that fronts a hollowed-out cavern, just upstream from Berry Creek Falls.*

Castle Rock Falls, *Castle Rock State Park, Los Gatos. This 50-foot cataract is a powerful surge of white, pounding water. The trail to the viewing platform is about a mile long.*

Carson Falls, *Marin Water District, Fairfax. A series of pools and falls rushing over giant boulders and leading to a 40-foot silvery chute. The round-trip is 3 miles over easy terrain.*

Diablo Falls, *Mount Diablo State Park, Danville. Hidden on the mountain's north flank are two falls forming a combined 85-foot drop. Reached by a steep and difficult hike, 9 miles round-trip.*

Triple Falls, *Uvas County Park, Coyote (Santa Clara County). A series of three cascades, about 40 feet in all, hidden in the foothills. Reached by a 2.5-mile hike from the trailhead.*

Cascade Falls, *Elliot Nature Preserve, Fairfax. Though not high, these falls are set in near-perfect surroundings of moss-lined rocks; also easy to reach, only 2 miles round-trip.*

Murrieta Falls, *Sunol Regional Wilderness, Livermore. At 100 feet this is the Bay Area's highest waterfall, but reaching it requires a long and strenuous hike (11 miles round-trip) from the trailhead at Del Valle Regional Park.*

In the area represented, you see not only San Francisco Bay, but also San Pablo Bay, the Carquinez Strait, and the Sacramento/San Joaquin Delta. That's a lot of ground—and water—to cover. In fact, you might be amazed how big the Delta is, with its 700 miles of waterways, sloughs, and bays. And there are other surprises, such as the size of Oakland's inner harbor and the amount of the bay already filled in, about 80%.

To re-create actual conditions, 185,000 gallons of water are mixed with seventeen tons of salt and pumped into the model at a precise rate, pouring through the Golden Gate, swirling around Alcatraz and into the bay. In seven and a half minutes the simulated tide rises and falls, compared with six hours in real life, and a day passes in about fifteen minutes. A year lasts just three and a half days; that's one hundred times faster than in nature.

Why go to all this trouble, you ask? Well, the bay and delta are both extremely important *and* extremely delicate, and the model has provided valuable data used to evaluate oil and chemical spills, dredging, the impact of landfill, and to study the mixing of fresh with saltwater.

Until the year 2000 the model was used chiefly as a laboratory, but computer simulations have taken over that role. Now its purpose is educational, and many hands-on and interactive displays enhance that purpose. For instance, you can "Take the Water Challenge" by trying to allocate California's precious water supply to competing interests—agriculture, industry, and cities—as politicians have to do. There is an excellent self-guided audio tour available, which takes about thirty minutes to complete.

The Bay Model, at 2100 Bridgeway (accessed via Marinship Way), is open Tuesday through Saturday (also Sunday during summer) from 9:00 A.M. to 4:00 P.M. Call (415) 332–3871 for further information.

Angel Island sits a mile offshore from the affluent Marin town of Tiburon. Though the bay's largest island (about 740 acres), it is often ignored by visitors eager to see that neighboring isle of ill repute—Alcatraz. Yet Angel Island is easily reached by ferryboat from Marin County or San Francisco.

You won't see any cars on board—except for staff vehicles, they're not allowed on the island—but there will be cyclists with their bikes, hikers with backpacks, boys with fishing rods, and families lugging picnic baskets (sorry, no dogs). After a short trip the ferry arrives at Ayala Cove, named for Spanish explorer Juan Manuel de Ayala, whose ship, the *San Carlos,* first anchored here in August 1775. Ayala used the island as a base for mapping the bay and named it *isla de los angeles.*

Ayala Cove faces Raccoon Strait and Tiburon, only a mile distant. When the same spot served as a quarantine station for ships with infected crews, it was nicknamed Hospital Cove. Now, under more pleasant circumstances, a ranger's kiosk stands at the dock and provides information and maps.

You can visit ***Camp Reynolds,*** a military garrison built during the Civil War to guard against the unlikely prospect of Confederate ships slipping into the bay. With seventeen structures standing, this is the nation's largest collection of Civil War–era army buildings. Much later, Angel Island felt the shadow of its notorious neighbor. At "Alcatraz Gardens" prisoners from "The Rock" raised vegetables to supplement their meager diet.

One trail leads to North Garrison, the "Ellis Island of the West," which was an immigration station for the expected waves of Europeans after the Panama Canal opened. But they never came; instead, tens of thousands of Asians (mostly Chinese) were held and interrogated before being admitted. The station operated until 1940, then was used to process enemy prisoners during the war. One of the old barracks has been restored as a museum, open weekends only. Here you can visit the cramped, dingy quarters where new arrivals were held for questioning. Look for Chinese writing scratched on the walls, bitter poems composed by disillusioned immigrants. Translations are on display in the visitor center.

But all is not history on Angel Island. Thin strips of sand are perfect for beachcombing and sunbathing (but not for swimming in the ice-cold bay). With 13 miles of trails and fire roads threading across the landscape, hiking is excellent. The trek up the North Ridge Trail is especially noteworthy, weaving through cool groves and across meadows to the top of 781-foot Mount Livermore, where a grandstand view of sailboats on the bay awaits. Along the way you might spot some of the 200 or so resident deer. Although there are many good trails, the island's "main street" is a 4.8-mile-long perimeter road, which is very popular with bicyclists. (Bicycles can be rented on Angel Island or brought over by ferry.) Campsites are available on weekends but often are booked weeks in advance.

At present "the backyard island" is entirely a state park. For more information call (415) 435–1915. Ferry schedules vary depending on the season. For details call (415) 773–1188 (from San Francisco) or (415) 435–2131 (from Tiburon).

Straits and Bays

If you like islands—and have a taste for the unusual and exclusive—don't miss tiny ***East Brother Island,*** home to a bed-and-breakfast inn built right inside a working lighthouse. Four rocky islands occupy San Pablo Strait where San Francisco and San Pablo bays meet: the Sisters, near the Marin coast; and the Brothers, just west of Point San Pablo. They can be seen from the Richmond–San Rafael Bridge (I–580), which links Marin County and the East Bay.

West Brother Island is uninhabited except for a few seabirds and waterfowl. The old Lighthouse Service built a station on East Brother back in 1873, and it was deemed the "Riviera Station" by keepers because of its favorable location—sheltered from winds, storms, and fog. After automation the old building was nearly razed, until a conservation group stepped in and offered to transform it into a profit-making venture. Today, the West Coast's only bed-and-breakfast lighthouse has five rooms to let.

You don't have to stay at the inn to visit the island, however. Lighthouse buffs can grab a picnic lunch and take the day excursion (11:00 A.M. to 4:00 P.M.) from Point San Pablo Yacht Harbor May through September, Saturday only, $15 round trip per person). After a ten-minute ride, you'll spot the carpenter's Gothic-style cottage—with its fish-scale shingles, gingerbread trim, and picket fence—perched on a lump of land less than an acre in size.

Inside, the rooms are furnished with antiques and provided with those extra touches you won't find elsewhere, such as a set of earplugs at bedside in case the foghorn is in use. The inn is open Thursday through Sunday; overnight rates are on the expensive side but include transportation, historical tour, and gourmet meals. For further information call (510) 233–2385.

The Carquinez Strait is a deep channel between San Pablo Bay and Suisun Bay that, in turn, leads to the Sacramento–San Joaquin River Delta. A vital shipping lane since the days when paddle wheelers plied these waters, the strait retains some of that bucolic atmosphere. You get there by heading east toward Sacramento on I–80, then taking the Crockett exit just before crossing the Carquinez Bridge.

The town of ***Crockett*** is a collection of aging homes scampering up a hillside right in the shadow of the bridge. The huge redbrick C&H sugar refinery dominates the scene as it has for decades. Nearby sits the Crockett

Historical Museum, open Wednesday through Saturday from 10:00 A.M. to 3:00 P.M. (no admission fee), with exhibits recalling the days when this company town was the West Coast's major sugar-refining center.

From Crockett take the Carquinez Bridge (I–80) across the strait into Solano County, then continue east on I–780 to the town of ***Benicia.*** As you enter this dreamy community, it's hard to believe that it served for a year as California's state capital and stood ready to challenge San Francisco as the Bay Area's chief port. Founded in 1847 the town was more accessible to the interior and also boasted a better harbor and climate. But the dreams proved to be delusions.

The heart of Benicia is First Street, lined with antiques and crafts shops, restaurants, and boutiques. Stop by the Chamber of Commerce at number 601 for a map listing forty historic sites. Centerpiece of the collection is the ***Old State Capitol*** on West G Street. This redbrick, Georgian-style building had its brief moment of glory back in 1853, when Benicians convinced California's new legislature to reside here. Legend has it that the politicians' wives demanded the move to Sacramento thirteen months later

Old State Capitol, Benicia

because of Benicia's licentious reputation. Now you can peek inside and see original whale-oil lamps, quill pens, and brass cuspidors. It's open daily from 10:00 A.M. to 5:00 P.M. Admission charged.

Trivia

Benicia was named for the wife of General Mariano Vallejo, Spain's last Commandant General in California.

Another notable historic site is the first Masonic Temple in California (1850) at 110 West J Street, made from lumber shipped around Cape Horn. There are dozens of restored Victorians, with a specially fine collection on East D Street.

First Street begins (at Military Road) with a lovely little park and a white gazebo, then slopes gently toward the strait. Benicia is a great town for walking, and its main street lends itself to browsing in shops and short detours to the historical sights, such as the state's first Protestant church on West K Street.

Captain Blyther's Restaurant (123 First Street) occupies an old clapboard house that at one time served as a brothel. It stands near the newly restored train depot. From here it's a short walk to a pier poking out into Carquinez Strait, almost within handshaking distance of passing vessels. Once upon a time Benicia was a key railroad crossing for the two largest train ferries ever built. Each carried thirty-six cars and two locomotives and crossed the strait to Port Costa from 1879 to 1930.

Benicia also attracts visitors with a Waterfront Trail (at the foot of Twelfth Street) along Southhampton Bay and a new marina and village just east of First Street. Farther along are a thriving port, where tens of thousands of Japanese autos are unloaded each year, and a large oil refinery, but neither is close enough to detract from the historic center.

In 1851 the U.S. Army built an important arsenal here that stored weapons and ammunition for troops fighting from the Indian campaigns through the Korean War. You can still visit the clock tower, commander's home, guardhouse, cemetery, and ***Camel Barns.*** These date from the army's ill-fated camel corps, seventy-seven beasts of burden brought from the Middle East in 1855 for use in the arid Southwest. One barn now houses the Benicia Historical Museum, open Wednesday through Sunday from 1:00 to 4:00 P.M. For information about tours call (707) 745–5435.

Benicia is renowned for its large artists' colony, dedicated to crafts such as glassblowing as well as the fine arts. Many artists have studios in former warehouses of the Arsenal and hold an open house in May. There is also an abundance of antiques stores and an annual fair in August. For further information contact the Benicia Chamber of Commerce at (707) 745–2120.

Contra Costa County

Cross Carquinez Strait again on the Benicia-Martinez Bridge (I–680) and enter little-visited Contra Costa County. Towns such as Concord, Walnut Creek, and Danville are known as long on subdivisions and shopping malls and short on visitor attractions. Yet there are several excellent regional and state parks that only locals seem to know about.

Everyone has heard of the great California Gold Rush, that crazy stampede for riches that hurled a sleepy territory onto a dazzling path of fame and fortune. But what about the great coal rush of the 1860s, which led to decades of mining "black diamonds"?

A few years after the glittering stuff turned up in the Sierra foothills, California's largest known coal deposit was opened for mining on the northern slope of Mount Diablo. From these foothills a cluster of mines disgorged $20 million worth of coal, about four million tons in all.

Square-jawed miners from around the world joined Americans for a life of hard work and long hours, occasionally relieved by a holiday or social event. Next to the mines small, dust-choked settlements—like Nortonville and Somersville—sprouted, thrived, then wilted when mining ceased after the turn of the twentieth century. There was a comeback of sorts during the 1920s and 1930s with the mining of silica sand.

This mining legacy lives on at ***Black Diamond Mines Regional Preserve*** south of Antioch, where about 4,000 acres have been carved out of the grassland and smoothly contoured foothills. Although most mines were long ago abandoned and sealed over, there is still plenty of evidence of the backbreaking life.

Black Diamond offers the chance to explore 40 miles of trails. As you wander the tracks, you'll see reminders from the mining days. Especially noteworthy is historic Rose Hill Cemetery, whose chipped and broken gravestones tell sad tales (some in Welsh) of the harsh lives of miners and their families, who died from epidemics, childbirth, mining accidents, or, if they were fortunate, from natural causes.

Miles of trails crisscrossing the preserve go past a number of abandoned mines, one of which has been converted into an underground museum. Open weekends, March through November from 10:00 A.M. to 4:30 P.M., the Greathouse Visitor Center displays photographs and artifacts from the period. Hundreds of feet of old mining tunnels are open for exploration, but bring a flashlight!

Black Diamond Mines Regional Preserve is open daily, from 8:00 A.M. to dusk; admission is $4.00 per car. To reach it take State Highway 4 to Antioch and exit at Somersville Road; then go 3 miles south. For information about naturalist programs, call (925) 757–2620.

Contra Costa is also home to the Bay Area's most majestic lookout point. A trip to the top of 3,849-foot ***Mount Diablo*** will have you singing "On a clear day you can see forever," especially if it really is a clear day. The view from the summit takes in 20,000 square miles in parts of more than thirty California counties. Because few other mountains lie nearby, Diablo stands like a lofty island amid the surrounding flatland. But one word of warning: Wait for a windy day or right after a storm, or you may find yourself peering down into thick layers of haze.

Local Indians considered Diablo a place of power, the only point not submerged by a primordial flood of tribal legend. The mountain was the center of the universe, home of the gods and a magical place to be respected—and feared. Presently the only thing to fear is the spine-jangling drive up a tortuous road.

As you ascend, you'll notice the wide range in vegetation caused by sharp differences in temperature, rainfall, and wind exposure. Mountain landscapes go from shady cottonwood canyons to open woodlands, erosion-carved gullies to wind-sharpened crags.

Mount Diablo State Park covers an 18,000-acre chunk of the mountain and is reached via Walnut Creek or Danville by one of two separate entrances. Where these roads join, at about 2,200 feet, sits a ranger station; stop for a detailed map of the hiking trails. From here you make the final ascent of 4.5 miles to the summit, where you'll find an observation tower that may inspire you to song, as you look out on the delta and Wine Country, the bay and San Francisco, Mount Tamalpais in Marin, and sometimes all the way to Lassen Peak in the Cascade Range.

Once you've tired of gaping, the trails beckon. In an hour's walk you can pass from grassland to bay-scented canyons strewn with wildflowers like the endemic globe lily. High above soar golden eagles, red-tailed hawks, and horned larks.

Mount Diablo State Park is open daily from 8:00 A.M. to sunset year-round; for more information call (925) 837–2525. There is a $5.00 day-use fee charged per vehicle. Camping is available.

The Mount Diablo area is a great place for horse lovers as well. You can rent a horse for solo riding or join a guided tour with Western Trail Ride Adventures; call (925) 946–1475. Summit Ranch in Alamo spreads over thirty-five acres near the mountain and is home to about 120 horses of twenty different breeds being boarded or trained. Visitors are welcome to see the facilities at 100 Summit Ranch Road, open daily from 8:00 A.M. to 6:00 P.M. Call (925) 945–0267 for directions from I–680.

The East Bay

What has come to be known as the East Bay lies directly across the water from San Francisco and is normally reached via the Bay Bridge or BART (Bay Area Rapid Transit). Along a narrow strip of land between the hills and the bay lie a string of communities with widely differing appeal. Most travelers concentrate on two: Oakland, with one of the world's largest ports; and Berkeley, the perennial home of excellence and eccentricity.

As you may have discovered already, wineries are a dime a dozen in Northern California. If you grow weary of the grape, you should weave over to the ***Takara Sake Brewery*** in Berkeley for a taste of the famous Japanese drink: "Happiness you can pour," as the company's motto says. Takara has been making sake—rice wine—in Kyoto for more than seventy years, and the brewery here now produces America's number one selling brand—Sho Chiku Bai.

Trivia

Oakland airport was the starting point for Amelia Earhart's final flight.

You will enter a serene, wood-paneled tasting room bathed in subtle light. Japanese poems and woodblock prints decorate the walls, shoji screens cover the windows, and bright lanterns hang from the ceiling. At a long bar you can imbibe seven kinds of sake, filtered or with rice residue, and three brands of sweet plum wine.

The making of sake is an ancient art. Early records show that the first batch was created more than 2,000 years ago. Techniques at the time were on the primitive side; fermentation was induced by villagers chewing rice and spitting the resulting wad into a wooden tub. Yet sake was once reserved for only the most sacred events, and the *toji* ("sake master") was revered as an artist.

Today the brewery tries to combine the wisdom of the *toji* with modern technology. All the rice used is grown in California's Central Valley, then milled and polished, soaked, and steamed. Next the rice is seeded with a special culture to make *koji,* which is combined with more rice, yeast, and water and allowed to ferment for about twenty-five days. After several filterings, the raw sake is pasteurized and aged for six months.

Many people believe sake hits you like the kick of a Japanese mule, but the drink contains only 16 percent alcohol, about the same as wine. But wine it is definitely not.

The Takara Sake Brewery, at 708 Addison Street in Berkeley (just off University Street near I–80), is open daily from noon to 6:00 P.M. Call (510) 540–8250 for information about group visits.

You could spend days visiting the University of California and its famous museums and libraries. One lesser known Berkeley sight lies south of the campus: the ***Judah L. Magnes Museum.*** Named for an Oakland rabbi who helped found the Hebrew University in Israel, this was the first Jewish museum in the western United States and is now the nation's third largest of its kind.

The collection is housed in a spacious three-story villa in a fashionable Berkeley neighborhood. In addition to a permanent collection, there are special exhibitions that change every three months, a historical archives and research library, and a rare book and manuscript collection. All bring out the same point—the universality of Jewish culture, with common threads stretching from biblical times to the present day. Imaginative exhibits reflect the vast scope of Judaic history and culture, whether in an embroidered velvet wedding dress from Turkey, a Persian illuminated manuscript, or an amber necklace from Yemen. Every object has a story. Take the gilded wood carving used by the Jews of Cochin, India; it served as an ark for the sacred Torah, the basic canon of the Jewish Scripture.

The permanent collection concentrates on textiles and ceremonial objects such as Hanukkah lamps made from pewter, bronze, silver, and stone; a large collection of Torah binders; framed *ketubbahs*—decorative calligraphic wedding contracts; and objects used at circumcisions. The rare book and manuscript library houses outstanding works by Jewish typographers and book designers. The manuscript collection of more than 5,000 items includes personal papers of such prominent individuals as Albert Einstein. On the third floor the Western Jewish History Archives is a research library dedicated to the role of Jews in the American West and has a fine collection of books, newspapers, and oral histories. A recent exhibition, "Hidden in the Walls," featured artifacts recovered from an early San Francisco synagogue.

The Judah L. Magnes Museum, at 2911 Russell Street in Berkeley, is open free of charge from 10:00 A.M. to 4:00 P.M., Sunday through Thursday; closed holidays. For information about current exhibits, call (510) 549–6950.

Trivia

Oakland is one of the few cities that can boast a natural saltwater lake at the core of its downtown. Lake Merritt is the largest saltwater body within a U.S. city.

Looking up the street from the museum, you'll see one of a handful of legendary California resort hotels—the Claremont. It's a big, white wedding cake of a place, with soaring towers, a steeply sloped roof, and dozens of gables, set amid twenty acres of palm trees, roses, swimming pools, and tennis courts.

Straddling the border between Berkeley and Oakland, high in the hills, the ***Claremont Resort Hotel*** has been a Bay Area landmark since its completion in 1915. Lots of mystique surrounds the old girl, like the story of how Frank Havens won the estate in a checkers game from millionaire miner Borax Smith at Oakland's Athenian Club. The old Claremont reached a zenith of popularity in the 1930s and 1940s with radio broadcasts from "High Atop the Hill" and big band dances in the Garden Room. (Lawrence Welk made his West Coast debut here.)

Each room is unique because of the building's curved shape: Some rooms have three walls, others five, and one suite boasts its own private sauna. But you don't have to stay there to enjoy it; take a stroll around the gardens or partake of the stirring views from the cocktail lounge. The hotel features a European-style spa, with a gym, weight room, whirlpool, and steam rooms. You can even get a "loofah scrub," warm almond or avocado oil blended with sea salt and applied to the body to remove dead skin. Now that's what you call luxury service!

The Claremont Resort Hotel is located at Ashby and Domingo Avenues in Oakland; for information call (510) 843–3000.

Another East Bay landmark clutching the hills is the ***Oakland Temple,*** one of just fifteen such sanctuaries worldwide run by the Church of Jesus Christ of Latter Day Saints, better known as the Mormons. This majestic structure stands out like a divine beacon, especially when illuminated by floodlights at night.

The design, contemporary with a slight oriental motif, features an exterior faced with Sierra white granite and topped with several pinnacle-like towers decorated with gold and blue mosaics. Two large sculptured panels grace the exterior. One depicts Christ in Palestine; the other shows him with the Indians of America shortly after his resurrection, an event accepted as fact by Mormons.

After pondering the temple's unusual design, outdoor fountains, pools, and palm-lined gardens, you can enter the visitor center for some background on the building and the church itself. Using a series of panels, the guide explains the story of how the angel Moroni visited Joseph Smith and delivered the Book of Mormon. Only church members can enter the temple, but visitors see a film showing the interior—peaceful and lily white, the same color worn by the faithful.

After the presentation your guide will escort you to the terraced gardens, a spectacular spot overlooking most of the Bay Area, tended impeccably by seven full-time gardeners.

The Visitors Center at the Oakland Temple, 4766 Lincoln Avenue, is open without charge daily from 9:00 A.M. to 9:00 P.M. There is also a genealogical library open Tuesday through Friday to the general public; for information call (510) 531–1475.

Trivia

Writer Jack London ran for mayor of Oakland on the Socialist ticket.

Another local landmark is the ***Paramount Theatre of the Arts,*** a former movie palace of the grand old style whose glamour refuses to fade. Built in 1931, it is an outstanding example of art deco architecture and decor, including carved walls of faux gold and softly lit ceilings. Guided tours (Saturday at 10:00 A.M.) provide a complete view of the 3,000-seat theater, which hosts a full schedule of musical and theatrical events, from Willie Nelson to Vladimir Horowitz. The Paramount Theatre is located in downtown Oakland at 2025 Broadway; for current program information call (510) 893–2300.

Trivia

"The Paramount Theatre is the prime example of the most exquisite restoration of a movie palace in the entire world."

—Bob Dorian, former AMC host

By all means take in Oakland's intriguing trio of major attractions: Jack London Square, Lake Merritt, and the Oakland Museum. But try to squeeze in a short stop at the ***Swans Housewives Marketplace*** downtown, a cavernous warehouse filled with small stands and shops selling everything that remotely resembles food. An Oakland institution for ninety years, the market is *the* place to find what no other store chooses—or dares—to carry: beef chitterlings and pork stomach, oxtail and baby goat, buffalo fish and fresh blood by the pint. If you're partial to pigs, you can find ears, snouts, tails, heads, and feet, with or without skin. Raccoon has been known to turn up from time to time.

But all is not bizarre at the Swans Housewives Marketplace. As you wander amid shouting shopkeepers and hard-bargaining locals, you start to see other delights: yams the size of footballs, fresh ginger, footlong plantains, slabs of bacon with the rind still on, jars of spices and herbs like fresh-ground cardamom, and barrels of smoked herring. It's the kind of place that will make you swear off processed food for the real stuff—or make you a vegetarian.

Swans Housewives Marketplace, at Ninth and Clay Streets, is open daily from 8:00 A.M. to 7:00 P.M. For information call (510) 832-9078.

As you continue south along I–880 through the East Bay, you may cringe at the endless urban development, the result of nearly continuous waves of settlers since 1850. What most people don't realize is that nearly a third of San Francisco Bay and four-fifths of its salt marshes have disappeared as a result of ceaseless filling and diking. What took 15,000 years to create has been destroyed in 150.

Even so, the bay still claims the West's largest marsh habitat, as well as the nation's largest urban wildlife refuge—23,000 acres in all. But the ***San Francisco Bay National Wildlife Refuge*** in Fremont remains underused and little known, even by locals. One reason for the lack of excitement is that the humble salt marsh was long regarded as a wasteland. It was the kind of place to be drained or diked if possible, but never visited or enjoyed, much less thought of as a valuable natural resource.

First-time visitors still find silence and not much scenery, a broad, flat, blackish-green expanse cut by a channel and dotted with salt ponds. But if you stop to listen, you will hear the tide trickling through the marsh grasses and a symphony of birdcalls. And if you pick up a handful of bay mud and study it, you'll find living creatures in that seemingly lifeless clump in your hand.

Trivia

More sourdough bread is produced in Oakland than in any other city in the world.

The refuge features a visitor center describing the habitat. Subject to the constant tidal action of intermingling fresh and saltwater, marshes contain no trees, yet teem with vegetation. Among the thirty main plant species, cord grass, salt grass, and pickleweed figure prominently. Within the refuge's jigsaw border you also see ponds, mudflats, and open water, providing a home to 250 bird species. This is a vital stop on the Pacific Flyway, and in fall tens of thousands of shorebirds rest along the lapping waters of the bay. Egrets, ducks, sandpipers, and herons are commonly seen.

About 30 miles of nature trails cross the refuge, among them the Tidelands Trail, which starts on high ground and descends to sea level, crossing two footbridges in the process. Within this one refuge, careful observers will glimpse the delicate chain of life from one-celled forms to mammals. Fish, crabs, and shrimp begin their lives in the estuary, and seals give birth on its protected banks. Soon you'll realize that this "wasteland" forms a productive living community.

Located at the east end of the Dumbarton Bridge, the San Francisco Bay National Wildlife Refuge is open for free daily from 7:00 A.M. to sunset. (Visitor center is closed Sunday and Monday.) Guided walks are conducted on weekends; for further information call (510) 792–0222.

If you follow Highway 84 from the Dumbarton Bridge up through Fremont, you will eventually reach an unusual corner of the East Bay. Before there was a Hollywood, there was ***Niles,*** the short-lived movie-making capital of California. On the side of a hill overlooking town, large white letters spell out NILES, just like that other place.

This evocative town at the mouth of Alameda Creek got started as a flour mill in 1842. The community was known as Vallejo Mills for more than twenty years, until the influential Western Pacific railroad renamed it after a company bigshot. Niles was an important link in the rail network between the Bay Area and Sacramento, and from there to the rest of the nation.

Essanay Film Studios started in 1912 and ran the show from offices at First and G Streets, producing one and two reelers starring Wallace Beery and Ben Turpin. Everyone thought the location ideal for making westerns because of the old frontier houses and the canyon's creek and forests. More than 450 movies were filmed here, including *The Tramp* with Charlie Chaplin. But fate and the film industry would shift south to a quiet district of Los Angeles, leaving Niles with only memories of what might have been.

Today, Niles still has a Wild West feel, with false-front buildings lining the main street on one side. Antiques shops abound, as do bare-knuckle bars like Joe's Corner, formerly owned by a local character named Bronco Billy, according to legend. There are many interesting shops to peruse, selling everything from Indian art to incense.

Alameda Creek slices through the hills behind Niles and forms 6-mile-long Niles Canyon, blessed with some of the area's most rugged and beautiful scenery. Along Niles Canyon Road you'll see rolling hills, grazing cattle, steep slopes, and idyllic places to stop for a picnic or to fish. The town of Sunol lies at the canyon's far end.

Nearby is a most unusual sight, the ***Sunol Water Temple.*** This neoclassical monument features fluted columns, a dome painted with exotic figures, and noble inscriptions chiseled in stone. Designed by famed architect Willis Polk, it pays tribute to a system that brings water all the way from the Sierra Nevada. To reach the temple, follow Niles Canyon Road until you see the sign for I–680, then take an immediate right through the gates. It's open weekdays only from 7:30 A.M. to 4:30 P.M.

The Peninsula

The San Francisco Peninsula is an arm of land south of the city, split by the coastal mountains into two distinct regions. The bay side has the airport, light industry, and a string of small towns that have melded into an uninterrupted suburban sprawl. Peninsula life is comfortably well-off (very comfortably in posh Hillsborough and Atherton) without the trendiness of Marin County. West of the mountains, the peninsula's ocean side (covered in the South Coast chapter) marches to the beat of a different drummer—a world of farms and fishing far removed from the Bay Area's hectic pace. The Peninsula extends south as far as Palo Alto, and beyond lies the Santa Clara Valley, or Silicon Valley, as it has come to be known.

Jets soar overhead, and all around humans have taken over the once pristine bay. Yet the ***Coyote Point Museum for Environmental Education*** tries to make people aware of the complex ecosystem disrupted in the process. The museum inhabits a spectacular site along the shore just south of San Francisco International Airport in San Mateo.

Outside are various "wildlife habitats," a kind of minizoo for animals formerly abundant in the area: bobcats and raccoons, scaly snakes and playful river otters, badgers and tree frogs. A walk-through aviary, with a huge tentlike net to keep the birds from escaping, is home to long-billed herons, owls, scavengers like turkey vultures, and a watchful golden eagle peering down on visitors from its perch.

Inside, the museum boasts an impressive architectural design of ascending ramps, lofty beamed ceilings, and redwood paneling. (How many trees were cut down for this, one wonders.) Exhibits stress man's intrusive role in the environment, which is based on a delicate balance between the many species sharing our planet. The message is clear: There are just too many people. But humans are not alone in greedy consumption; an eye-catching pyramid of ersatz dead animals (stuffed snakes, rats, etc.) demonstrates how just one hawk will eat about 1,200 other creatures in a year, which is something not even the most voracious human can manage.

Other interesting exhibits include the cranium of a giant sperm whale and a hive cutaway to show thousands of bees at work producing honey (the queen is marked by a green dot). You can listen to the hum of their wings, in the original key of E when the bees are tired and A when they speed up!

The Coyote Point Museum, 1651 Coyote Point Drive, San Mateo (650–342–7755), is open Tuesday through Saturday from 10:00 A.M. to 5:00 P.M. and from noon on Sunday. Admission is charged.

The ***Hiller Aviation Museum*** in San Carlos is dedicated to humanity's dream of flight, as well as one man's stunning achievements in the field. Stanley Hiller, Jr., was only eighteen when he built his first successful helicopter, the XH-44 (on display), and he went on to found Hiller Aircraft Corporation in the Bay Area. Over the years he became involved in all sorts of interesting projects, like a one-man flying platform (used in a James Bond film) and the 290-pound collapsible Rotorcycle. Small enough when folded to carry in a pod under an aircraft's wing, it could become a full-sized helicopter in a matter of minutes.

Last of the Yana Indians

Ishi, the last known Stone Age survivor in North America and the last wild American Indian, is entombed in Olivet Memorial Park in Colma, just south of San Francisco. His story is told in a famous book, Ishi in Two Worlds, *by Theodora Kroeber.*

Ishi was first glimpsed in 1911 hiding near Oroville and was taken into custody. Anthropologists soon learned of his existence, and he was taken to live in a San Francisco museum, from the most primitive of existences to a place of clocks and calendars, money and newspapers. But Ishi chose to stay on as janitor rather than go to a reservation, and he lived happily in the museum until his death in 1916. He was cremated along with a bow and arrows, a basket of acorn meal, and other personal items, and the ashes were placed in a black clay urn inscribed "Ishi, the last Yana Indian, 1916."

Because land was so expensive in the city, Colma in San Mateo County became the burial place for most San Franciscans. At present there are seventeen cemeteries here with the grave sites of historical personages such as Wyatt Earp (Hills of Eternity) and a lineup of millionaire tycoons: Crocker, Flood, Spreckels, and Hearst (all at Cypress Lawn Memorial Park). To learn more about visiting famous grave sites, contact the Colma Historical Association at (650) 757–1676 or stop at the museum at 1500 Hillside Boulevard, Colma.

If you're in need of a drink after a day of cemetery hopping, drop by Old Molloy's Tavern, a former 1920s speakeasy, at 1655 Old Mission Road, Colma.

Mr. Hiller was also the driving force behind this fine museum, which is like a mini-Smithsonian in layout and quality of exhibits. Greeting visitors is the whalelike Avitor, which made its first flight in 1869—by which time only one Wright brother had been born—right up the peninsula near San Francisco. This was the very first motor-powered, unmanned plane in the world, designed and built by an Englishman. The Hiller collection, mostly original restored aircraft, contains many other aviation landmarks: first controlled glider, first experimental wind tunnel, first plane to fly from the Pacific to the Atlantic (across the Isthmus of Panama in 1913), and first takeoff and landing from a ship (the Curtiss Pusher in 1911). The Condor robotic spy plane, fully automated and capable of flying at 67,000 feet, cost $300 million to create and made a grand total of eight flights before being abandoned by the government. The only surviving example of the massive plane, with a wingspan of 201 feet, lords over the entire collection.

One of the collection's rarest pieces is the Gonzales plane, designed by two fifteen-year-old brothers in San Francisco. Indeed, it seems that inventive prodigies have always been attracted to airplanes and the dream of flying higher and faster than before. Among the most enthusiastic visitors to the museum are groups of young schoolchildren, who wander awestruck among the aircraft and may well design a plane of their own at some future date.

The Hiller Aviation Museum is located next to San Carlos Airport at 601 Skyway Road (take the Redwood Shores exit off Highway 101). Open daily from 10:00 A.M. to 5:00 P.M.; admission charged. For information call (650) 654–0200.

While on the Peninsula, take a trip south to Palo Alto to visit "The Farm." At one time a trotting-horse ranch in the middle of nowhere, ***Stanford University*** has a beautiful, sun-drenched campus filled with palm trees and Romanesque-style buildings of sandstone and red-tile roofs. Getting there involves taking Highway 101 south to the University Avenue exit and heading west until it becomes Palm Drive.

A visitor information center in Memorial Hall is open daily from 9:00 A.M. to 5:00 P.M with tours available. Call (650) 723–2560 for schedules. An outstanding overview is available from the fourteenth-story platform of nearby Hoover Tower.

One highlight is ***Memorial Church,*** which dominates a central courtyard called the Inner Quad. Outstanding features are the luminous stained-glass windows and a mosaic reproduction of Cosimo Rosselli's

Last Supper fresco behind the altar. Supposedly, Mrs. Stanford received papal permission to have it copied. Master stonecutters carved the inscriptions in the transepts using ancient religious symbols. The church is open from 8:00 A.M. to 5:00 P.M. weekdays and from 10:00 A.M. to 6:00 P.M. on weekends. (Free tours Friday at 2:00 P.M.)

The university's sterling visitor attraction may be the ***B. Gerald Cantor Sculpture Garden.*** Here, twenty works by Auguste Rodin reside in a formal outdoor setting. Counting some 160 pieces housed inside the adjacent museum (the Cantor Center for the Visual Arts), Stanford now has the world's second-largest collection of Rodin sculpture, surpassed only by the Musée Rodin in Paris, although most works here were cast after the artist's death.

Quarks and Charms

A century ago scientists believed that the eternal and indestructible atom was the smallest thing in nature. Then the nucleus was discovered: ten thousand times smaller than an atom and composed of neutrons and protons surrounded by whizzing electrons. Surely that was the ultimate building block, it was thought. Not for particle physicists. At the Stanford Linear Accelerator Center near the famous university, top scientists (with 150 Ph.D.s among them) struggle to unlock the ultimate secrets of the universe.

The linear accelerator here is like a giant electron microscope in allowing physicists to see particles smaller than light waves—except that this "microscope" is a 2-mile-long copper tube buried 30 feet underground in a tunnel. Inside this tube tiny particles are hurtled toward one another at nearly the speed of light, the collisions producing energy and even smaller particles. Electrons and positrons "surf" along waves of electromagnetic radiation created by giant microwave power generators 600 times more powerful than your average oven. The accelerator can emit electron beams with energy up to fifty billion volts, which makes for one heck of a power bill!

Extremely dense subatomic particles called quarks and leptons, each with its own name and "flavor" (mass and electrical charge) are now considered the smallest things in nature. Physicists here have discovered the psi *(a new quark called a "charm") and the* tau *(an exotic lepton). But all this is no laughing matter. The discoverers of those particles were rewarded with the Nobel prize in physics. Meanwhile the search for even smaller particles goes on.*

The Visitor Center of the Stanford Linear Accelerator is open weekdays from 8:00 A.M. to 5:00 P.M., and free tours take about two hours; reservations required. Contact the Public Affairs Office at (650) 926–2204 for schedules.

Crowning the outdoor display is *The Gates of Hell*—whimsical 21-foot-tall bronze doors considered the sculptor's greatest public work. Rodin toiled for two decades on this creation of 180 writhing figures, which represents a hell of unfulfilled dreams and passions. Another major work is titled *The Burghers of Calais.*

The sculpture garden is open continuously, with tours offered on Saturday at 11:00 A.M. and Sunday at 3:00 P.M. Call (650) 723–4177 for details.

Trivia

- *The San Francisco Peninsula is home to a couple of oddball collections: the American Antique Slot Machine Museum (San Bruno) and the Museum of Pez Memorabilia (Burlingame).*
- *The Pulgas Water Temple in Woodside, modeled after temples of ancient Greece, celebrates the arrival of San Francisco's drinking water from the Sierra Nevada.*
- *Hillsdale Shopping Center in San Mateo opened in 1954 as the country's first mall-style shopping complex, "one-stop city shopping."*

Driving Highway 101 gives the impression that the Peninsula is not much more than an endless sprawl of suburbia, but taking I–280 to the west presents a much different picture—wooded hills, lakes, and splendid vistas. An even more scenic route follows ***Skyline Boulevard*** (Highway 35), a two-lane road about 2,200 feet above sea level hugging the spiny backbone of the Santa Cruz Mountains. Along the route you are treated to pleasant, wooded countryside and those great views again, this time of both the Bay Area and the Pacific.

You can reach Skyline Boulevard via Highway 92 from San Mateo, passing Crystal Springs Reservoir, which contains San Francisco's main water supply and is built atop the San Andreas Fault. Don't let the word *boulevard* fool you; this 23-mile scenic route is really a well-maintained country road. The sights are pleasant if not spectacular: Christmas tree farms, nurseries growing rhododendrons, a few private homes, parks, and open-space preserves laced with hiking trails and picnic areas.

Purisima Creek Redwoods Preserve (4.5 miles south of the Highway 92 junction) takes in 2,500 acres of the big trees and surrounding watershed. Views of the coast are exceptional, and there are some great footpaths, such as Soda Gulch Trail.

Two excellent county parks are ***Huddart,*** just below Skyline at King's Mountain Road, with nature trails and limited facilities, and even less-known ***Wunderlich,*** near the junction of Woodside Road, which is popular with equestrians. The two are linked by the Bay Ridge Trail. ***Portola State Park*** off Alpine Road offers camping and impressive stands of redwoods, and ***Windy Hill Preserve*** has two good trails and allows dogs.

The most unusual of the parks is ***Los Trancos State Preserve,*** located about 1.5 miles off Skyline Boulevard along Page Mill Road. Here you can follow the San Andreas Fault Trail and study the seismic history of the past two million years. A self-guided tour along the path includes fourteen marked stops along the one-third-mile-wide fault, pointing out earthquake evidence such as sag ponds, benches, and scarps, as well as a spot where a fence jumped 6 feet during the 1906 temblor. (The Pacific Plate normally moves about 1 inch per year.) You'll also see boulders that at one time lay 23 miles to the southeast, according to geologists. The most striking view is from a high point near the parking lot, from which you can trace the fault by eye all the way to San Francisco. Los Trancos is open daily from dawn to dusk.

Farther along Skyline Boulevard lies Long Ridge Preserve, featuring a beautiful little pond hidden in a stream-cut canyon. The park covers almost 1,000 acres, with trails in a variety of arboreal settings and views of Big Basin, Butano Ridge, and Devils Canyon.

Santa Clara Valley

Skyline Boulevard intersects Highway 9 at the Saratoga Gap, marking the end of the scenic driving route. You can turn right and proceed to Santa Cruz, passing Big Basin State Park and the old railroad town of Felton. Stay on Highway 35 and continue 11 winding miles to I–880 and the more direct route to Santa Cruz and San Jose. Or turn left on Highway 9 and drive to the town of Saratoga in the Santa Clara Valley, home to a main street of quaint shops and quality restaurants, plus little-known ***Hakone Gardens*** (7 miles from Highway 35).

This lushly planted slice of the Orient, spread over sixteen acres of gentle hills, is considered the most authentic example of Japanese gardens in America. Four different gardens display the art form—harmonious placement of plants, rocks, and water—and there are several discreet structures built without nails, including a cultural center modeled on a tea merchant's house.

Open daily to the public, Hakone Gardens (21000 Big Basin Way) also provides docent tours and tea service for groups. It's open from 10:00 A.M. to 5:00 P.M. No admission charged, but there is a $7.00 parking fee. Call (408) 741–4994 for information.

The Santa Clara Valley is justly famous for its high-tech industry and also boasts a few well-publicized attractions, such as the Tech Museum of

Innovation, Great America amusement park, and the Winchester Mystery House. Although receiving its fair share of visitors, San Jose's excellent ***Rosicrucian Egyptian Museum*** deserves more attention. Dedicated to the allure and romance of ancient Egypt, the museum is just one building in a complex that forms the American Grand Lodge of the Rosicrucian Order. This nonsectarian, fraternal group explores subjects such as occult knowledge from antiquity and expanding human potential.

Covering an entire square block, the grounds are an oasis of fountains, palm trees, a garden growing papyrus, hieroglyphics-covered shrines, stone sphinxes, and a carved obelisk. Buildings seem to have been transported from the banks of the Nile. The sand-colored administration building is a copy of the great temple of Medinet Habu in upper Egypt, and the planetarium was built to resemble a Moorish castle in North Africa. The shrine to Pharoah Akhnaton is a replica of the original in Luxor, and the temple of Amon at Karnak was inspiration for the museum itself.

A double line of kneeling rams flanks the entry walkway. Between them stands an 8-foot stone statue of Taurt, a hippopotamus symbolizing fertility. Entering through enormous bronze doors, you lift the veil of time as you pass into evocative galleries, where the distant past seems alive. The museum conveys an almost childlike enthusiasm for the exotic and strange with its extensive collection of mummies—not just humans but also fish, falcons, cats, snakes, and a crocodile.

There's also a rare mummy of a baboon from Sakkara, where sacred temple animals were entombed, a set of X rays of a mummy inside its sarcophagus, and canopic jars, in which the deceased's vital organs were placed for the trip to the next world. (The brain was discarded.) The most remarkable mummy is ***Usermontu,*** a priest whose body lies stretched out with folded arms and is eerily preserved right down to the teeth and fingernails. His metal leg pin is believed to be one of the first known examples of knee surgery.

There are enough exhibits to fascinate for hours: a skillfully re-created rock tomb with inscriptions and false doorways copied exactly from the famous tombs of Beni Hasan; small carved figures called *Ushabti,* which acted as servants of the departed; and personal collections of toys, jewelry, papyrus scrolls, and musical instruments. One of the most prized pieces is a black granite statue of Cleopatra, still beautiful after all these years.

The Rosicrucian Egyptian Museum, at Park and Naglee Avenues in San

Rosicrucian Egyptian Museum

Jose, is open daily except Monday from 10:00 A.M. to 5:00 P.M.; admission charged. For information call (408) 947–3636.

A block away lies the San Jose Municipal Rose Garden, five acres featuring 3,500 rose shrubs from nearly 200 varieties. A new flush of roses blooms every six to eight weeks. Located at Naglee and Dana Avenues, the garden is open daily from 8:00 A.M. to sunset; no admission charged.

At 4,200 feet ***Mount Hamilton*** dominates the Santa Clara Valley, and it can be reached via Highway 130 off Alum Rock Road. After 19 miles and a couple hundred curves past hills covered with oak and chaparral, you reach ***James Lick Observatory.***

Named for the gold rush entrepreneur whose $700,000 donation made it all possible, the observatory was finished in 1888. Early visitors had to take a horse-drawn stagecoach to see the famous 36-inch refractor telescope. Weighing fourteen tons, it's still the world's second-largest of its kind. Today you can see this early telescope up close and watch the rotating dome's hydraulic floor rise 17 feet to accommodate star-gazing from different angles. Lick himself is entombed under the oak floorboards.

Another dome (one of eight on the mountain) houses a newer, 120-inch reflector telescope that weighs an awesome 275 tons and is used for important research by University of California astronomers. But don't expect to see them on duty—they all sleep by day and work by night, when the stars are out.

The Lick Observatory Visitors Center is open daily from noon to 5:00 P.M. and the 120-inch telescope gallery from 10:00 A.M. to 5:00 P.M. Daily tours; call (408) 274–5061 for information.

PLACES TO STAY IN THE BAY AREA

MARIN COUNTY

Best Western Corte Madera Inn,
56 Madera Boulevard,
Corte Madera;
(415) 924–1502

Casa Madrona Hotel,
801 Bridgeway,
Sausalito;
(800) 567–9524

Gerstle Park Inn,
34 Grove Street,
San Rafael;
(800) 726–7611

Hotel Sausalito,
16 El Portal,
Sausalito;
(888) 442–0700

The Inn Above Tide,
30 El Portal,
Sausalito;
(800) 893–8433

Lindisfarne Guest House,
1601 Shoreline Highway,
Sausalito;
(415) 383–3134

Mill Valley Inn,
165 Throckmorton Avenue,
Mill Valley;
(800) 595–2100

Mountain Home Inn,
810 Panoramic Highway,
Mill Valley;
(415) 381–9000

Tiburon Lodge,
1651 Tiburon Boulevard,
Tiburon;
(415) 435–3133

EAST BAY

Best Western Inn at the Square,
233 Broadway,
Oakland;
(510) 452–4565

Hotel Durant,
2600 Durant Avenue,
Berkleley;
(510) 845–8981

Inn at Benicia Bay,
145 East "D" Street,
Benicia;
(707) 746–1055

Jack London Inn,
444 Embarcadero,
Oakland;
(510) 444–2032

Lake Merritt Hotel,
1800 Madison Street,
Oakland;
(510) 832–2300

Marina Village Inn,
1151 Pacific Marina,
Alameda;
(800) 345–0304

Washington Inn,
495 Tenth Street,
Oakland;
(510) 452–1776

PENINSULA/SOUTH BAY

Briar Rose Bed & Breakfast Inn,
897 East Jackson Street,
San Jose;
(408) 279–5999

Campbell Inn,
675 East Campbell Avenue,
Campbell;
(800) 582–4449

Coxhead House Bed & Breakfast,
37 East Santa Inez Avenue,
San Mateo;
(650) 685–1600

Embassy Suites,
150 Anza Boulevard,
Burlingame;
(650) 342–4600

Granada Inn–Silicon Valley,
2515 El Camino Real,
Santa Clara;
(408) 241–2841

Homestead Studio Suites Hotel,
1830 Gateway Drive,
San Mateo;
(650) 574–1744

Hyatt Rickeys,
4219 El Camino Real,
Palo Alto;
(650) 493–8000

Madison Street Inn,
1390 Madison Street,
Santa Clara;
(408) 249–5541

Millwood Inn,
1375 El Camino Real,
Millbrae;
(800) 345–1375

Places to Eat in the Bay Area

Marin County

Dipsea Cafe (American),
200 Shoreline Highway,
Mill Valley;
(415) 381–0298

Guaymas (Mexican),
5 Main Street,
Tiburon;
(415) 435–6300

Lark Creek Inn (American),
234 Magnolia Avenue,
Larkspur;
(415) 924–7766

Marin Joe's Restaurant (American),
1815 Casa Buena Drive,
Corte Madera;
(415) 924–2081

Panama Hotel & Restaurant (Californian),
4 Bayview Street,
San Rafael;
(415) 457–3993

Scoma's (seafood/Italian),
588 Bridgeway,
Sausalito;
(415) 332–9551

East Bay

Autumn Moon Cafe (American),
3909 Grand Avenue,
Oakland;
(510) 595–3200

Blackhawk Grille (American),
3540 Blackhawk Plaza Circle,
Danville;
(925) 736–4295

Cafe Rouge (Continental),
1782 Fourth Street,
Berkeley;
(510) 525–1440

Chez Panisse (Californian),
1517 Shattuck Avenue,
Berkeley;
(510) 548–5525

Cuckoo's Nest Cafe & Restaurant (American),
247 Fourth Street,
Oakland;
(510) 452–9414

The Fat Lady (steakhouse),
201 Washington Street,
Jack London Square,
Oakland;
(510) 465–4996

Soizic (French),
300 Broadway Avenue,
Oakland;
(510) 251–8100

Yoshi's (Japanese),
510 Embarcadero, West
Jack London Square,
Oakland;
(510) 238–9200

Peninsula/South Bay

Bella Mia Restaurant (Italian),
58 South First Street,
San Jose;
(408) 280–1993

Bella Vista Restaurant (Mediterranean),
13451 Skyline Boulevard,
Woodside;
(650) 851–1229

Bertolucci's (Italian),
421 Cypress Avenue,
South San Francisco;
(650) 588–1625

Blake's Steakhouse (American),
17 North San Pedro Square,
San Jose;
(408) 298–9221

Cafe La Scala (Italian),
1219 Burlingame Avenue,
Burlingame;
(650) 347–3035

California Cafe (Californian),
2855 Stevens Creek Boulevard,
Santa Clara;
(408) 296–2233

Eulipia (cosmopolitan),
374 South First Street,
San Jose;
(408) 280–6161

Evvia (Greek),
420 Emerson Street,
Palo Alto;
(650) 326–0983

Gordon Biersh Brewing Co.
(American),
640 Emerson Street,
Palo Alto;
(650) 323–7723

Hong Kong Flower Lounge
Restaurant (Chinese),
51 Millbrae Avenue,
Millbrae;
(650) 692–6666

Max's Opera Cafe
(American),
1250 Old Bayshore
Highway,
Burlingame;
(650) 342–6297

Taxi's (American),
2700 South El Camino
Real,
San Mateo;
(650) 377–1947

Vivace (Italian),
1910 Ralston Avenue,
Belmont;
(650) 637–0611

Helpful Web Sites in the Bay Area

Angel Island:
www.angelisland.org

Bay Model:
www.spn.usace.army.mil/bmvc

Benicia Chamber of
Commerce:
www.ci.benicia.ca.us

Berkeley Convention
& Visitors Bureau: www.berkeleycvb.com

Coyote Point Museum:
www.coyoteptmuseum.org

East Brother Lighthouse:
www.ebls.org

Hakone Gardens:
www.hakone.com

Hiller Aviation Museum:
www.hiller.org

Judah L. Magnes Museum:
www.magnesmuseum.org

Marin County Convention
and Visitors Bureau:
www.visitmarin.org

Marin Headlands:
www.nps.gov/goga

Mount Diablo State Park:
www.mdia.org

Oakland Convention &
Visitors Bureau:
www.oaklandcvb.com

Rosicrucian Egyptian
Museum:
www.egyptianmuseum.org

San Jose Convention
& Visitors Bureau:
www.sanjose.org

San Mateo County
Convention and Visitors
Bureau: www.sanmateocountycvb.com

Santa Clara Chamber of
Commerce: www.santaclara.org

Tiburon Peninsula
Chamber of Commerce:
www.citysearch.com/sfo/tiburon

Worth Seeing/Doing in the Bay Area

Filoli Mansion
(Woodside)

Jack London Square
(Oakland)

Lake Merritt
(Oakland)

Marineworld/Africa USA
(Vallejo)

Muir Woods/Mount
Tamalpais (Marin)

Oakland Museum of
California

Paramount's Great
America (Santa Clara)

Tech Museum of
Innovation (San Jose)

University of California
(Berkeley)

South Coast

The South Coast (some would say California's northern Central Coast) is a world apart from San Francisco and the Bay Area. But whatever you call it, the southern coastline of Northern California (and its interior valleys) evokes wonderful travel images—barking sea lions and fresh fish dinners, primeval wildlife refuges and sunbaked adobes, ghostly cypress trees and coastal fog stretching to the horizon like strips of gauze.

The South Coast encompasses all or part of Monterey, San Benito, Santa Cruz, and San Mateo Counties and is reached and explored via Highway 1 or Highway 101. Although several small towns dot the area, it is overwhelmingly devoted to such nonurban pursuits as fishing and agriculture. The atmosphere is infectious, and you just might find yourself leaving with a string of garlic or a box of artichokes crammed into your trunk. You may even glimpse a bit of Old California (the Spanish period) as it was before American settlers changed life forever.

San Mateo/Santa Cruz Coast

Your magic carpet to the South Coast is Highway 1, whose various incarnations along the Pacific provide some of Northern California's most memorable sight-seeing. The stretch between San Francisco and Santa Cruz, although busy at times, is relatively unheralded when compared with Highway 1 through Big Sur or along the Mendocino coast. Yet, on a clear day (fog is a frequent visitor) the scenery is a stunning marriage of land and sea.

You can reach the coast of San Mateo and Santa Cruz Counties from San Francisco by heading south on I–280, then taking Highway 1 exit to Pacifica, a fog-shrouded bedroom community. South of town, the road narrows and snakes along rugged terrain. (The road is subject to closure at Devil's Slide.) You will pass gnarled cypress trees, the golden sands and sheer cliffs of Montara State Beach, and the old Montara Lighthouse (1875), now doubling as a youth hostel (650–728–7177).

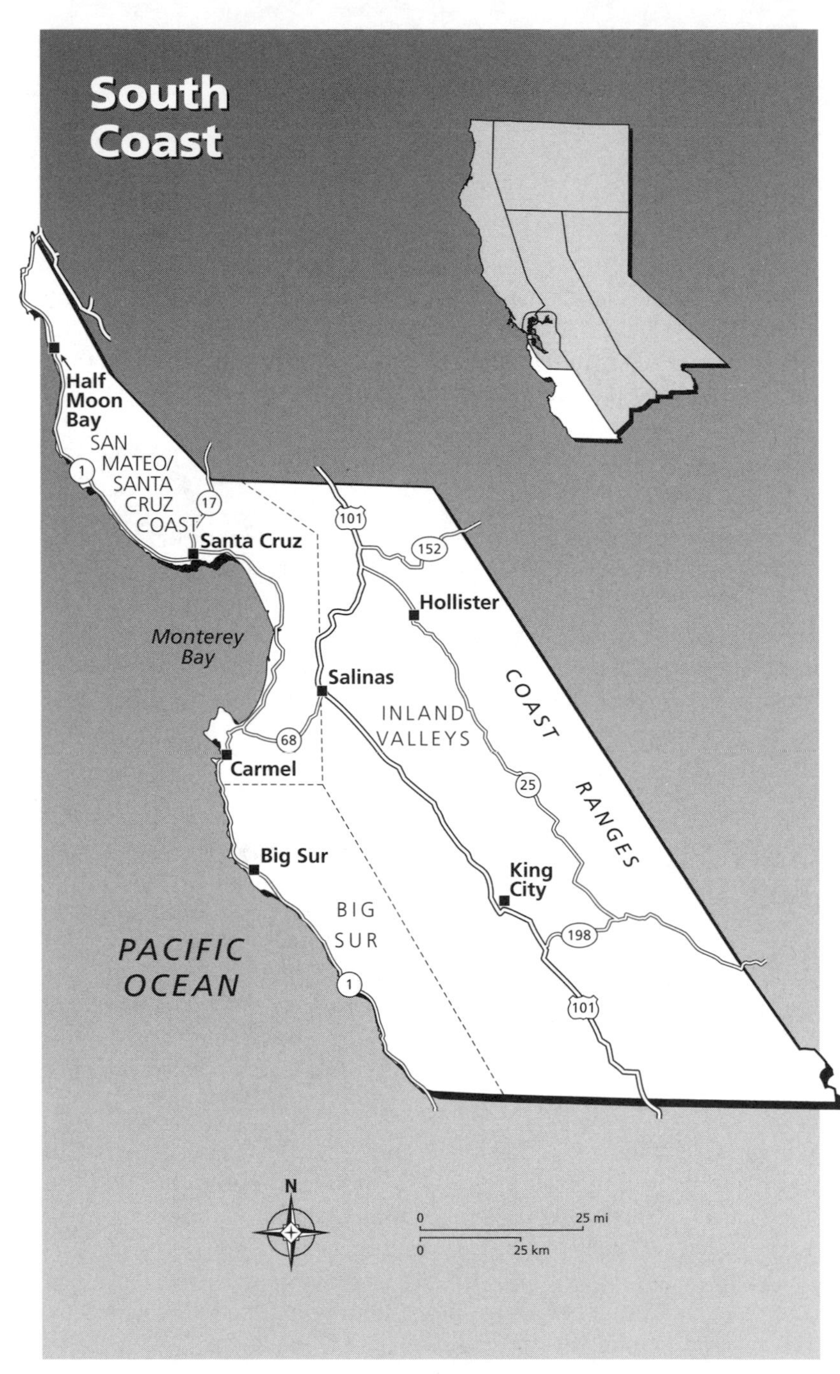
South Coast
Half Moon Bay
SAN MATEO/ SANTA CRUZ COAST
1
17
Santa Cruz
101
152
Hollister
Monterey Bay
Salinas
COAST RANGES
INLAND VALLEYS
68
Carmel
25
Big Sur
King City
BIG SUR
198
PACIFIC OCEAN
101
N
0
25 mi
0
25 km

SOUTH COAST

Author's Top Ten on the South Coast

Pescadero

Pigeon Point Lighthouse

Pacific Grove

Carmel Valley

Big Sur

San Juan Bautista

National Steinbeck Center Museum and Archive

Salinas Valley wineries

Pinnacles National Monument

Mission San Antonio de Padua

Our first stop is little ***Princeton-by-the-Sea*** and Pillar Point Harbor, the only port between the Golden Gate and Santa Cruz. According to local lore the village was named by an early developer for his dog, Prince. The harbor, on the north side of Half Moon Bay, was the site of shore-based whaling and sardine fishing that peaked during the 1940s. But just as in Monterey, the industry went belly up when the sardines mysteriously vanished. Ignored for years, Princeton finds itself riding the crest of a comeback.

The turnoff from Highway 1 is Capistrano Road, a semicircular route gliding past Princeton Inn (1906) and the harbor. ***Pillar Point*** has a breakwater, a marina with berths for hundreds of commercial and pleasure craft, and lots of opportunities for fishing. Walk to the end of Johnson Pier and watch fishmongers selling their catch. You can surf cast from the beach (license required), drop a line from the pier, or fish for lingcod or rockfish offshore. Two excursion outfits operate daily, weather permitting: Captain John's Fishing Trips (650–726–2913) and Huck Finn Sportfishing (650–726–7133).

If you're fortunate and here at the right time, you can spot gray whales migrating south from Alaska (November to January) or returning from Baja California with newborn offspring (March and April). Whale-watching cruises along the coast also leave from the harbor.

Naturally, there is ample opportunity to sample the fruits of the sea. The Shore Bird Restaurant (390 Capistrano Road) is tucked in a New England–style cottage overlooking the harbor and features a separate oyster bar. Just across the road is Barbara's Fish Trap, a cheap and friendly place to eat. In the port itself Princeton Seafood Co. serves chowder in a sourdough bread bowl, and the Ship to Shore Fish Market has an outdoor grill.

For ambitious hikers a wonderful trail leads around the tip of Pillar Point (beyond the radar tower) to a primeval world of sea lions, cormorants, pelicans, tide pools, and clusters of offshore rocks. Surfers flock here to a spot called "Maverick's" to take on some of California's most challenging waves, reaching heights up to 30 feet during winter storms.

The coast's character begins to change noticeably after the growing community of ***Half Moon Bay,*** famous for its Pumpkin Festival every October. (It's also the terminus of Highway 92 from San Mateo, an

Trivia

The Monterey Bay National Marine Sanctuary covers 5,312 square miles. At its center is an underwater canyon twice as deep as the Grand Canyon.

alternate route to the coast.) After this, the coastal strip becomes thinly populated and heavily planted, the rocky shoreline giving way to long stretches of sandy beach.

To the south lie several excellent beaches for day use. At San Gregorio State Beach you can drive inland 1 mile on Highway 84 to see the hamlet of San Gregorio, with its historic Spanish-style general store and post office and the funky Stage Stop Cafe on Stage Road.

Back on the coast, Pescadero State Beach has sand dunes, tide pools, and a creek where steelhead run. Right across the road is ***Pescadero Marsh Natural Preserve,*** habitat for 235 species of resident and migratory birds, including blue heron with 6-foot wingspans. Two trails loop through the marsh along nearly level ground (dogs not allowed). For information about guided walks, call (650) 879–2170.

An authentic slice of rural small-town California awaits 2 miles inland at the hamlet of ***Pescadero,*** set amid verdant vegetable fields with the hazy coastal range as a backdrop. It's a place of country stores and woodframe houses, white-steepled churches and front-porch rockers. Founded by Portuguese whalers in about 1850, the town prospered and once boasted two first-class hotels.

Although the name *Pescadero* means "fisherman," most residents are farmers, and the town seems to float amid fields of artichokes, brussels sprouts, beans, and lettuce. Stage Road is the closest thing to a main street, and ***Duarte's Tavern*** at number 202 has a reputation for the best food and drink in these parts. For sixty years this raucous, down-to-earth establishment has served up Portuguese linguica sausage, fried artichoke hearts, crab cioppino, oysters, abalone, corned beef hash, and other delights. For reservations call (650) 879–0464. Also on Stage Road you'll find the old Arcangeli Grocery (1929), now called Norm's, and the First Congregational Church (1867).

If possible, come to Pescadero in May, when residents of the port community take to the streets en masse for the Chamarita Festival of the Holy Ghost. Several area farms offer "pick your own" opportunities for fruits and vegetables.

More beach parks line the shore south of Pescadero, but for a change of pace try ***Butano State Park,*** 2,200 acres of dense redwoods and Douglas fir a few miles inland. *Butano* is an Indian word meaning "a gathering place for friendly visits," and this little-known park features forty campsites, including one for backpackers atop a 1,600-foot grade, a creek, a small fern canyon, and several crowd-free trails. To get there take Pescadero Road to Cloverdale Road, or enter on Gazos Creek Road off Highway 1 about 10 miles south of the Pescadero turnoff. For further information call (650) 879–2040.

A few miles south of Pescadero State Beach stands ***Pigeon Point Lighthouse,*** the second tallest in the United States and the quintessential coastal beacon. This 115-foot, white-brick sentinel thrusting up from a dramatic promontory has guided ships away from a shallow reef since 1872. Ironically, the point was named for a clipper ship called *Carrier Pigeon,* which sank here twenty years earlier. Later it became a favorite unloading spot for bootleggers.

The double-walled brick lighthouse has survived several major earthquakes and still has its original Fresnel lens in the glass-enclosed lantern room at the top. On weekends only, tours take visitors up 144 steps for a

Sunbathing au Naturel

Free-spirited Northern California offers several beaches where nude sunbathing is the accepted norm. Be sure to bring lots of sunscreen and apply it liberally to areas not accustomed to the light of day. Here's a list of some personal favorites along the South Coast—or places to avoid if this is not your taste.

San Mateo/Santa Cruz Area:

- *Devil's Slide, along Highway 1 about a mile north of Montara State Beach. A steep trail leads to the beach.*
- *San Gregorio Beach, 9 miles south of Half Moon Bay, marked by orange rocks along roadside.*
- *Panther Beach, about 11 miles north of Santa Cruz. Park between Highway 1 and railroad tracks; follow steep path to beach.*
- *Four Mile Beach, 7 miles south of Panther, near the junction of Highway 1 and Baldwin Creek. Follow a dirt road winding past a marsh to nude area.*
- *Bonny Doon Beach, 2 miles south of Davenport at intersection of Bonny Doon Road. Take footpath over the railroad tracks down to a cove.*

Monterey Area:

- *Pfeiffer Beach, in Los Padres National Forest 12 miles north of the Esalen Institute on Highway 1. Take Sycamore Canyon Road to beach parking lot, then follow path across stream.*
- *Molera State Beach, just north of Big Sur where the river meets the ocean. Cross a footbridge over the lagoon and walk south to a series of coves.*

gum-swallowing view of the coast. For real lighthouse buffs, three former Coast Guard bungalows now serve as a youth hostel; for reservations call (650) 879–0633. For those pea-soup days when the light can't be seen, there's also a fog signal that can be heard up to 5 miles away.

Continuing south along the coastal highway, you reach Santa Cruz County, where the scenery changes abruptly. Here the cliffs drop sheer to a road that hugs a narrow ledge overlooking the ocean. Look for the sign marking Waddell Creek Beach and pull over. On the other side of the road is Rancho del Oso State Park, where there's a trailhead for a wonderful hike few people know about. About half a mile up a paved road sits a ranger station (open weekends only from noon to 4:00 P.M.) where further information and trail maps are available. Call (831) 459–3800.

For anyone in a hurry, the short marsh trail offers glimpses of the usual coastal fauna and flora, but the real attraction here is the ***Skyline to the Sea Trail.*** This scenic route along Waddell Creek is actually two trails—one for walkers and another for horses and bicycles—and it winds all the way to Big Basin State Park in the hills, about 5 miles away. The trail is like an old ranch road with few difficult stretches, so it's perfect for Sunday hikers. Along the way you may see California quail and other birds, deer, and even an occasional mountain lion (rangers recommend making noise as you walk to frighten them).

Waddell Creek is a pleasant stream that attracts steelhead in winter, and about 6 miles from the trailhead you reach beautiful Berry Creek Falls amid a redwood forest (see the Bay Area chapter). There are several campsites along the trail, but reservations are strongly recommended; call (831) 425–1218 for information.

Just north of the town of Santa Cruz, at the water's edge and flanked by fields of brussels sprouts, lies the ***Joseph M. Long Marine Laboratory.*** Spread over forty acres of wetlands and seashore, this is primarily a research center for the University of California, Santa Cruz. But visitors are welcome, and unlike the famous Monterey Aquarium on the other side of the bay, it's rarely crowded and it's cheap.

At the Seymour Marine Discovery Center, a small aquarium has excellent exhibits of local shells and fish, hermit crabs, starfish, monkey-face eels, and other marine life from Monterey Bay, including pint-size sharks. A touching tank for the youngsters swarms with creepy creatures from below.

Every few minutes docents lead brief tours to the outdoor tanks where sea lions, dolphins, and other marine mammals are studied and trained.

You will not only be entertained by the frisky critters, but you'll learn such obscure details as how to tell a seal from a sea lion (check the ears), and the eating habits of a dolphin. And speaking of eating, there's an 85-foot skeleton of a blue whale that weighed about 130 tons when alive. As others of the species, it ate four tons of krill shrimp a day just to survive!

To reach the Long Marine Laboratory, take Swift Street off Highway 1, turn right at Delaware Street, and continue to the end. It's open daily except Monday; no admission charged. Call (831) 459–3800 for information.

Two miles east of Swift Street along West Cliff Drive, at the north tip of Monterey Bay, is a small, brick lighthouse containing the ***Santa Cruz Surfing Museum.*** Started by a few barnacled old veterans, the museum traces sixty years of the sport through breathtaking photos and an exciting video, rubber fins, and an array of surfboards.

You can trace surfing's evolution from redwood boards weighing a hundred pounds to the shorter, lighter present-day variety, made from foam and fiberglass. There's even an exhibit on sharks and the mangled wet suit of a surfer attacked by a great white.

The Santa Cruz Surfing Museum is open every day except Tuesday and Wednesday from noon to 4:00 P.M., with no admission charged. Call (831) 420–6289 for information. You can conclude your visit with a short walk to Steamer Lane, a popular beach where the surf is usually up.

Top Annual Events on the South Coast

Whalefest, *Monterey (mid-January)*

Monterey Wine Festival *(early April)*

Artichoke Festival, *Castroville (mid-May)*

San Juan Bautista Early Days & Grand Ball *(mid-June)*

California Rodeo, *Salinas (mid-July)*

Carmel Bach Festival, *Carmel-by-the-Sea (mid-July to early August)*

Steinbeck Festival, *Salinas (early August)*

Capitola Begonia Festival *(early September)*

Monterey Jazz Festival *(late September)*

Pacific Coast Fog Fest, *Pacifica (late September)*

California International Airshow, *Salinas (late September)*

Butterfly Parade, *Pacific Grove (early October)*

Art & Pumpkin Festival, *Half Moon Bay (mid-October)*

Christmas in the Adobes, *Monterey (mid-December)*

While visiting this typical California beach town, take in ***Santa Cruz Harley-Davidson, Inc.*** It's Northern California's largest dealership and features a unique museum of antique motorcycles and factory memorabilia, including one of the first motorized bikes from 1929. This rare JDH "two-cam twin" has been called "the greatest motorcycle ever built." Other bikes on display included early models with sidecars and the 1947 Harley that introduced the famous twin flathead engine, used for the next six decades of these fine machines.

Though you might see a Hell's Angel cruise in to have his "hog" repaired, the museum does not develop this theme. The focus of most historic photos is on the "wholesome" image of couples and families having fun on their motorcycles, heading off to Sunday picnics and the like. Both traditional and "outlaw" biker gear, featuring the world-famous Harley-Davidson logo, is on sale as well. The museum is open daily except Monday from 10:00 A.M. to 6:00 P.M., at 1148 Soquel Avenue, Santa Cruz; (831) 421–9600.

Monterey Bay

Leaving the Santa Cruz area on Highway 1, you enter Monterey County, renowned for its outstanding visitor attractions. But first there's an unscheduled stop at a most unlikely place. As you approach the weather-beaten fishing village of ***Moss Landing,*** the first thing you'll notice are the two hideous smokestacks of a huge, belching power plant. This may inspire you to push the accelerator to the floor, but that would be a mistake.

Moss Landing is the one town on Monterey Bay that still looks like a rough-and-tumble fishing port. There are tuna and shellfish canneries, hundreds of chipped and rusting vessels, boats up on blocks, vacant lots filled with weeds—the kind of thing John Steinbeck saw when he wrote about Monterey decades ago.

Trivia

Monterey County has been ranked the world's number one golf destination by Golf Digest.

The Monterey Jazz Festival in September is the oldest of its kind in the world.

This seaside settlement claims a curious history. A Frenchman named Paul Lezare founded "the city of St. Paul" in the 1850s. Two decades later, Captain Charles Moss built some docks, and Moss Landing boomed with grain shipments, sardine canneries, whaling, and boat building—before the inevitable decline. Now it's a center for oceanographic research as well as a threadbare working port. Several restaurants and antiques shops have also cropped up along the main drag.

Elkhorn Slough, nearby, shelters a world of salt marshes and tidal flats inhabited by hundreds of species of birds and waterfowl, invertebrates and fish, not to mention sea otters, seals, and salamanders. This 2,500-acre estuary (where freshwater and saltwater meet) is one of the nation's most biologically productive habitats. Nearly 90 percent of California's wetlands have been destroyed by "progress," and Elkhorn is second in size only to the shores of San Francisco Bay. The slough straddles a 7-mile-long river channel windi through marshland blanketed with mustard plant, filaree, and lupine.

Elkhorn Slough National Estuarine Research Reserve forms about half of the entire slough and is open regular hours for visitors. The main channel outside the reserve is open continuously for fishing, kayaking, and the like.

Begin at the visitor center, which is well stocked with maps and interpretive displays. Five miles of wide trails crisscross the sloping terrain leading down to the slough. Along the way you may spot a golden eagle or a peregrine falcon hunting for lunch among the impressive stands of eucalyptus or live oak. Patches of mugwort, lavender-colored wild radish, and hundreds of other botanical delights crowd the estuary banks and provide sustenance for the countless migratory and resident birds. (Late fall, winter, and early spring are the best times for birding.)

The stillness at Elkhorn is overwhelming, just as it must have been when the planet's first life oozed forth from a place like this. At present highly developed species such as the snowy egret share the marsh with one-celled life forms, spanning eons of evolutionary history. If you're lucky, you may find as many as fifty seals lounging on the mud banks or spot the pattern of a leopard-shark's fin as it cuts the surface of the water.

Trivia

Scotsman David Jacks was known for marketing a popular local cheese, which henceforth became known as Monterey Jack.

Elkhorn Slough Reserve is open year-round Wednesday through Sunday from 9:00 A.M. to 5:00 P.M., with guided tours on weekends at 10:00 A.M. and 1:00 P.M. You can reach the reserve via Dolan Road (next to the power plant), heading east about 3 miles to Elkhorn Road, then another 2 miles north to the visitor center. For information call (831) 728–2822.

A company called Elkhorn Slough Safari out of Moss Landing offers nature tours aboard a 27-foot pontoon boat. The two-hour excursion is led by jocular Captain Yohn Gideon and a naturalist, who share an uncanny ability to spot the abundant wildlife as it appears. They also provide loads of information and anecdotes about the animals. This is one of the nation's top places for bird-watching: More than 300 species have been spotted here, many using the slough as a stopover on their migrant flyways. Cruising along the inland waterway, visitors help count the playful otters, constantly grooming themselves, and large numbers of harbor seals (almost 200 seen on a recent visit). For details on the pontoon-boat excursion, call (831) 633–5555. Don't forget the camera and binoculars!

You can "celebrate the thistle" a few miles away at ***Castroville,*** a town owing its entire identity to one thing—artichokes. The area's soil and mild climate create a kind of artichoke heaven, and Castroville claims about 90 percent of the total U.S. production. It's a one-vegetable town and isn't shy about proclaiming itself "The Artichoke Center of the World" in a sign fixed above Main Street. This town of about 5,000 lies at the western edge of the famous Salinas Valley, home to some of the nation's most fertile farmland.

Founded back in 1863 by Juan Battista Castro, the town witnessed some bad times. Then, about 1920, Italian immigrants appeared with a curious Mediterranean plant and the crazy idea of cultivating it. The rest, as they say, belongs to artichoke history.

Castroville boasts a 20-foot-tall, 16-foot-wide artichoke made of reinforced concrete that has become an icon of American roadside kitsch. This local treasure marks the location of ***The Giant Artichoke Restaurant.*** Here you can discover a multitude of tasty ways to prepare the thistle—boiled, marinated, sautéed, in soup, bread, cake, salad, omelets, quiches, pasta, and the restaurant's specialty—french-fried artichoke hearts.

In May, Castroville hosts its annual ***Artichoke Festival,*** and visitors can discover even more ways to eat the beloved thistle, as well as take part in a full-blown celebration that includes a parade, 10K run, and artichoke cooking and eating competitions. And there's one interesting footnote to it all: Back in 1947, none other than a budding starlet named Marilyn Monroe reigned as Castroville's first "California Artichoke" queen. Today, Norma Jean's Club on Merritt Street honors the star with weekly drag shows.

Castroville lies at the junction of Highways 156 and 183, about 7 miles from Salinas and 2 miles from Highway 1. You can visit from the Monterey Peninsula or stay in Castroville at the Artichoke Inn; (831) 633–3300.

Monterey and its well-known neighbors hardly require an introduction. Renowned indeed are the world-class golf, outstanding aquarium, Cannery Row, Fisherman's Wharf, and Carmel's quaint shops and restaurants. One lesser-known attraction, ***Monterey's Path of History,*** begins just a few steps from the wharf, yet few visitors find it.

Monterey is one of California's most historic places, with its best collection of Spanish colonial-period architecture. After early explorers made claims for the crown (Vizcaino named the area for the Count of Monte Rey), the peninsula was finally settled in the 1770s. Monterey became

Alta California's liveliest town, not to mention a provincial capital under both Spanish and Mexican flags.

About forty buildings remain from before 1850, when the gold rush and San Francisco stole most of Monterey's thunder, and about a dozen are open along the Path of History. Ironically, they were less a product of any Spanish or Mexican influence than of Yankee settlers such as Thomas Larkin, who tried to build a New England–style house using local materials and created the "Monterey-style" two-story adobes with balconies, overhanging roofs, beamed ceilings, and plank floors.

The ***Custom House,*** at 1 Custom House Plaza, is the oldest surviving government building on the Pacific Coast (1827). Cargo was inspected and taxed here before it could be sold. Researchers have used an old ship's manifest to cleverly re-create a feeling for the times, with kegs of whisky,

The Truth about Artichokes

One of the oldest foods known, artichokes were cultivated in the Mediterranean region thousands of years ago. Catherine of Medici introduced them into France in the mid-1500s. In present-day France les artichauts *are prepared in dozens of ways, including baked hearts au gratin.*

Italian immigrants first brought artichokes to California in the 1920s, and today the state accounts for 99.9 percent of all American production, more than three million cartons annually valued at nearly $50 million. About three-fourths of this crop is grown in Monterey County, where the climate and soil are considered ideal.

Artichokes belong to the thistle group of the sunflower family, and the "vegetable" we eat is really a flower bud. If allowed to bloom, the violet-blue blossom would measure 7 inches in diameter.

The artichoke is a thistlelike spheroid sheathed in tough, pointed leaves, what one food critic described as "an organic hand grenade." Yet within the tough exterior is palatable flesh with a subtle taste. It's said that eating artichokes makes other food taste sweeter and helps cheap wine resemble the vintage stuff.

Artichokes are high in folic acid, vitamin C, and fiber; low in calories and sodium; and contain no fat or cholesterol. They are also high in snob appeal and reputed to be an aphrodisiac.

Somewhat challenging to consume, artichokes are one of the last holdouts in an age of fast food. But aficionados swear all the effort is worth it. They can be steamed, boiled, baked, french-fried, marinated, and stir-fried with seafood, pasta, and so on. For some classic recipes send an SASE to the California Artichoke Advisory Board, P.O. Box 747, Castroville, CA 95012; or call (831) 633–4411.

tallow candles, sacks of flour, and piles of "California banknotes," the cowhides used for bartering at the time. All this loot is lorded over by a gabby parrot. One historical note: At the Custom House the U.S. flag was officially raised for the first time in California—on July 7, 1846, during the Mexican-American War.

The Pacific House, 8 Custom House Plaza, was used for military storage and later as a tavern. Now it's a museum covering the Costanoan Indians through the early American period. The Casa del Oro, corner of

It's a Dog's World

My bouncy Samoyed and I often have trouble finding places—parks, trails, beaches, and motels—that let us enjoy the facilities together. Not so Carmel-by-the-Sea, which welcomes dogs and "their people" with open paws.

Start with the city beach, a gorgeous swath of white sand bordered by cypress trees and a nice walking trail, located at the end of Ocean Avenue. Here my dog can join dozens of other pooches frolicking leashless with the full protection of the local law. This innocent play often turns into an authentic canine circus with all the normal instinctual behavior, so watch where you step. It's the only beach for many miles that allows such freedom (leashed pets are permitted at Carmel River State Beach south of town).

When we walk around Carmel, I can go into any shop without worry; there are special doggie hitching posts outside for pets to relax in the shade while waiting for their masters. (Many shops will allow them to enter.) A woman named Gale Wrausmann runs "Carmel Walks," a foot-and-paw tour of the quaint little town that not only allows dogs (on leash), but encourages them to come along. There's a special segment of the tour called "the canine culture of Carmel, past and present." Call (831) 642–2700 for information.

Finally, we know there will always be some place to sleep and eat while in Carmel. The Cypress Inn is an elegant Mediterranean-style hostelry replete with antiques and feather beds. It's part-owned by famous dog-lover Doris Day, which means your pooch will get the V.I.D. treatment, including his or her pet bed and an invitation to "Yappy Hour" each afternoon. But the Cypress Inn is very popular, and reservations are essential; call (800) 443–7443. Pets are also welcome at the Happy Landing Inn and the Wayside Inn.

After a day of romping, my dog often likes to turn in early, but when we go out there's the chic Porta Bella Restaurant, where we can sit outside in a candlelit courtyard with other dogs and owners. For reservations call (831) 624–4395. If it's booked, we can dine in the patio of Le Bistro or the Plaza Cafe and Grill, and sometimes the chefs will even find a little treat to slip their special guests. Now that's something to bark about!

Scott and Olivier Streets, contains a general store featuring novelty items and gifts. You can see the old safe where gold was stored (*oro* means "gold" in Spanish) and an herb garden outside.

California's First Theater, corner of Scott and Pacific Streets, is entered through rough-hewn Jack Swan Tavern, where you can still order anything from beer to sarsaparilla. Mr. Swan was an English sailor who settled here and opened a boardinghouse. In 1850 a stage show was put on to entertain the restless soldiers stationed in Monterey (they also served as actors). You can still see the Troupers of the Gold Coast perform hiss-the-villain-style productions. (The theater was undergoing restoration throughout 2003.)

Colton Hall, 522 Pacific, was built by a navy chaplain who became the town's first American mayor. The neoclassical building in Friendly Plaza became the site of California's constitutional convention in 1849. You can see the tables where delegates sat, their notes, inkwells, and wire-rimmed spectacles. The realistic cells at Old Monterey Jail next door look ready for the next prisoner to arrive (it was used until 1956).

The ***Larkin House,*** 510 Calle Principal, remains the best example of the Monterey style. It was built in 1835 by the future U.S. Consul to Mexico, Thomas Larkin. The Cooper-Molera Adobe, corner of Polk and Munras Streets, has been beautifully restored, right down to matching the original wallpaper, and houses an interpretive center with historical exhibits and an otter pelt. At the ***Stevenson House*** (under restoration), 530 Houston Street, author Robert Louis Stevenson paid 25 cents per week in rent while visiting his wife to be, Fanny Osborne. Poor, unknown, and in frail health, he wrote articles for local newspapers and a book entitled *The Old Pacific Capital,* an account of Monterey in the 1870s.

These and other buildings on the Path of History are open at various times throughout the week. For further details pick up a map at the Custom House, open daily from 9:00 A.M. to 5:00 P.M., or call (831) 649–7118.

If history is your thing and money is no object, try staying at the ***Old Monterey Inn,*** an imposing Tudor-style home (built by a former mayor) transformed into a quality bed-and-breakfast inn. Each of ten rooms features a different motif, and all are incredibly cozy; call (831) 375–8284 for reservations.

The tiny community of ***Pacific Grove*** may be the best-kept secret on the Monterey Peninsula. Clutching a finger of land immediately west of Cannery Row, it embraces a 4-mile stretch of spectacular coastline dotted with rocky beaches, tide pools, and seaside parks ablaze with the pink blossoms of iceplant. A cool blanket of fog often hangs over its

Trivia

Seventeen-Mile Drive through Pebble Beach is the only private toll road west of the Mississippi River.

quiet streets, lined with small cottages and inns replete with bay windows, gables, and stained-glass windows.

In 1875, 450 Methodists arrived here by horse and wagon to camp out and "sing praises to God in open air." Every summer the Methodist Seaside Retreat became a tent city, but before long visitors became residents and built modest homes in this nature-blessed spot. The retreat was something of a curiosity to its ripsnorting neighbors along The Row. For nearly a century liquor was outlawed and required a prescription. Not until 1969 did California's last "dry" town fall off the wagon. Laws also banned gambling, dancing, swimming without a proper costume (i.e., doubled crotched), fishing on Sunday, and fast buggy-driving.

As far as anyone can tell, the mysterious monarch butterflies started arriving in Pacific Grove about the same time as the Methodists. Each fall tens of thousands of these orange-and-black creatures wing it from as far away as Alaska and the Canadian Rockies for a winter sojourn in "Butterfly Town USA." From early October (when there's a festive Butterfly Parade) through early March, you can see butterflies hanging together in clusters on the branches of cypress and eucalyptus trees. One spot in particular is a butterfly haven: the Butterfly Sanctuary on Ridge Road, behind the Butterfly Grove Inn. You can look, but don't touch; there's a $1,000 fine for anyone caught "molesting butterflies."

A special exhibit explains the monarch phenomenon at the ***Pacific Grove Museum of Natural History,*** once voted the finest of its size in the country. Excellent displays showcase the peninsula's animal and plant life, from univalves and giant oysters to wild boars and playful sea otters. One highlight is a relief map of Monterey Bay, which plummets 8,400 feet to the ocean floor—deeper than the Grand Canyon. The museum, at 165 Forest Avenue, is open daily except Monday from 10:00 A.M. to 5:00 P.M. No admission charged. For information call (831) 648–5716.

At the Pacific Grove Chamber of Commerce across the street, you can pick up a map of a walking tour of eighteen historical sites, including old St. Mary's Church and the ***Point Pinos Lighthouse.*** This coastal beacon is the oldest in continuous operation on the West Coast, marking the entrance to Monterey Harbor since 1855, when it used a lard-oil lantern. A historical museum inside is open Thursday through Sunday from 1:00 to 4:00 P.M.

From the adjacent Point Pinos Reservation, you can spy sea otters frolicking offshore in the kelp beds and hear the sharp crack of an abalone shell being opened for lunch by one of these delightful creatures. Once thought extinct, otters have staged a remarkable comeback. You can watch them year-round from numerous points along Ocean View Boulevard, especially between the Hopkins Marine Station and the lighthouse.

Pacific Grove is also famous for its bed-and-breakfast inns, housed in creaky, charming Victorians amid storybook settings. Among the best are the Gosby House Inn, Green Gables Inn, the Seven Gables Inn, and the ultimate Victorian, the old Centrella Hotel. For further information call the Pacific Grove Chamber of Commerce at (831) 373–3304.

The village of Carmel, next to Pacific Grove, is cute indeed. But cuteness alone does not suffice when tourist crowds swarm into town. When that happens, it's time to head for the valley.

Point Pinos Lighthouse

Trivia

San Francisco artists and writers flocked to Carmel after the 1906 earthquake left them homeless, and a tradition was born.

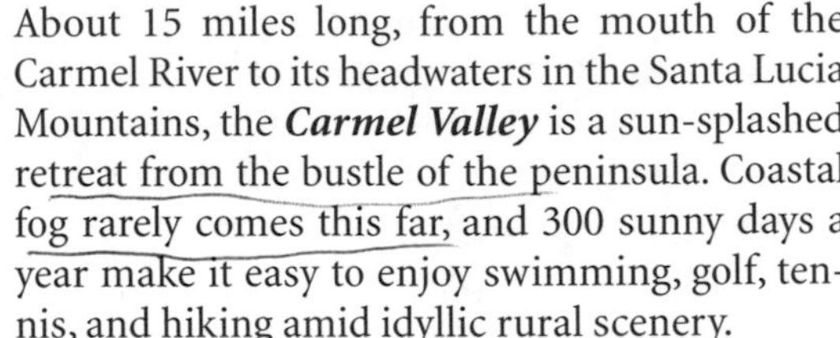

About 15 miles long, from the mouth of the Carmel River to its headwaters in the Santa Lucia Mountains, the ***Carmel Valley*** is a sun-splashed retreat from the bustle of the peninsula. Coastal fog rarely comes this far, and 300 sunny days a year make it easy to enjoy swimming, golf, tennis, and hiking amid idyllic rural scenery.

Just south of Carmel, Carmel Valley Road heads inland from Highway 1 and follows the river toward the hills. Along the way you will pass fields of artichokes and strawberries, fruit orchards, and grazing horses. The entire Monterey Peninsula is a golfer's paradise, and the valley claims some of the finest courses. The ***Rancho Canada Golf Club,*** a thirty-six-hole public facility about a mile inland, features one scenic course leaping the river five times. The ***Carmel Valley Golf and Country Club*** is open to guests of ***Quail Lodge*** and reciprocating private clubs. One of the country's highest-rated resort hotels, it occupies a pastoral setting on 245 acres of lakes, woods, and meadows. Another private course at the ***Carmel Valley Ranch Resort*** features nine holes along the river and the back nine climbing the hills, in addition to twelve tennis courts.

Although money definitely talks in the valley, fun is not the exclusive domain of high rollers. ***Garland Ranch Regional Park*** provides picnic sites and more than 7 miles of trails through alluring hills and meadows. The park is especially beautiful in April and May with a fantastic array of wildflowers.

Right in the neighborhood is ***Château Julien Winery,*** housed in a beautiful replica of a French estate, with an elegant tasting room where six varieties of wine are sampled. The place is small enough that the wine maker himself sometimes assists with the tour. Château Julien is open from 8:00 A.M. to 5:00 P.M. weekdays and from 11:00 A.M. to 5:00 P.M. weekends. For information about tours call (831) 624–2600.

Other wineries with tasting rooms in the Carmel Valley are: Bernardus, 5 West Carmel Valley Road, (831) 659–1900; Chateau Sinnet, 13746 Center Street, (831) 659–2244; Galante, 18181 Cachagua Road, (831) 659–2649; Georis, 4 Pilot Road, (831) 659–1059; Heller Estate, 69 West Carmel Valley Road, (831) 659–6220; Joullian, 2 Village Drive, (831) 659-8100; and Robert Talbot, 53 West Carmel Valley Road, (831) 659–3500.

The valley is one place you can still get away from it all. Take ***Stonepine,*** for instance, a secluded country estate set in the hills just beyond Carmel Valley Village. At one time the home of the fabulously wealthy Russell and Crocker families, the former Double-H Ranch claimed the most s cessful thoroughbred breeding west of the Mississippi. Centerpiece the 330-acre estate is Château Noel, a Mediterranean-style mansion wi a priceless collection of art and antiques. Galas and special events have become a specialty at Stonepine; for example, for $5,000 (not counting food and drink) you can throw a "Gone with the Wind" party that features members of the National Civil War Association in costume fighting a mock battle! For information call (831) 659–2245.

Seclusion of a very different kind can be found at the ***Tassajara Hotsprings Resort.*** Operated by the Zen Mountain Center as a monastic community, Tassajara is open to the public part of the year for overnight stays. Seventeen hot mineral springs have been attracting bathers here since Indian days, and the spot was a fashionable resort in the early 1900s. Tassajara is open during summer, but closed in winter for student training. Call (831) 659–2229 for information.

There are numerous shopping spots, accommodations, and dining possibilities throughout the area, especially at Carmel Valley Village. For information contact the Chamber of Commerce, P.O. Box 288, Carmel Valley, CA 93924; (831) 659–4000.

The busy four-lane section of ***Carmel Valley Road*** between Highway 1 and Laureles Grande gives way to a twisty two-lane blacktop that winds through vineyards and oak groves, narrow canyons, and green pastures. Allow about two hours for the one-way journey from Carmel Valley Village to the town of Greenfield on Highway 101.

For information about the entire area, write the Monterey Peninsula Chamber of Commerce and Visitors and Convention Bureau, P.O. Box 1770, Monterey, CA 93942–1770 or call (888) 221–1010.

Big Sur

Highway 1 south of Carmel, also known as the Cabrillo Highway, ranks as one of the America's great scenic roads—the greatest, say some. It winds for 90 miles along the high cliffs of Big Sur toward San Simeon and San Luis Obispo County, regarded as the start of Southern California. Along the way are jagged mountains rising from the Pacific, grassy promontories sprinkled with wildflowers, rushing streams, and dense pockets of redwoods. Yet few people realize how wild Big Sur and the coastal mountains remain, despite their immense popularity with visitors.

The Esselen Indians once inhabited this land, but whites did not settle here until after 1850, and the highway was not completed until 1937. During the 1950s novelist Henry Miller became the focus of an artists colony, and a decade later, hippies arrived in droves, spurred on by tales of good vibes and beautiful scenery. But the hippies went again, and even now only about 1,500 permanent residents call Big Sur home. Amenities are few, just a smattering of resorts and campgrounds, and the sense of escape is compelling. To capture this feeling of quiet intimacy, try staying at ***Deetjen's Big Sur Inn,*** a collection of simple cabins built by Norwegian immigrants in the 1920s. Call (831) 667–2377 for information.

The dramatic 30-mile drive from Carmel to Big Sur takes about an hour, along a road that clings desperately to the seaward face of the Santa Lucia Mountains. Along the way (about 15 miles south), you will pass the massive, 714-foot-high Bixby Bridge, with a grace and grandeur almost equal to the natural wonders of Big Sur. It was built during the 1930s by prisoners eager to work off time on their sentences. A bit south, the historic Point Sur lighthouse sits perched 361 feet above the boiling surf. For information on guided tours, call (831) 625–4419. Farther along (30 miles south of Carmel) are the world-famous Nepenthe Restaurant and the ***Henry Miller Memorial Library,*** with documents and artifacts on the life of the feisty writer and painter. For information call (831) 667–2574.

If you are seeking solitude, stay away from Pfeiffer–Big Sur and Julia Pfeiffer Burns State Parks in summer or on weekends. On the other hand, ***Andrew Molera State Park*** remains an adventurer's hideaway within easy reach of the main road, about 5 miles north of Big Sur.

The park rises from the oceanfront and hugs the Big Sur River at about 3,400 feet above sea level. Within its 5,000 acres of cottonwood, oak, and redwood forests is a network of more than 20 miles of hiking trails. To the delight of most visitors, the only thing missing is a road. People come for the excellent hiking, and the trails traverse the beachfront, bluffs, meadows, and banks of the Big Sur River. You might spot harbor seals and sea lions at the shore or mule deer and bobcat farther inland. One of the better trails follows the river to the lagoon for about a mile, emerging on a rocky beach watched over by egrets, gulls, surf scoters, and black oyster catchers.

After you've whetted your appetite for adventure, it's time to take on nearby ***Ventana Wilderness.*** This 167,000-acre refuge forms part of the vast Los Padres National Forest and represents the southernmost realm of the coastal redwoods. Wild boar, mountain lion, raccoon, California condor (see sidebar) and dozens of other species call it home. Within its

For the Birds

The rare and regal California condor has lived in the Santa Lucia Mountains for at least ten millennia and once roamed as far north as British Columbia. They are North America's largest land bird, with a 10-foot wingspan and a range of 150 miles per day.

However, by the late 1980s these magnificent creatures were close to extinction due to hunting and egg collecting, and urgent action was required. The last known wild condor was taken into captivity to join twenty-six others. Working together, the U.S. government and Ventana Wilderness Society began a careful breeding program followed by reintroduction into the wilderness, and plans call for about fifty releases over the next ten years. Fingers and claws are crossed, but so far the program seems to be working.

The Ventana Wilderness Society has a research and education center beside the entrance to Andrew Molera State Park and can be reached at P.O. Box 894, Carmel Valley, CA 93924; (831) 624–1202.

rugged, chaparral-covered confines are 237 miles of hiking trails, such as Botchers Gap–Devil's Peak Trail, a steep, 4-mile hike offering spectacular views of the coast. For overnighters the preserve has fifty-five rustic campsites available on a first-come basis. For information on Andrew Molera State Park and the Ventana Wilderness, call (831) 667–2315.

Inland Valleys

One route for the adventurous leaves Highway 1 near Lucia, south of Big Sur. Scenic Nacimiento Road switchbacks over the rugged coastal mountains all the way to bucolic San Antonio de Padua Mission near Jolon. You are more likely, however, to enter the coast's interior valleys on Highway 101. If arriving from the north, you will leave the Bay Area outside of San Jose, then pass Gilroy, famous for its annual Garlic Festival. Just about anything related to "the stinking rose" can be found at ***Garlic World:*** braids, gifts, souvenirs, and gourmet items like garlic ice cream. It's located off Highway 101 at 4800 Monterey Highway, about 3 miles south of Gilroy; (408) 847–2251.

Gilroy's agricultural roots are in full bloom at ***Bonfante Gardens*** theme park, with its forty rides and attractions geared for families and mature visitors (rather than the scary, thrill-packed rides of Great America). There's a steam train and Quicksilver Mine Coaster, the Pinnacles Rock Maze, and a fistful of rides like the Mushroom Swing, Artichoke Dip, and Garlic Twist (like Disney's teacups but with giant garlic bulbs doing the spinning). All in a lush horticultural wonderland that includes a vast greenhouse called Monarch Garden and the park's highlight: about twenty-five bizarrely woven and sculpted sycamores called "circus trees." Bonfante Gardens is open April through September; call (408) 840–7100 for further information.

Trivia

The sapphire blue gemstone called Benitoite is found at only one place in the world: the Diablo range of San Benito County.

You are leaving the Santa Clara Valley and entering San Benito County; follow Highway 101 south to Highway 156 and take it 2 miles east to ***San Juan Bautista.*** The town is a quiet place, with the feel of an old frontier community that time passed by. This tranquility belies the fact that San Juan, as locals call it, sits smack on the San Andreas Fault. At least one tremor a week rattles residents, with a good jolt several times a year.

The town's site, on an escarpment overlooking the San Benito River Valley, was handpicked by Franciscan missionary Fermin de Lausen on the feast day of John the Baptist, June 24, 1797. San Juan is alive with the dreamy feel of Old California, with a nicely restored mission, a main square where Mexican soldiers used to drill, and the Yankee town that later grew up around it. Before Spaniards arrived the valley was home to the Mutsun Indians, but despite the missionaries' efforts to "civilize" them, the natives were wiped out. The last full-blooded Mutsun died in 1930 and lies buried in the mission cemetery, along with about 4,000 other Indians, mostly in unmarked graves.

The mission's spacious church features a double row of arches, somber religious art, and flickering candles. Particularly noteworthy are the 40-foot-high altar paintings (called *reredos*), done by one Thomas Doaks in 1816. This Boston sailor had jumped ship to become the first American to settle in California. Now, the fading paintings are lit dramatically and spruced up with some scarlet curtains and statues. San Juan boasts the only mission church open continuously since its founding, and the original chapel bells still call parishioners to Mass. The museum displays the standard collection of worn-out vestments, kettles, rawhide thongs, and such curiosities as gaming sticks used by local Indians. The mission is open daily, from 9:30 A.M. to 4:30 P.M.; call (831) 623–4528 for details.

After Mexico lost California in 1846, San Juan became a trading center for livestock, and hotels, saloons, and stables sprouted up. It was also a key stop on the old stagecoach lines, with as many as a dozen stages a day trundling in and out of town on the San Francisco–Los Angeles run.

Weary travelers would stay the night at ***Angelo Zanetta's Plaza Hotel,*** converted from a soldiers' barracks. It was supposed to be a refined place (the future general William T. Sherman slept there), but two men died of gunshot wounds in the bar.

A self-guided tour of the two-story hotel costs $1.00. On it you'll see a table set for dinner, a portrait of nefarious local outlaw Tiburcio Vasquez, and a marvelous old barroom complete with card tables and spittoons. It's still the liveliest place in town whenever the Butterfly Bloomers, a group of high-kicking can-can girls, put on a show.

Right next door sits the ***Castro-Breen House,*** built by the prefect of northern Alta California, a man who even changed the town's name briefly to San Juan de *Castro.* The house is completely furnished, down to the kerosene lamps and chamber pots, just as it was when the Breen family resided there. This remarkable bunch (the parents and seven kids) were stranded in the high Sierra with the infamous Donner party for 111 days, but all of them miraculously (or suspiciously) managed to survive. After being rescued, they made a fortune in the goldfields and settled in San Juan.

Across the square is Plaza Stable, a hive of activity in the old stagecoach days. On display are numerous carriages and wagons, including a fringed surrey and an elegant black barouche. Out back is the blacksmith's shop, and next door you'll find a fourth historic building—Plaza Hall, once used as a dormitory by Indian maidens. The state historic park is open daily from 10:00 A.M. to 4:30 P.M.; call (831) 623-4881 for further information.

The ***Salinas Valley,*** one of the world's richest farming regions, lies to the southeast. Sometimes called "The Salad Bowl of the Nation," this 85-mile-long valley grows an astounding 60 percent of America's fresh vegetables. The town of Salinas, about 20 miles east of Monterey, has another claim to fame as birthplace of novelist John Steinbeck. Though largely scandalized by his writings at the time, now the town embraces the Steinbeck legacy with passion—understandably, as few places can claim a Nobel Prize winner as a native son.

One reason for the outrage was that Steinbeck borrowed liberally from the people and places encountered in his youth, and they often reappeared as thinly disguised fiction. The town was definitely the setting for *East of Eden.* One passage reads: "It was an immaculate and friendly house, grand enough but not pretentious, and it sat inside its white fence surrounded by a clipped lawn and roses." Steinbeck was describing his

Trivia

Almost 250,000 tons of sardines were processed on Cannery Row in 1945, the year John Steinbeck's novel of the same name was published.

own house, the two-story Victorian where he was born in 1902 and spent his first eighteen years.

At present the prim ladies of a local society have taken over the ***Steinbeck House*** and run it as a restaurant, serving luncheon amid turn-of-the-twentieth-century furnishings. The front bedroom, where the author was born, is now a reception area. John later occupied an upstairs bedroom and lived at home until after graduation from Salinas High School. The ***Steinbeck House Restaurant,*** at 132 Central Street, offers lunch daily except Sunday and is available for private parties. Call (831) 424–2735 for reservations.

Steinbeck died in 1968, and his remains rest in the Garden of Memories at 768 Abbott Street. After much heated discussion the town named its main library in his memory. Outside is an odd statue of the author smoking a cigarette (which vandals keep breaking off).

Just 2 blocks from his birthplace, the ***National Steinbeck Center Museum and Archive,*** filled with clever interactive exhibits, encapsulates just how creative contemporary museums have become. Ironically, the center sits facing Old Town Salinas and its tree-lined Main Street, where *The Grapes of Wrath* was publicly burned by local prudes shortly after publication. A stroll through the museum is like an intimate journey into the author's life and work, which were often interchangeable. But the collection is not merely for loyal readers or professors; complete novices will come away entertained and informed.

The self-guided tour through a series of vignettes begins with the "Growing Up East of Eden" room, which evokes the feel of turn-of-the-twentieth-century Salinas, including John's attic room with books he read as a child. You feel the cool air coming from a boxcar for lettuce (which figures prominently in the *Eden* novel), a reminder that young Steinbeck worked in the valley's fields and factories. The "Grapes of Wrath" room features migrant workers' cabins, and you can try your hand at washing laundry amid the sound of Woodie Guthrie tunes. Monterey's Cannery Row is re-created in precise detail, right down to the smell of sardines piped in from above.

If all this sounds kitschy, somehow it works, and visitors who might never dream of picking up a Steinbeck book could be inspired to do so. The writer's oeuvre was widely popular in his day and adapted by Hollywood, and film clips flicker among the various exhibits. You can sit on a bale of hay and watch *Of Mice and Men* or see Henry Fonda acting his heart out in *The Grapes of Wrath.* Steinbeck himself wrote a few scripts, including the highly successful *Viva Zapata!,* which is screened here in an ersatz Mexican plaza.

In another room you hear the author's moving Nobel Prize acceptance speech and see the actual camper-truck, nicknamed "Rocinante" (for Don Quixote's horse), that Steinbeck used to tour America for his book *Travels with Charley.* Another prized item is the original manuscript of his novelette *The Pearl,* just one of more than 30,000 items housed in the archival collection. These include letters, personal artifacts, oral histories (interviews), galley proofs with handwritten corrections, movie

Padre with a Mission

Father Junípero Serra was the George Washington of the California Missions, founding the first several in a chain of twenty-one along El Camino Real *("the royal road") from San Diego to Sonoma. He was a daring man of steadfast convictions, yet he is surrounded by controversy; some people want him canonized as a saint, but others say he helped destroy the California Indians.*

Serra was born on the Spanish island of Mallorca in 1713 and became a Franciscan priest at a young age. In 1749 he went to Mexico as a missionary and was so successful he was put in charge of a new project to explore and convert the inhabitants of distant California. He established the first mission at San Diego in 1769 and, a year later, sailed to Monterey. Here he founded Mission San Carlos Borromeo del Rio Carmelo near the banks of the Carmel River. Serra settled down at Carmel, and this mission became the flagship of the Catholic fleet in California. Thousands of Indians were baptized in its chapel, and they provided cheap labor for a thriving mission economy.

A statue of Serra presides serenely over a shaded garden of the old adobe building. Inside the church is a memorial to the padre, a replica of his living quarters with a simple plank bed and other furniture, as well as a leather thong he used to tame temptations of the flesh through self-flagellation. On a wooden table is a reliquary containing some splintered remains from his original coffin.

Father Serra, who died in 1784, lies buried outside in the mission cemetery beside his colleagues and thousands of converted Indians. Within fifty years of his death, mission life was gone forever, and the native population was decimated by disease and cultural trauma.

In 1988 Serra was beatified by the Catholic Church and awaits the highest of all honors—sainthood. Yet opponents say that while his motives may have been sincere, his ultimate legacy was disastrous.

posters and scripts, and rare first editions. Finally, the "Art of Writing Room" lets visitors explore their own creativity with CD-ROMs and other modern gimmicks Steinbeck could never have imagined.

Steinbeck called Salinas "The Valley of the World," and the new Valley of the World Agricultural History and Education Center explores this phenomenon. If farming is your thing, you can examine unique tools or take part in interactive activities like designing your own crate labels or "taking the long haul" (feel what it's like to be a truck driver).

The National Steinbeck Center, One Main Street, Salinas, is open daily from 10:00 A.M. to 5:00 P.M.; admission charged. For details call (831) 775–4728.

The Steinbeck Festival, a four-day event held each August, celebrates the author with speakers, films, special events, and tours. Another good month to visit Salinas is July, when California's largest rodeo erupts in a fury of bucking bulls and broncos, and cowboys roping calves, wrestling steers, and racing around barrels. For further information contact the rodeo at (800) 771–8807 or the Salinas Valley Chamber of Commerce, P.O. Box 1170, Salinas, CA 93902; (831) 424–7611.

If you plan to continue south through the valley, an idyllic alternate route along the ***River Road*** takes you through fields of vegetables and grapevines. This scenic trip starts about 5 miles west of Salinas off Highway 68 and follows the course of the Salinas River south to Soledad. Historic sites along the way include farmhouses, an early mission (at Soledad), and hot springs.

Monterey County, and the Salinas Valley in particular, has emerged as the country's leading wine-grape-growing region, with about 35,000 acres under cultivation. The valley owns the distinction of being the world's first premium grape-growing region developed through scientific study. Back in the 1930s, two University of California professors found that parts of it exactly matched the climate of prime growing regions in Europe. But not until the 1960s was the potential realized. Now there are about a dozen ***Salinas Valley wineries*** with many offering tastings and tours.

One pleasant detour from the River Road is to the ***Blackstone Vineyard*** in Gonzales. Tours take you to see where the grapes are crushed and through warehouses lined with giant barrels used in fermentation. You end up in the tasting room, right next to a deli and gift shop, to sample the winery's outstanding vintages. One added bonus here is a priceless collection of Ansel Adams photos entitled "The Story of a

Winery," which show wine making from the first bud on the vine to the final drink. The Monterey Vineyard, at 800 South Alta, is open daily from 10:00 A.M. to 5:00 P.M.; call (831) 675–4000 for information.

There are other outstanding wineries in the valley. ***Jekel Vineyards*** in Greenfield is open daily from 11:00 A.M. to 4:00 P.M. for tastings and tours by appointment; call (831) 674–5522. ***Smith & Hook Winery*** near Soledad overlooks the spot where missionaries planted the first grapes. Tasting is offered daily from 11:00 A.M. to 4:00 P.M. with tours by appointment; call (831) 678–2132. (A stop at this winery and Soledad Mission makes a nice conclusion to the River Road tour.) ***Chalone Vineyards,*** the patriarch of Monterey wineries, bottles some of the most respected American wines. Tastings on weekends are from noon to 5:00 P.M., weekdays by appointment; call (831) 678–1717.

Chalone Vineyards lies near ***Pinnacles National Monument,*** whose western side is reached via Highway 146 (east from Highway 101) at Soledad. An alternate route to the Pinnacles' eastern side is via State Route 25 through Hollister and the San Benito Valley. The route dips and rolls through fields and vineyards, passing sleepy hamlets like Tres Pinos and Paicines. This is ranch and farm country free from urban blights, the air scented with a strange mixture of flowers and fertilizer—a place where things are grown rather than made.

English explorer George Vancouver discovered this incredible geological showcase back in 1794, and the Pinnacles became one of America's first national monuments. What you see are remnants of an ancient volcano, carved and hammered by the elements over eons of time into jagged stone spires. Rocky peaks and solitary minarets rise against the sky to 1,200 feet above a canyon floor, pockmarked with talus caves and deep clefts cut by seasonal streams. The starkly angular shapes form a striking contrast with the soft rolling hills of the Gabilan range, making the place seem otherworldly. The barren, craggy landscape would make this a great place to film a movie about another planet.

But the Pinnacles has another side—spring wildflowers sprouting in the crevices, golden eagles and prairie falcons wheeling across the sky, miles of superb hiking trails through awe-inspiring terrain. It's a place that challenges the spirit as well as the body.

Incredibly, the Pinnacles sits about 200 miles north of its original location. About twenty-three million years ago, a volcano in what is now Southern California spewed forth countless tons of rock and lava through fissures in the surface. As most people know, the state straddles the 600-mile-long San Andreas Fault, a juncture of two large sections of the earth's crust. The Pacific Plate, moving north about 2 inches per year, has carried half of this lava flow with it. The Pinnacles' geological twin east of the fault remains where it was originally formed, buried beneath some hills near Lancaster in the south.

One reason the 4-by-6-mile park remains so wild is that it is not crossed by any road. Entry is from the west side at Chaparral Ranger Station or from the east, where park headquarters is located. Each side has its own personality and attractions: The west is better for basic camping or one-day visits. The more developed eastern side has a visitor center, as well as a private RV park and a small store. Both sides provide picnic sites and rest rooms.

A series of scenic trails link the two sides of the Pinnacles. Hiking and rock climbing are extremely popular, and trails of all skill levels lead you through some inspiring scenery. ***Bear Gulch Caves,*** for example, are rimmed with red cliffs splashed with green lichens. The popular caves are actually narrow canyons roofed over by fallen boulders. Balconies Cave, on the west side, was similarly formed, and you'll have to crawl, duck, and squeeze in pitch black along a few hundred feet of the trail (flashlight required).

You will likely spot animals common to the dense chaparral-brush habitat, such as black-tailed deer, and, if you're lucky, prowling bobcats or wild boars scavenging for acorns. Be sure to bring water; you can work up quite a thirst in this desiccated country. Late fall through spring is the best time to visit, because summer heat can be brutal. For more information contact the park rangers at (831) 389–4485.

One final treat awaits adventurous travelers: ***Mission San Antonio de Padua,*** near King City, marooned in the nineteenth century as if history and modern California had passed it by. Other missions in the string of Spanish colonial outposts may be prettier, but here a sense of isolation is pervasive, as it must have been when Father Serra founded it back in 1771. One good reason why the mission seems so cut off from the world: It sits completely surrounded by a U.S. Army base, Fort Hunter-Liggett. In fact, you will have to pass through an M.P. checkpoint to enter the mission lands.

Spaniards picked their sites well; this splendid valley, leeward of the Santa Lucia Range, is well watered and filled with grassy, oak-dotted hills. By the year 1800 Mission San Antonio was known for its wheat and livestock, with thousands of head of cattle, sheep, and horses. Some 1,300 Indians worked the fields under the watchful eyes of the Catholic padres.

Sitting on a piece of flat ground, the nicely restored mission (with some of its original roof tiles) looks as if its inhabitants simply walked away one day. A small chapel anchors one corner of the compound, its three-bell campanario reaching skyward as if in prayer. The adjacent quadrangle includes a museum, guest rooms for the occasional religious retreat, and narrrow passageways musty with the smell of bat droppings.

In the museum you can wander through several dark rooms displaying the best of mission life: handmade hymnals on sheepskin parchment, irons used to press the hosts for Holy Communion, and simple musical instruments that the padres taught their wards to play. Outside is further evidence that civilization passed this way: remains of an aqueduct, a water-powered gristmill, tanning pits, an oak stump for slaughtering livestock, and the original oak wine vat. But above all there is the quiet solitude of the place, broken only by a twittering bird or the splash of water in an old stone fountain.

Mission San Antonio de Padua is reached from the town of Jolon, via County Roads G–14 (north) or G–18 (south) a few miles off Highway 101. It is open daily from 9:00 A.M. to 4:30 P.M. (noon to 5:00 P.M. Sunday), with a small admission charged.

PLACES TO STAY ON THE SOUTH COAST

SAN MATEO/ SANTA CRUZ COAST

Beach House at Half Moon Bay, 4100 North Cabrillo Highway 1, Half Moon Bay; (800) 315–9366

Costanoa Coastal Lodge, 2001 Rossi Road, Pescadero; (650) 879–1100

The Darling House, 314 West Cliff Drive, Santa Cruz; (831) 458–1958

Harbor View Inn, 51 Avenue Alhambra, El Granada; (650) 726–2329

Old Thyme Inn, 779 Main Street, Half Moon Bay; (650) 726–1616

MONTEREY PENINSULA/ BIG SUR

Bay Park Hotel, 1425 Munras Avenue, Monterey; (800) 338–3564

Big Sur Lodge, Pfeiffer Big Sur State Park; (800) 424–4787

Captain's Inn, Moss Landing, (831) 633–5550

Carmel Mission Inn, 3665 Rio Road, Carmel; (800) 348–9090

Carmel Valley Lodge, Carmel Valley Road/ Ford Road, Carmel; (800) 641–4646

Casa Munras, 700 Munras Avenue, Monterey; (800) 222–2446

Colton Inn, 707 Pacific Street, Monterey; (800) 848–7007

Hotel Pacific, 300 Pacific Street, Monterey; (800) 554–5542

La Playa Hotel,
Camino Real at Eighth,
Carmel-by-the-Sea;
(800) 582–8900

Monterey Peninsula Inns,
1100 Lighthouse Avenue,
Pacific Grove;
(800) 525–3373

Pine Inn,
Ocean and Mount Verde,
Carmel-by-the-Sea;
(800) 228–3851

Ventana Inn & Spa,
Highway 1 South,
Big Sur;
(800) 628–6500

Victorian Inn,
487 Foam Street,
Monterey;
(800) 232–4141

INLAND VALLEYS

Casa de Fruta Orchard Resort,
6680 Pacheco Pass Highway,
Hollister;
(408) 842–9316

Country Rose Inn,
455 Fitzgerald Avenue,
San Martin (Gilroy);
(408) 842–0441

Good Nite Inn,
545 Work Street,
Salinas;
(800) 648–3466

Inn at the Pinnacles,
32025 Stonewell Canyon Road,
Soledad;
(831) 678–2400

Laurel Inn Motel,
801 West Laurel Drive,
Salinas;
(831) 449–2474

Paraiso Hot Springs Resort,
Paraiso Springs Road,
Soledad;
(831) 678–2882

Posada de San Juan,
310 Fourth Street,
San Juan Bautista;
(831) 623–4030

San Juan Inn,
410 Alameda Street,
San Juan Bautista;
(831) 623–4380

PLACES TO EAT ON THE SOUTH COAST

SAN MATEO/SANTA CRUZ COAST

The Anchorage (seafood),
4210 Pacific Coast Highway,
Half Moon Bay;
(650) 726–2822

Caddy's (American),
2 Miramontes Point Road,
Half Moon Bay;
(650) 726–6384

Casa Blanca Restaurant (Continental),
101 Main at Beach,
Santa Cruz;
(831) 426–9063

Gilbert's Seafood Grill,
Municipal Pier,
Santa Cruz;
(831) 423–5200

Miramar Beach Restaurant (American),
131 Mirada Road,
Half Moon Bay;
(650) 726–9053

Montara Beach Outrigger (American),
8150 Cabrillo Highway,
Montara;
(650) 728–7366

Moss Beach Distillery (seafood),
Beach Way and Ocean Boulevard,
Moss Beach;
(650) 728–5595

Sanderlings (Continental),
1 Seascape Resort Drive,
Aptos;
(831) 662–7120

MONTEREY PENINSULA/ BIG SUR

Brick's Steakhouse (American),
Lincoln and Fifth,
Carmel;
(831) 626–1999

Casa Linda, (Mexican),
638 Wave Street,
Monterey;
(831) 372–1032

Domenico's on the Wharf (seafood),
50 Fisherman's Wharf,
Monterey;
(831) 372–3655

Fandango (seafood),
223 Seventeenth Street,
Pacific Grove;
(831) 372–3456

Il Fornaio (Italian),
Ocean Avenue and Monte Verde,
Carmel;
(831) 622–5100

India's Clay Oven (Indian),
150 Del Monte Avenue,
Monterey;
(831) 373–2529

La Scuola (Italian),
10700 Merritt Street,
Castroville;
(831) 633–3200

Lugano Swiss Bistro (Continental),
3670 The Barnyard,
Carmel;
(831) 626–3779

Massaro & Santos (Californian),
32 Cannery Row,
Monterey;
(831) 649–6700

The Mucky Duck (British pub),
479 Alvarado Street,
Monterey;
(831) 655–3031

Nepenthe (American),
Pacific Coast Highway,
Big Sur;
(831) 667–2345

Pasta Mia (Italian),
481 Lighthouse Avenue,
Pacific Grove;
(831) 375–7709

Rappa's Restaurant (seafood),
101 Fisherman's Wharf,
Monterey;
(831) 372–7562

Inland Valleys

The Elegant Touch (American),
601A San Benito Street,
Hollister;
(831) 637–6246

Harvest Time (Italian)
7397 Monterey Street,
Gilroy;
(408) 842–7575

Salinas Valley Fish House (seafood),
172 Main Street,
Salinas;
(831) 775–0175

The Steinbeck House,
132 Central Avenue,
Salinas;
(831) 424–2735

Helpful Web sites on the South Coast

Big Sur Chamber of Commerce:
www.bigsurcalifornia.org

Carmel Walks:
www.carmelwalks.com

Elkhorn Slough:
www.elkhornslough.org

Henry Miller Memorial Library:
www.henrymiller.org

Joseph M. Long Marine Laboratory:
www.2.vcsc.edu/seymour center

Mavericks:
www.maverickssurf.com

Monterey Bay Aquarium:
www.mbayaq.org

Monterey Peninsula Visitors & Convention Bureau:
www.montereyinfo.org

Monterey State Historic Park:
www.mbay.net/ mshp/

National Steinbeck Center:
www.steinbeck.org

Pacific Grove Museum:
www.pgmuseum.org

Pinnacles National Monument:
www.nps.gov/pinn

Salinas Valley Chamber of Commerce:
www.salinaschamber.com

San Benito County Chamber of Commerce:
www.sbccc.org

San Mateo County Convention and Visitors Bureau:
www.sanmateocounty cvb.com

Santa Cruz County Visitors Council:
www.scccvc.org

Ventana Wilderness Society:
www.ventanaws.org

Worth Seeing/Doing on the South Coast

17-Mile-Drive (Carmel)

Año Nuevo State Reserve (San Mateo Coast)

Cannery Row (Monterey)

Fisherman's Wharf (Monterey)

Monterey Bay Aquarium

Mystery Spot (Santa Cruz)

Pebble Beach Golf Courses

Santa Cruz Beach Boardwalk

North Coast

The North Coast stretches almost 400 miles from Marin County to the Oregon border. Within this huge domain, nicknamed "The Redwood Empire," you will find some of California's outstanding scenery—sheer cliffs and craggy coastline, weathered fishing villages and square-jawed lumber ports, wine-country vineyards, and groves of redwoods as majestic as Gothic cathedrals.

You reach the North Coast via the twisting, incredibly picturesque Highway 1 or the faster and less scenic Highway 101. Numerous country roads connect the two before they join at Leggett in the heart of redwood country. Using both roads, you could make a loop tour taking in the lion's share of the scenic wonders.

Marin County

To reach the North Coast, take Highway 101 north from the Golden Gate Bridge and exit at Mill Valley/Stinson Beach (Highway 1). After reaching Muir Beach proceed 8 miles north to ***Audubon Canyon Ranch,*** which shelters a rookery of great egrets and great blue herons, huge birds with wingspans of up to 6 feet. The sanctuary is open mid-March to mid-July, weekends only.

Audubon Canyon Ranch sits on the east shore of Bolinas Lagoon, a shallow sheet of water enclosed by a sandpit that is home to an abundance of bird and marine life. On the inlet's other side is the curious village of ***Bolinas,*** 2 miles west of the highway at the end of Olema-Bolinas Road. But don't look for a sign pointing the way; reclusive residents keep tearing it down to confuse would-be visitors.

At the turn of the twentieth century, Bolinas was filled with hotels and saloons but then declined. During the 1960s hippies flocked here, and many stayed; you can see their legacy in funky shops such as Women's Crafts Collective, redolent with incense, and Bolinas People's Store, featuring organic foods. Artists and craftspeople abound, and their work appears at a tiny museum on Wharf Road, open weekend afternoons.

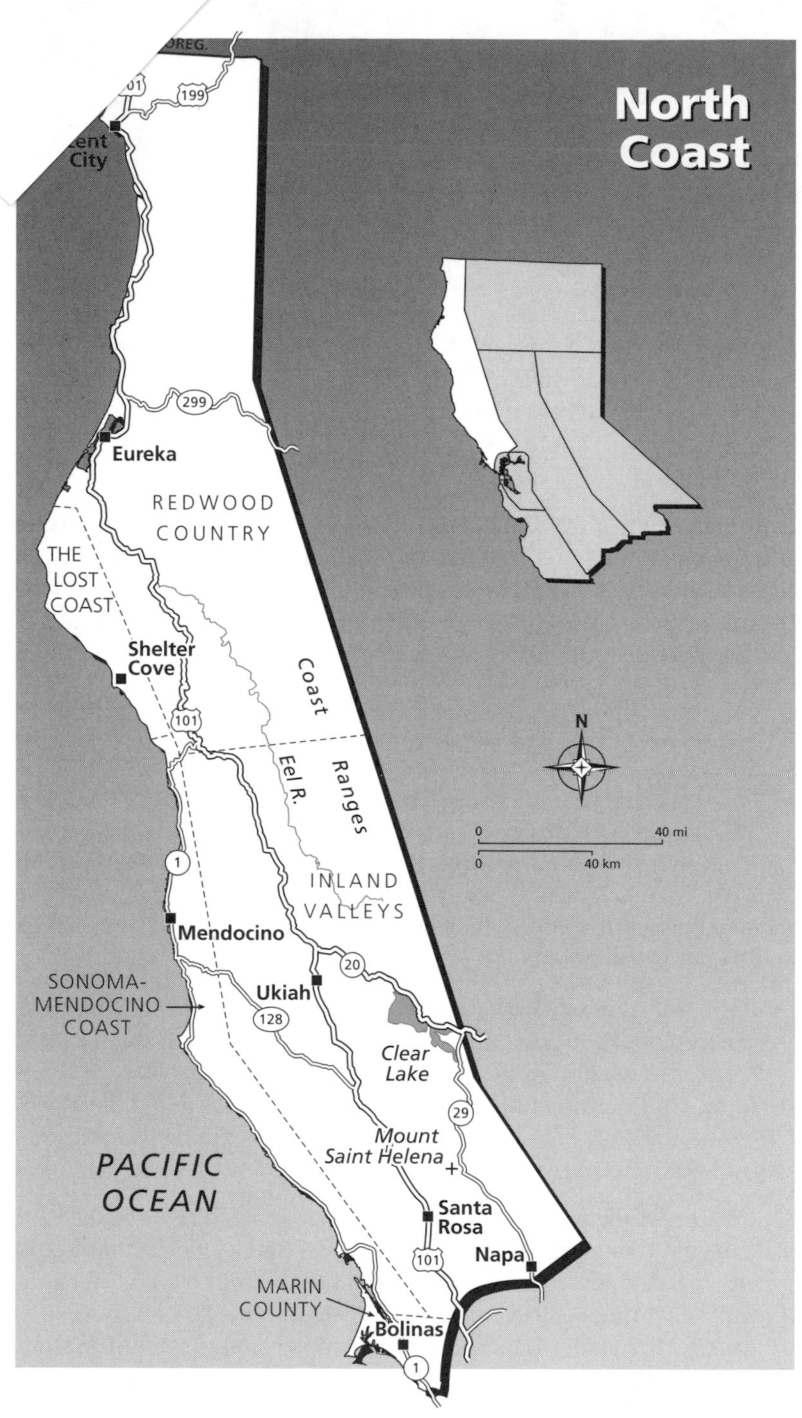
North Coast
199
101
299
Eureka
REDWOOD COUNTRY
THE LOST COAST
Shelter Cove
Coast Ranges
Eel R.
101
1
INLAND VALLEYS
Mendocino
20
Ukiah
SONOMA-MENDOCINO COAST
128
Clear Lake
29
Mount Saint Helena
PACIFIC OCEAN
Santa Rosa
Napa
101
MARIN COUNTY
Bolinas
1
N
0
40 mi
0
40 km

The main street also features a couple of good places to eat such as Bolinas Bay Bakery and Cafe, a gift shop and art gallery, and refreshments at Smiley's Schooner Saloon, a local hangout with live music on weekends. Some wealthy retirees live here, too, and there's an impressive collection of clapboard homes along Brighton Avenue, which leads down to the ocean past Calvary Church (1874).

Author's Top Ten on the North Coast

- *Point Reyes National Seashore*
- *Fort Ross State Historic Park*
- *Mendocino coast*
- *The Lost Coast*
- *Ferndale*
- *Redwood National Park*
- *Boonville*
- *Sonoma Plaza*
- *Jack London State Historic Park*
- *Mount Saint Helena*

According to U.S. Weather Bureau statistics, the Point Reyes Peninsula ranks as the foggiest and windiest spot on the entire Pacific Coast. Although Point Reyes lies in Marin County, only about 40 miles from San Francisco, it seems completely separated from the Bay Area. And even though visitors love the peninsula, especially Texans for some reason, it is large enough and wild enough to offer miles of untouched beaches and hundreds of hideaways. Most of the roughly triangular landmass belongs to one of ***Point Reyes National Seashore***'s two distinct areas: the wind-lashed beaches, treeless hills, and dairy farms to the north, or the forested slopes of Bear Valley to the south (near Olema and park headquarters).

La punta de los reyes (kings' point) owes its name to Spaniard Sebastian Vizcaino, who sailed past on January 6, 1603, the Feast of the Three Kings. But even he was a Johnny-come-lately—more than twenty years earlier, Sir Francis Drake had arrived aboard *The Golden Hinde* and claimed these lands for Queen Elizabeth. According to legend the rollicking seafarer nailed a brass plaque to a tree near the inlet we now call Drake's Bay.

History of quite another sort created Point Reyes. The infamous San Andreas Fault splits Olema Valley and Tomales Bay, separating the peninsula from the mainland geologically. Point Reyes sits perched on the Pacific Plate, which is moving about 2 to 3 inches a year northward and has its own distinctive plant life and minerals. For example, redwoods thrive on Bolinas Ridge to the east, but not on the peninsula.

The epicenter of the great 1906 San Francisco earthquake was just a half mile from where park headquarters now stand. (The only casualty was a cow that fell into a gash in the earth and had to be pulled out by its tail.) You can walk the Earthquake Trail and see where "The Big One" moved a wooden fence 15 feet. (Some geologists claim the epicenter was offshore near San Francisco.)

Also near the visitor center is *Kule Loklo,* a re-created ***Coast Miwok Indian Village.*** Sitting in a quiet meadow, the settlement consists of huts made tepee style from rough planks or thatched reeds, a granary for storing acorns, a ceremonial dance house, and a sweat house—all built using aboriginal tools and methods.

Searching for *Nova Albion*

In the summer of 1579, Sir Francis Drake anchored his ship The Golden Hinde *somewhere along the coast of northern California. This rollicking English buccaneer, who served Queen Elizabeth I, had been raiding Spanish American outposts, and his leaking vessel was overloaded with treasure and in need of repairs. Upon disembarking he named the land* Nova Albion *and claimed it for England a full forty-one years before the first Pilgrims landed at Plymouth Rock.*

However, the exact site of Drake's landfall is uncertain and is hotly debated by local historians and mariners. Unfortunately, the ship's logs describing important details were lost after being turned over to the queen. According to the journal of Chaplain Fletcher, a landing party went ashore and set up tents along the beach as curious Indians watched. One man hammered out a metal plate detailing Drake's claims, which was nailed to a post stuck in the sand and, by the logic of the day, "this kingdome . . . Nova Albion*" became property of England.*

The brass plate Drake left behind was found in 1936 and authenticated, but it turned up at an inland site, obviously moved during the ensuing centuries. The puzzle is further complicated by a confusing chart of the Golden Hinde*'s landing site drawn by a Dutch cartographer. It seems to be a treasure map, recording the site of several tons of silver bars buried by Drake and his men. Later, several expeditions failed to recover the buried treasure due to the faulty records. (According to another theory one ship did find it around 1600, but it sank under the weight off Duxbury Point Reef nearby.)*

Now a historical marker honoring the landing sits above the beach at Drakes Estero, a small estuary within Drakes Bay at the southern end of Point Reyes National Seashore. Along its leeward curve white cliffs, much like those in Dover, England, protect the bay, and these may have inspired the name New Albion. Enthusiasts of the local Drake Navigators' Guild also claim that shards of Chinese porcelain found here pinpoint the exact spot of Drake's camp at the entrance to the estuary.

But other people challenge the claim, proposing alternate sites like Agate Beach in Bolinas, 10 miles to the south. Here black rock ballast and stone cannonballs, along with a mariner's dial and other artifacts, have surfaced. Some other people say the landing took place within San Francisco Bay or as far south as Half Moon Bay. So until other evidence is unearthed, the debate will rage on.

Bear Valley Trail (named for the once numerous grizzlies) cuts through Inverness Ridge from the visitor center to the ocean. The 4.4-mile path is the park's most popular, passing through woods and meadows to an agate-strewn beach, tide pools, and Arch Rock—carved by crashing Pacific waves.

But Point Reyes is not for hikers only. You can drive through the little town of Inverness, founded by a judge who noted the area's resemblance to the Scottish Highlands, or out Limantour Road to a long, sandy spit. Facing almost due south, Drake's Bay has a flat, sandy beach abutting sandstone bluffs. Very different is Ten Mile Beach, a seemingly endless swath of sand pummeled by high winds and swirling surf and loaded with driftwood riches.

The most popular drive takes you 21.5 miles out to ***Point Reyes Lighthouse,*** cowering from the elements at the tip of the peninsula. Before the lighthouse went up in 1870, about forty ships had been smashed into kindling against the rocks here. To keep below the fog ceiling, the lighthouse sits at 294 feet above sea level and is reached from an even higher platform via a vertiginous staircase of 308 steps.

A catwalk and railing around the lighthouse provide an outstanding vantage point for whale watching in season. The big gray ones, as many as eighty a day during the mid-January peak, can pass within a few hundred yards. It's fortunate for whale watchers that there's nothing to see in summer, when this spot becomes the foggiest in the United States. The only time you *can* see anything is when the winds are so strong you may get blown out to sea; gusts up to 133 miles per hour have been recorded. The lighthouse is open Thursday through Monday from 10:00 A.M. to 4:00 P.M., but may be closed during high winds.

Point Reyes is packed with sightseeing options, but one highlight is the ***Tule Elk Preserve,*** reached by a jaw-dropping drive along a wooded ridge top. Elk calves and young bulls begin to appear in May, and by late summer the dominant males start to gather their "harems" for breeding.

Top Annual Events on the North Coast

Napa Valley Mustard Festival *(February–March)*

Mendocino Coast Whale Festivals, *Mendocino/Fort Bragg (March)*

Redwood Coast Dixieland Jazz Festival, *Eureka (March)*

Spring Wildflower Show, *Boonville (April)*

Great Arcata to Ferndale Kinetic Sculpture Race *(May)*

Arcata Bay Oyster Festival *(June)*

World's Largest Salmon Barbecue, *Noyo Harbor (July)*

Wildwood Days, *Rio Dell (August)*

Fort Humboldt Days, *Eureka (August)*

Paul Bunyan Days, *Fort Bragg (September)*

Mendocino County Fair and Apple Show, *Boonville (September)*

Festival of Lights, *Yountville (December)*

Trivia

More than two million people visit Point Reyes National Seashore annually.

Sometimes the bulls battle by locking horns to secure their territory and favorite females.

For further information about activities and camping throughout the park, call the Bear Valley Visitor Center at (415) 464–5100. The entire Point Reyes area enjoys an abundance of atmospheric hotels and bed-and-breakfast inns, though they tend to be pricey. The Blackthorne Inn in Inverness floats among the trees like a sailing ship, and one room called the Eagle's Nest is reached by climbing a narrow spiral staircase. Among other choices are the Olema Inn (Olema), Ten Inverness Way (Inverness), Holly Tree Inn (Point Reyes Station), Thirty-Nine Cypress (Point Reyes), and MacLean House (Inverness). Contact Point Reyes Lodging for a full list of area hostelries at (800) 539–1872.

Due to its shallow inlets and cool water, this area is ideal for raising oysters, which feed on the abundant plankton found here. At special oyster farms they are strung together and hung on racks in the bay to grow into mature clusters ready for harvest. Pioneer of this technique is the Johnson Oyster Company on Drake's Estero, located within the national seashore just off Sir Francis Drake Boulevard. Oysters are rough on the outside but tasty inside, and here you can buy them shucked or in the shell to eat on the spot or take home. Open daily except Monday from 8:00 A.M. to 4:30 P.M.; (415) 669–1149.

Tomales Bay tends to be warmer and less windy than the peninsula, and the eastern shoreline along Highway 1 is home to several more oyster farms. Best of the bunch may be Hog Island Oyster Company in the historic town of Marshall (20215 Highway 1). Here you can feast on oysters live in the shell or barbecued (bring your own sauce and napkins) as well as clams and mussels.

Sonoma–Mendocino Coast

Highway 1 between Bodega Bay and Fort Bragg offers stunning seaside scenery, as well as nineteen state and county parks with delightful opportunities for hikers, campers, anglers, and photographers. The stretch south of Jenner, at the mouth of the Russian River, traverses a gentle shelf fringed by sandy beaches, then bucks and snakes through a landscape of sheer cliffs and pounding waves.

A recommended side trip from the coast starts at the village of ***Bodega,*** setting for Hitchcock's thriller, *The Birds* (you can see the old Potter School used in the film). Farther east along Highway 12 is Freestone,

Trivia

San Francisco Solano Mission in Sonoma was California's twenty-first and final mission (1823).

where you can partake of a unique Japanese-style enzyme bath and massage at a spa called Osmosis; (707) 823–8231. Turn north here onto the Bohemian Highway to reach the town of ***Occidental,*** following an old railroad route through thick stands of redwood trees. Area residents flock here for the scenic location and collection of family-style restaurants, coffeehouses, and shops. Particularly appealing for an outdoor lunch is the patio restaurant at the Union Hotel. Continue north 6 miles to the Russian River and turn west on Highway 116 toward a small settlement called ***Duncans Mills,*** with a sign boasting POPULATION 85, ELEVATION 26. Several historic buildings and railway cars form part of an outdoor museum in this sleepy village, at one time the last stop on the Russian River line from San Francisco, 77 miles to the south. (The old train depot and ticket office are being restored to their turn-of-the-century condition.) Good places to eat include the Gold Coast Bakery and Cape Fear Cafe, and an interesting shop to browse in is called Worldly Goods. Return to the coast and the town of Jenner at the mouth of the Russian River by driving west on Highway 116.

Trivia

The Russian trading post at Fort Ross enabled the Russians to explore the northern California coast while hunting for seals and otters.

The Russians were here! The Russians were here! ***Fort Ross State Historic Park,*** sitting on a bluff overlooking the Pacific, re-creates the substantial Russian colony located here in California's early days. The setting, about 12 miles north of Jenner in Sonoma County, is a dramatic one—a weathered gray fortress with the sea at its feet and a backdrop of forested hills. Fort Ross was the largest Russian settlement outside Alaska and caused the Spanish much heartburn about the safety of Alta California. But in the end, neither nation would control this rich land.

In 1812 Ivan Kuskov and a shipload of colonists landed to establish a beachhead on the Pacific coast for the powerful Russian American Trading Company. Raising food was one objective, but most of the Russians and native Alaskans arrived eager to exploit the lucrative sea otter pelt trade. Over the next few years, the outsiders, using two-man kayaks and harpoons, slaughtered the otters nearly to the point of extinction.

The Russians remained almost thirty years, and during its heyday Fort Ross became the centerpiece of a sizable community. Despite intense rivalry a lively trade developed with the Spanish, and products from Fort Ross were highly prized by *Californios.*

Fort Ross

Fort Ross today is a careful reconstruction with some original elements intact, such as the Rotchev House, home of the last commandant and his gracious wife, Princess Helena. The domed chapel is the most interesting building architecturally; built in 1824, it was completely destroyed by a fire in 1970. One of the original bells, which melted in the blaze, was recast for display outside the church. Inside, where the Russians once prayed, you see religious icons and flickering candles.

But the Russian experiment did not last. By the 1830s sea otters were thought to be extinct, and gophers were destroying the crops. In 1841 the colonists tried unsuccessfully to sell the fort to Mexico. Later it was unloaded for $30,000 to none other than John Sutter of Sacramento, who would have his own rendezvous with history several years later when he discovered gold. In a few months the Russians were gone, and the future of California changed course.

Trivia

The tallest totem pole in the United States (160 feet) is found at McKinleyville in Humboldt County.

Fort Ross State Historic Park is open daily from 10:00 A.M. to 4:30 P.M.; entry fee is $4.00 per car. For information call (707) 847–3286.

One final site before leaving Sonoma County (29 miles north of Jenner) is ***The Sea Ranch,*** a high-end residential and vacation development famed for its innovative architecture: highly modern yet clad in sea-weathered wood. Back in the 1960s, developers purchased 5,000 acres, a 10-mile stretch of coastline, and began to build amid some controversy. Yet the final product is a fine example of low-impact development. There is a luxury hotel, golf course, and even a chapel, not to mention incredible ocean views.

The ***Mendocino coast*** is steeped in a kind of sleepy beauty—with emerald forests cooled by ocean mists, the blue-green water and white surf of the Pacific, and weathered redwood barns and fences. Sheep graze languidly on the hillsides while seals splash offshore. The whole coast is so scenic that television and movie crews flock to places like Mendocino (used to simulate New England for the TV series *Murder, She Wrote*).

Highway 1 enters Mendocino County at ***Gualala*** (pronounced wa-LA-la), a relatively balmy village where the wealthy and famous have been known to hang out. To the north sits stately ***Point Arena Lighthouse,*** and you can huff and puff up the 115-foot tower to eye-popping views of the coastline. It's open daily from 10:00 A.M. to 3:30 P.M.; $4.00 admission charged. ***Manchester State Beach,*** a 5-mile sweep of sand and surf, is the first in a string of fine state parks along this magical coast.

Lumber profoundly shaped Mendocino's modern history. In 1850 an expedition seeking a foundered ship brought back reports of vast redwood forests—just the kind of news needed by the lumber-hungry boomtown of San Francisco. Whenever a river or stream met the ocean, a mill and small town sprouted, each with a "doghole port" just large enough for a ship to anchor. Though most mills shut down by the 1960s, you can still see remnants of docks and piers running out into cramped coves. The village of ***Elk,*** about 15 miles south of Mendocino, is a classic doghole port town, sprawling on a high bluff overlooking a rock-strewn cove where lumber was once king.

Little River is another photogenic coastal hamlet with its fair share of country-style inns. Among them is the Inn at Schoolhouse Creek on the site of a former Coast Guard lookout station, where each room has a personal touch. Nearby Little River Cove (2 miles south of Mendocino) is a favorite spot for scuba and skin divers, who brave the frigid waters to

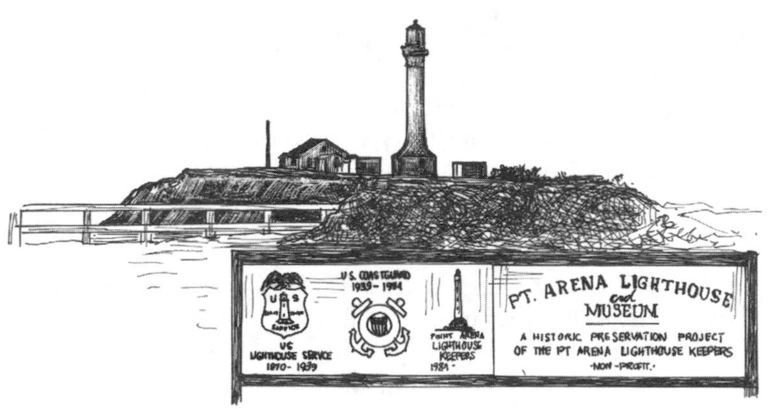

Point Arena Lighthouse

harvest abalone. Just opposite lies ***Van Damme State Park,*** where nature is practicing its own curious form of bonsai with the native cypresses and pines.

In the Pygmy Forest fully mature trees range from just 6 inches to a few feet in height, stunted by shallow root penetration, a lack of nutrients, and the world's most acidic soil. The contrast with the giant stands of redwoods nearby is unnerving. Van Damme also offers a delightful hike up to Fern Canyon, where a junglelike profusion of lush foliage crowds the banks of Little River. The park is open daily from dawn till dusk for a $4.00 per car day-use fee; for information call (707) 937–5804.

Another nearby park is definitely worth a stop. ***Jughandle State Reserve*** offers a special nature trail called The Ecological Staircase on which hikers can trace half a million years of geological history along five wave-cut terraces. Going from the shoreline inland, each one is a hundred feet higher and a hundred thousand years older and features different rock formations and flora.

The town of ***Mendocino*** (population 1,050) is a real charmer, with a white-steepled church and clapboard houses, unique shops (like one selling only local jams and preserves) and cozy country inns, and sitting right next to scenic Mendocino Headlands. Downtown contains an intriguing collection of galleries, some selling crafts and others (like Gallery One and William Zimmer) offering sophisticated fine art. You can pour a Guinness and sample pub grub at Patterson's or dine out in style at one of several gourmet restaurants. For all these reasons, on weekends Mendocino can become overrun with tourists, so try to come during the week. But while everyone talks about how it looks "just like" a New England fishing village, it really does not. The streets are too wide and straight, and the houses are set too far apart and don't have shutters.

Rough-and-tumble ***Noyo Harbor,*** on the other hand, could have been lifted from the Maine coast. This little fishing port just south of Fort Bragg is chock-a-block with trollers, drag boats, and Boston whalers tied up two and three deep along the wharves. Weathered canneries, warehouses, and salty-dog restaurants jostle for position along the waterfront with marine hardware stores and fish markets. A handful of shops sell things like smoked salmon and burl art, a world apart from Mendocino.

Quaintness comes hard in Noyo. This is a place of scavenging gulls and marine shortwaves, cannery workers in rubber boots and derelict trailers, battered pickups and rotting nets. A sign on the door of the local grocery says it all: ABSOLUTELY NO WETSUITS OR MUDDY FEET! Many of the muddy feet come from divers for sea urchins, those spiny purple creatures whose private parts are in great demand for Japanese sushi. But there are no sushi bars in Noyo, nor does fish come served with delicate sauces of garlic and herbs; most likely it will arrive breaded and deep-fried, served in a basket with tartar sauce and fries. For good food try Sharon's by the Sea or Cap'n Flints. Noyo also serves home to the self-proclaimed World's Largest Salmon Barbecue, a giant fish feed every Fourth of July weekend.

If you like to catch your own, try one of several charter boat services, which also do whale watching trips in season. There are shops to outfit you for the trip, and others to freeze, can, or smoke your catch. Noyo Harbor lies 1 mile south of Fort Bragg at the end of North Harbor Drive. Noyo River Lodge (707–964–8045) overlooks the harbor and river.

Fort Bragg got its start as part of the Mendocino Indian Reservation, then became a military post. Charles Russell Johnson built the first mill in 1885, and he later launched the Skunk Railroad (named for the smell of its original gas engines), at present Fort Bragg's number one visitor attraction. From a frontier-style depot, the train, powered by a mint-condition 1924 Baldwin steam engine, takes visitors on an inspiring trip to Willits on the other side of the densely forested coastal mountains.

Lumber has always counted here, and the town puts on its best face for events like Paul Bunyan Days on Labor Day weekend, when big crowds gather to watch loggers throwing axes, climbing poles, and rolling logs. There's even a chainsaw art competition, an event that makes Mendocino artists cringe.

Fort Bragg's historic downtown section along Main and Franklin Streets has antiques shops, art galleries, restaurants, and hostelries, including a growing number with overtly cute names—"For the Shell of It" (souvenirs) and "Understuff" (ladies lingerie). The North Coast Brewing Company has taken over the 400 block of North Main Street with towering vats, a store, and a restaurant; brewery tours are available.

Trivia

The California gray whale measures up to 50 feet in length and weighs up to 40 tons.

Several miles of beachfront north of Fort Bragg belong to MacKerricher State Park, which offers the rare chance to explore pristine coast with large sand dunes and crashing waves. It's open without day-use fee to picnickers, beachcombers, and horseback riders.

For further information contact the Fort Bragg–Mendocino Coast Chamber of Commerce; (800) 726–2780.

The Lost Coast

After Rockport, 28 miles north of Fort Bragg, Highway 1 turns inland, merging with Highway 101 at Leggett. The reason is simple—coastal mountains called the ***King Range*** thrust out to sea like a clenched fist, rising from sea level to 4,000 feet in just 3 miles. This precipitous climb caused construction engineers to shake their heads and change direction, and the resulting slice of highway-free terrain (about 50 miles long) is called the ***Lost Coast.***

Adventurous travelers can explore some of California's wildest landscapes—wave-battered sea stacks and wrecked steamers, jagged cliffs and talus piles—and see an abundance of wildlife including mink, deer, river otter, and black bear. The King Range is one of the wettest spots on the Pacific coast, with about 100 inches annually (mostly between October and April) and almost twice that amount in a really wet year.

Trivia

The King Range is one of the most geologically active ranges in the United States. It has risen 66 feet over the last 6,000 years.

The heart of the Lost Coast is the ***Sinkyone Wilderness,*** one of the most remote pockets in the nation. Usal Road, north of Rockport (at milepost 90.9), is the unpaved route into this area, and it continues in a generally northward direction along the top of a steep ridge. From the crest you can catch glimpses of the uninhabited coast, with its tiny "ghost ports," such as Wheeler at the mouth of Jackass Creek, now just a pile of bleached timbers. There are also some rugged trails and camping facilities for the backpacking set.

A Whale of a Show

Each year more than 15,000 giant whales weighing up to forty tons—grays and other species—travel thousands of miles between the Bering Sea (Alaska) and warm lagoons in Baja California to mate and give birth to 15-foot calves. Along the craggy coast of northern California, whale watchers gather to see the parade of these magnificent mammals, who often come close to the shore.

When: *The trip south starts in late November and peaks in January; the return takes place in March and early April, by which time the calves have grown to 20 feet and more. The best viewing time is early morning with the sun at your back, when the water is calmest.*

Where: *The best observation sites are high on cliffs, where the land juts out and lighthouses often stand. Among the best spots (by county from south to north):*

- *Marin: Point Reyes National Seashore, especially the lighthouse and Drakes Bay*
- *Sonoma: Salt Point State Park near Jenner and Bodega Head in Sonoma Coast State Beach*
- *Mendocino: Gualala Head, Point Arena lighthouse, Noyo Harbor entrance, Mendocino Headlands State Park, Laguna Point in MacKerricher State Park*
- *Humboldt: Shelter Cove and Clam Beach (north of Eureka)*
- *Del Norte: Castle Rock and Endert's Beach in Redwood National Park (south of Crescent City)*

What: *You may see just one mother and her calf or a hundred whales traveling in a pod, swimming (at 3 to 4 mph) and frolicking merrily. Among the behaviors to watch for: breathing (approaching the surface to take several breaths before diving); spy hopping (poking the head above the surface and holding the pose as if for a photo op); blowing (exhaling water and air through the top of the head in a V-shaped spout); sounding (diving at a steep angle so that the fluke, or tail, is thrust out of the water); and breaching (leaping from the water and twisting the entire body dramatically in the air). Experts are most puzzled by breaching, but many believe whales do it just for fun!*

Trivia

At Humboldt Redwoods State Park is the Travel-log, a 1915 mobile home crafted from a single tree, in which impresario Charles Kellogg traveled the nation to preach the importance of preserving the redwood forests.

The quiet village of Shelter Cove nestles on a small bay between the two main wilderness areas comprising the Lost Coast. Reached by a tortuous, 24-mile road from Garberville (on Highway 101), it is a special place with a palpable sense of isolation and a rare black-sand beach. At one time a vital shipping point, Shelter Cove now draws campers, whale watchers, and fishermen. Nearby are miles of pristine beaches and small parks, perfect for a getaway picnic, and the shoreline offers an abundance of crab, shellfish, and driftwood.

Much of the Lost Coast belongs to the ***King Range National Conservation Area,*** stretching north of Shelter Cove about 25 miles to the mouth of the Mattole River. There are a handful of drivable roads and a leg-stretching trail leading to the summit of King Peak. Baden-Powell types rate the Lost Coast Trail as outstanding; it's primarily a beach route, passing waterfalls, relics of early shipwrecks, an abandoned lighthouse, Indian shell mounds, and abundant marine life. (Be careful; rattlesnakes often hide in piles of driftwood.)

Trivia

"When a tree takes a notion to grow in California nothing in heaven or earth will stop it."
—Lillian Leland, 1890

For information about the King Range National Conservation Area, contact the Bureau of Land Management, 1695 Heindon Road, Arcata, CA 95521. For Sinkyone State Park call (707) 986–7711.

The easiest way to explore the north part of the Lost Coast is by taking a spectacular 70-mile detour from Highway 101. Mattole Road in Humboldt Redwoods State Park leads to wide-open country of wooded slopes and into the Mattole River Valley, where locals raise livestock, apples, and strange substances not currently considered legal. The hamlet of Honeydew consists of a gas station, post office, and a few refugees from the sixties. Fifteen miles farther on is Petrolia, site of California's first oil strike and today a sleepy village with sleepy residents and a white-steepled church.

Follow the road a few more miles and the ocean suddenly leaps out in all its splendor. That pile of rocks to the north is ***Cape Mendocino,*** the most westerly point in California. Cattle and sheep graze on the hillsides and along the shore, where sand sprays the beach like shrapnel during storms. After about 3 miles the road takes a steep turn back into the mountains.

(The approach is even more impressive coming down this grade from the direction of Ferndale.) It's a thrilling drive not to be missed.

Redwood Country

Although not really "off the beaten path," a drive along the ***Avenue of the Giants*** in Humboldt Redwoods State Park forms an essential part of any visit to the Redwood Empire. This popular 33-mile scenic alternate runs generally parallel with Highway 101 and the South Fork of the Eel River, and it's a slow-down-and-look kind of road without any heavy trucks or high-speed traffic. The south entrance lies 6 miles north of Garberville, and the two-lane road then tunnels through several dozen different groves (the park was acquired piecemeal). An auto-tour brochure is available at either end of the avenue.

Trivia

Sixty percent of the world's tallest trees can be viewed along the 31-mile Avenue of the Giants Scenic Drive.

Numerous turnouts allow for neck craning, and trails lead to tranquil glens and riverbanks. The giant pillars of redwood form a green canopy overhead, penetrated only by solitary shafts of sunlight filtering down to a lush carpet of mosses and ferns clutching the forest floor.

California can claim two native giants—the mighty Sierra Redwood, or Giant Sequoia, with diameters up to 35 feet, and the taller, more slender *Sequoia sempervirens,* or Coast Redwood, found here. These are the bluebloods of the tree world, whose ancestors date back to the dinosaur age—"ambassadors from another time," as John Steinbeck put it.

Trivia

The Smith River (Del Norte County) is California's last undammed river.

The victory of conservationists in saving the trees is honored at ***Founders Grove*** near Weott, where an inviting pathway takes you to Founders Tree, 346 feet tall and about 1,500 years old. Among the redwoods live other species such as Douglas fir, madrone, and tan oak, but mainly ferns or fernlike plants survive in the shadowy world below. The most abundant is the redwood sorrel, a cloverlike ground cover lining the pathways. This vegetation creates a kind of damp twilight mood whatever the time of day; the air is heavy and musty, and the only sounds you hear are the twitter of birds, the trickle of a small stream, or the crunch of humus beneath your feet.

You can exit the Avenue of the Giants at a number of spots within the state park, which is Northern California's largest. One detour goes to

Trivia

Rockefeller Forest in Humboldt Redwoods State Park boasts ten of the sixteen tallest trees on earth.

Rockefeller Forest, a vast expanse of virgin redwoods untouched by logging. That in itself is miraculous, because just one specimen, called the Tall Tree, would yield 235,000 board feet of lumber. Another, the Giant Tree, is one of the largest Coast Redwoods, with a height of 363 feet, circumference of 53 feet, and crown spread of 62 feet. There is an excellent visitor center near Founders Grove that provides details about out-of-the-way trails and attractions. For further information contact Humboldt Redwoods State Park Visitors Center at (707) 946–2263; open daily from 9:00 A.M. to 5:00 P.M.

If you want to see what Small Town U.S.A. *ought* to look like, stop by ***Ferndale,*** the best-preserved Victorian town in California. Throughout this picturesque village grand old wood-and-shingle ladies have been meticulously renovated and painted in outrageously bright color combinations. Naturally, all this provides a startling counterpoint to the wild Lost Coast immediately to the south and to every merely ordinary town.

Founded in 1852 by Seth Lewis Shaw, Ferndale sits snugly at the base of a forested ridge above the Eel River Valley, 4 miles west of Highway 101. All around are dairy farms, with green pastures, red barns, and white farmhouses. There was a time when Ferndale was dubbed "Cream City," and successful local dairymen erected mansions known as "Butterfat Palaces," done up with gingerbread trim and surrounded by white picket fences. Farming still helps Ferndale to prosper, and nobody here wants subdivisions replacing open space and cows. But times do change, and Ferndale is now hoping to milk some of the tourist trade whizzing past on the way to redwood country.

Trivia

The Humboldt County Fair, held each August in Ferndale, is California's oldest.

The town's top attraction is a perfect version of Main Street, with no parking meters or traffic lights and a fine collection of shops. Painted ladies stand cheek-by-jowl up and down the street, showing off their bay windows, cupolas, false fronts, and dazzling color combos. Except for the cars this could be a nineteenth-century American street.

There's plenty to see along Main Street, Ferndale: historic relics such as Danish Hall and the Hotel Ivanhoe, recently restored to its 1870s glory. There's an old-fashioned barber shop and Rexall drugstore and shops galore, like the Emporium and The Gazebo, selling everything you never knew you wanted, from stained glass to antique dolls. By mid-morning the Palace Saloon (1890) is doing a thriving trade (it claims to be the most westerly in California). There's an abundance of unpretentious eating spots, Curley's Bar & Grill, the Candystick, and Cream City Cafe among them. For a special treat, take the horse-drawn carriage tour of Ferndale and imagine yourself in another era.

Trivia

The entire Victorian village of Ferndale has been declared a State Historic Landmark.

Victoriana is hardly restricted to Main Street; one of Northern California's most photographed charmers, the ***Gingerbread Mansion,*** stands a couple of blocks away. This yellow-and-peach fantasy of jigsawed woodwork, turrets, and gables belongs to the Queen Anne–Eastlake style. A prim and proper English garden adorns the exterior, and inside is one of

Monarchs of the Forest

*For millions of years before the last Ice Age, redwood trees stretched across the entire Northern Hemisphere, including Europe and Asia. Now they thrive exclusively in the mists of northern California. The Coast Redwood (*Sequoia sempervirens*) grows along a narrow coastal strip about 450 miles long by 25 miles wide from just north of the Oregon border to Big Sur. This belt is defined by a Pacific climate of mild, foggy summers and cool, wet winters, which is ideal for the trees.*

A typical coastal redwood lives several hundred years and can reach 2,000 years and more. Mature trees average 200 to 250 feet, but the tallest among them surpass 350 feet. That's twice the height of Niagara Falls. Though not as massive as their arboreal cousins, the Giant Sequoia of the southern Sierra Nevada, some coastal redwoods grow up to 20 feet in diameter.

Despite these superlatives, however, redwoods are delicate in many ways. Their cones are quite small, and it takes more than 100,000 seeds to make one pound. Their root systems are broad and shallow, no more than 13 feet deep, which means they can be toppled by strong winds. (This happened in 1991 to the venerable Dyerville Giant in Humboldt Redwoods State Park.)

Yet redwood trees are strong. The soft, reddish bark, from 6 to 12 inches in thickness, acts like asbestos in protecting them from fire. Tannin in the bark makes them resistant to fungus and insects such as termites. For these reasons the heartwood, bright cherry to dark mahogany in color, has been highly prized in building since Americans first arrived. Of two million acres of original old-growth forest, fewer than 100,000 remain today.

Founded in 1918, the Save-the-Redwoods-League has been instrumental in protecting the species by purchasing large tracts of old-growth forest. At present the trees are sheltered in thirty-two California state parks and Redwood National Park.

Trivia

The M.V. Madaket, *the oldest passenger-carrying commercial vessel in the United States (1910), still cruises Humboldt Bay.*

Some 90 percent of the oysters produced in California are harvested from Humboldt Bay.

the most highly rated bed-and-breakfast inns in Northern California, prettied up with lace curtains and floral wallpaper, ceiling mirrors, and old claw-foot bathtubs. Another Victorian charmer, complete with gazebo, is the Shaw House Bed and Breakfast Inn.

For the best overall view of this idyllic community, drive or walk to the top of the city cemetery, filled with moss-covered tombstones. A bit farther out the same road lies ***Russ Park,*** a bird-watcher's dream, where you will find tranquility and the ubiquitous ferns whence Ferndale got its name. For information write the Ferndale Chamber of Commerce, P.O. Box 325, Ferndale, CA 95536 or call (707) 786–4477.

Humboldt County seat ***Eureka*** makes a good base for exploring redwood country without roughing it. The spectacular ***Carson House*** on Second Street is the ultimate Victorian. Its architect took all the design elements to their whimsical extremes and created a monument to pomposity (in the eyes of some), but it's the most-photographed building in town. Surprisingly, most of the "wood carving" is actually done with plaster. Today the Carson House is a private club and cannot be visited without an invitation. Right across the street is another gem built for the Carson family, affectionately called "the pink lady." The Carter House, a remarkably good re-creation built using 1884 blueprints, sits at the corner of Third and L Streets and forms part of the Carter House Victorians bed-and-breakfast complex.

Eureka's Old Town near the waterfront is a trove of Victorians, many restored to mint condition, including the Vance Hotel and Oberon Saloon. The new ***Eureka Boardwalk*** between C and M Streets provides splendid views of Woodley Island and Humboldt Bay, where pelicans dive and harbor seals frolic. Dotted with signal flags and nautical banners, it makes a great place for a stroll. The bay is a haven for wildlife, and a small ferry called *The Madaket* provides a narrated cruise. Operated by the Maritime Museum, the boat has the smallest licensed bar in California. The ferry docks at the foot of L Street; for details call (707) 445–1910.

Trivia

Eureka was named "Best Small Art Town in America" in 1996. More than 8,000 artists call Humboldt County home.

The heart of Old Town is a gazebo at Second and F Streets, site of many local cultural events such as "Arts Alive" on the first Saturday of each month. Eureka has become the arts capital of northwest California, with an abundance of working artists and many fine galleries and museums. The district's centerpiece is the ***Morris Graves Museum of Art,*** housed in a refurbished Carnegie Library at 636 F Street. It features exhibits in seven galleries and an innovative outdoor sculpture garden. Look for Humboldt County's guide, *The Palette,* for current details.

Trivia

Eureka has more Victorian buildings per capita than any other city in California, including the most photographed of all: the Carson Mansion.

Want to find a wooden rain gutter for your house? For an inside look at how Victorians are restored, be sure to visit the ***Blue Ox Millworks and Historic Park,*** dedicated to preserving the skilled craftsmanship involved in transforming raw wood into fine architectural details. The mill features a collection of vintage machinery and human-powered tools that even the Smithsonian would salivate over, among them a bicycle-like velocipede and rare scroll saws and tenoners. This amazing complex of buildings and workshops is a thriving business, not just a museum, and a self-guided tour takes you to a lathe room, sawmill, blacksmith shop, and a vintage print shop with the oldest press in California. Here Blue Ox's owner, the Bunyanesque Eric Hollenbeck, prints his own newspaper when not involved in countless other activities, from boatbuilding to making resins from tree sap. A true monument to American self-reliance, the Blue Ox is located at First and X Streets; for information call (707) 444-3437. Open daily except Sunday from 9:00 A.M. to 4:00 P.M.; admission charged.

Eureka has many gourmet restaurants, but for a different experience be sure to sniff out the ***Samoa Cookhouse,*** the last survivor of its kind in the West. Open for three meals a day, seven days a week, the cookhouse continues the two-fisted tradition of serving huge mounds of hearty food for a fixed price, lumber-camp style. For dinner your rosy-cheeked, well-scrubbed waitress might serve up soup and two salads, baked cod and roast beef, Spanish rice and green beans, apple or cherry pie, milk or juice, and buckets of steaming coffee. You reach the Cookhouse by taking Samoa Bridge across Humboldt Bay to Samoa, about five minutes from Eureka.

Redwood National Park, about an hour's drive north, claims one of the world's tallest trees, as well as some fine scenic and recreational spots spread over 106,000 acres of prime forest and 33 miles of coastline. Park headquarters is located in Crescent City near the Oregon border, but the main visitor center lies to the south at Orick. Try not to get confused, but within the national park

Trivia

Battery Point Lighthouse in Crescent City (1856) is the state's oldest working lighthouse.

Trivia

The Willow Creek Museum, in the mountains 50 miles east of Eureka, contains the world's largest collection of Bigfoot artifacts. According to local lore, the hairy giants are spotted along Highway 299, the "Bigfoot Scenic Byway."

are three California state parks, each floating in a sea of federal land. But no matter who's in charge, every corner of the vast expanse has something to offer, whether Roosevelt elk weighing up to 1,200 pounds, a kayak trip along a mountain stream, or groves of redwood skyscrapers reaching to the heavens.

At ***Orick*** you learn why these Goliaths of the plant world can live more than two millenia. Unfortunately, the same things that make a redwood "everlasting" also make its lumber highly prized by the builders of cities. Already by 1940 about half of California's virgin forests were gone.

Nevertheless, here you can still recapture the feel of a primeval redwood forest. A lush green carpet of ferns and other small plants contributes to the almost fairyland quality found along many trails. Among the more popular are the Redwood Creek Trail to the Harry Cole Tree, an overachiever measuring 366.3 feet from crown to base, taller than a thirty-five-story building. (The grove, near Orick, is accessible year-round.)

Another exceptional stand is fog-drenched Lady Bird Johnson Grove, where a trail passes one tree hollowed out by fire and used as a goose pen. The Penthouse Tree, just a shattered hulk after a storm ripped through the area, now serves as fertile home for a plethora of forest life. Even the heavily damaged trunk sprouts tiny branches again, a noble testimony to the tenacity of redwoods.

Trivia

The "burl art" capital of the world is the town of Orick, southern gateway to Redwood National Park.

Prairie Creek Redwoods State Park offers a spine-twanging excursion along 4 miles of gravel road to Gold Bluffs Beach, where you might spot elk wading into the surf amid huge piles of driftwood. About 2,000 wild elk live here in the park. (Exit at Davison Road from Highway 101; trailers are prohibited.) Four miles farther on, Fern Canyon's nearly vertical walls, set just 15 feet apart in some places, are completely covered with ferns and other plants. Though not awe-inspiring like the redwoods, Fern Canyon provides a startling contrast in scale.

Trivia

Ulysses S. Grant served as an army captain during 1853 at Fort Humboldt, where he was known as "Sam Grant."

The Redwood Information Center in Orick is open from 9:00 A.M. to 5:00 P.M. daily; for information call (707) 464–6101.

For information on the entire area, contact Humboldt County Convention & Visitors Bureau, 1034 Second Street, Eureka, CA 95501; (800) 346–3482.

Inland Valleys

As mentioned, State Highway 1 is the more scenic choice for exploring the North Coast's lower regions. ***The Redwood Highway*** (Highway 101) is faster and more direct, but by no means shabby in the scenery department. And its tributaries lead to one of the region's top draws—Wine Country. You can drive the highway as an alternate to the coastal route or combine the two in a loop; remember that they join at Leggett, about halfway to the Oregon border from San Francisco.

Heading north from Marin, your first stop should be ***Petaluma Adobe State Historic Park*** in Sonoma County. This was the heart of Vallejo Country—General Mariano Vallejo to be exact, whose rancho sprawled over 66,000 acres. The Mexican commandant founded Sonoma and lived part-time on his country estate, a portion of which forms the historic park.

Construction on the adobe house began in the mid-1830s and took a decade to complete. Bricks of adobe (water and straw mixed with clay and then sunbaked) went into 3-foot-thick walls surrounding a central courtyard. Today about 80 percent of the walls are original, and the two-story house has been restored to a working rancho, right down to the crowing roosters, grazing livestock, and hides hanging out to dry. You'll find a pit where adobe bricks are made, a horse-powered millstone, a cast-iron pot filled with bubbling paraffin for candles, a candle-dripping device, wooden looms, and clay ovens for baking bread.

Trivia

At least 370 species of birds have been spotted traveling the Pacific Flyway along the North Coast.

The rancho's brief halcyon era was shattered with the American takeover of California in 1846 and the discovery of gold two years later. Vallejo himself became a living symbol of the romantic days, reluctantly resigned to the inevitable changes. The park is open daily from 10:00 A.M. to 5:00 P.M.; admission charged. For information call (707) 762–4871.

The town of ***Petaluma*** also merits a visit, if only to see the curious blend of ornate Victorians and silos. Bisected by a river and surrounded by rich farmland, Petaluma has been a dairy and poultry center ever since the incubator was perfected here. (There's still an annual Butter and Eggs Day celebration, not to mention the World Wrist Wrestling Championships.) In an earlier era the town was also one of the nation's foremost carriage-building centers, and all the prosperity left a 4-block core of historic structures that went unscathed by the 1906 earthquake. Parts of Petaluma were used in filming *American Graffiti.*

Northwest of Petaluma, the town of ***Sebastopol*** is the heart of Sonoma County's apple district. More specifically the Gravenstein variety, green-yellow in color with red streaks. According to one story, Russians from Fort Ross brought Gravensteins to Sonoma back in the early 1800s. Another has botanical wizard Luther Burbank planting them here about a century ago (he had a farm nearby). In any case Sebastopol is one of few places growing them today, accounting for 90 percent of the entire U.S. crop. Gravensteins are like the Model-T of apples, with thin skin and too short a shelf life for modern markets. But oh, what taste!

From Highway 101 follow Highway 116 (west) at Cotati. "The Gravenstein Highway" meanders through hilly countryside dotted with farms and orchards and crisscrossed by unpaved country lanes. Sebastopol lies about 10 miles west and is a pleasant enough town, with an abundance of antiques stores. But people come for the many farms and roadside fruit stands selling tasty apples, Gravensteins starting in late July and other varieties in autumn. Ratzlaf Ranch, Kozlowski Farms, Walker Apples, Twin Hill Ranch, and dozens more are listed on the ***Sonoma Farm Trails Map,*** available by calling (800) 207–9464.

The season opens each spring with the Apple Blossom Festival. During Sebastopol's ***Gravenstein Fair*** in mid-August, apple mania descends on the area as the fruit appears in every conceivable form: fresh and dried; in pies, cakes, bread, and apple butter; in jam, jelly, juice, and sauce; in apple wine and, of course, pure, delicious apple cider. You can take a horse-and-surrey ride through the orchards and even meet the Apple Queen, whose cheeks are bound to be, well, come see for yourself.

From Sebastopol take Highway 12 northeast to fast-growing ***Santa Rosa,*** a town with a nice historic district and a couple of attractions from a time when the area, as described by Luther Burbank, was "the chosen spot of all the earth as far as nature is concerned." The famous Massachusetts-born horticulturist lived here for more than fifty years and lies buried beneath a cedar of Lebanon he planted next to his home.

The ***Luther Burbank Home and Memorial Gardens*** honors the genius who spent a lifetime trying to improve the quality of plants. You can join a guided tour of the Burbank house, including a visit to a greenhouse and stroll through the gardens.

Burbank's record is written in the hundreds of new plant varieties he developed that now grow in almost every country on earth. Armed with elaborate scientific theories and an uncanny green thumb, he startled contemporaries by creating, among many others, the Shasta daisy; the Russet potato; a spineless cactus for animal fodder; an edible raspberry; large, modern varieties of rhubarb and corn on the cob; and the "plumcot," a cross between apricot and plum. Burbank was fond of grafting the branches of one tree to another, and you can see the elm he created to provide more shade and a single apple tree that produced thirty-six varieties of the fruit. Once challenged by a skeptic to make a "white blackberry," he proceeded to do just that to prove it could be done!

The Burbank Home and Gardens, 204 Santa Rosa Avenue, is open April through October, Tuesday through Sunday from 10:00 A.M. to 4:00 P.M.; admission charged. The Memorial Gardens are open year-round at no charge. For information call (707) 524–5445.

Snoopy, Charlie Brown, and Lucy of the *Peanuts* comic strip are the stars of the new ***Charles M. Schultz Museum*** and Research Center. Born in Minnesota, the humble genius who coined "Happiness is a warm puppy" and other gems was a Santa Rosa resident for many years before his death in 2000. The museum is located across the street from the ice rink where he ate two meals a day, and it has the feeling of a large house.

Peanuts was the most widely circulated comic strip in history (read by 355 million people worldwide), inspired many TV specials, and is the only such feature given a retrospective at the Louvre in Paris. Yet it took time for the innovative concept to catch on: kids faced with the tribulations of childhood in ways every adult could identify with. Originally called *Li'l Folks,* the strip first appeared in 1950 amid *Superman, Prince Valiant,* and other traditional comic fare, and it met with some hostility (critical letters denouncing *Peanuts* as boring and stupid are on view). About one hundred original four-panel storyboards are on display from an archive of 7,000. The most remarkable exhibit is a mural in the Great Hall made from 3,500 *Peanuts* strips reproduced on tiles, which forms a giant image of Charlie Brown and Lucy. The Charles M. Schultz Museum, 2301 Hardies Lane, Santa Rosa, is open daily except Tuesday. For hours and admission charges, call (707) 579–4452.

North of Santa Rosa, shopping malls and tract homes give way to a rustic landscape of woods and vineyards interspersed with a few small towns like Healdsburg and Geyserville. One delightful side trip from the main highway takes you into bucolic Anderson Valley, which looks more like parts of Germany than tourist-poster California. There's something "foreign" about the residents here as well. Some still speak a strange local dialect called *Boontling*, designed to confuse outsiders decades ago. (See below.)

Heading west from Cloverdale take Highway 128, a road with a thousand curves that passes through deep-green hills and pastureland, fruit orchards and vineyards. The road flattens out around the town of Boonville, a good place for a break at Anderson Valley Brewing Company and Buckhorn Saloon, voted one of the country's top small breweries. On weekends (11:00 A.M. to 4:00 P.M.) the ***Anderson Valley Historical Museum,*** housed in a little red schoolhouse, displays an unusual collection of bear traps and Indian baskets, loggers' saws and old gingham dresses.

Trivia

Lake County grapes produce more award-winning wines per acre than those in any other area in the world.

Boonville is the linguistic home of Boontling, which is a hodgepodge of English, Scottish, Pomo Indian, and made-up words, "a deliberately contrived jargon," according to one Cal State University professor, who has compiled a dictionary of the "language." For example, *bahl gorms* means "good eats," and a pay telephone is called a *bucky walter.* Though spoken mostly from around 1880 to 1920, you can still spot signs on Main Street written in Boontling like one for the cafe *Horn of Zeese,* which means a good "cup of coffee."

Cut by the Navarro River, 16-mile-long Anderson Valley was originally devoted to logging and livestock, but farmers soon discovered it was perfect for raising apples and wine grapes. There are several good wineries here with crowd-free tasting rooms; among them, Roederer Estate Winery in the hamlet of Philo is open daily from 11:00 A.M. to 5:00 P.M.; for information call (707) 895–2288.

From here you can continue along Highway 128 to the Mendocino coast, about thirty minutes away, or double back to Boonville and take Highway 235 northeast to the town of ***Ukiah,*** where you can rejoin Highway 101. *Ukiah* is a Pomo Indian word meaning "deep valley." This is precisely the setting for the Mendocino County seat about halfway between Santa Rosa and Leggett. One good reason to stop is ***The Sun House,*** a State Historic Landmark, and the adjacent ***Grace Hudson Museum,*** erected by townsfolk devoted to the memory of this inspired artist.

In 1891, soon after Grace Carpenter married Dr. John Hudson, she painted a portrait of a Pomo Indian child called *National Thorn,* the first in a numbered series of 684 oils, mostly of Native American subjects. The Ukiah museum boasts only a few of the paintings, however. Most hang in museums and private collections all over the United States; even Kaiser Wilhelm of Germany owned one.

Trivia

Clear Lake, California's largest natural lake (43,000 acres of surface, 100 miles of shoreline), is known as "The Bass Capital of the West."

The collection derives chiefly from the work of John Hudson, a physician by trade, who became so enchanted with the Pomos that he gave up his practice to gather artifacts. For the next forty years, he amassed such a large collection that both the Field Museum and the Smithsonian share part of it today, with plenty left for Ukiah. Included are superb basketry, flutes and clapper rattles, a mush paddle, a modern-looking handbag with abalone pendants, and the scalp of a black mallard.

Other exhibits focus on the Hudsons' personal lives. Grace, for example, came from quite a remarkable family: Her newlywed parents spent four bumpy months traveling to California in an oxcart in 1857, and her mother became an artist of note. The Grace Hudson Museum, 431 South Main Street, is open Wednesday through Sunday. For more information call (707) 467–2836.

The Sun House next door was the Hudsons' dream home for many years. Over the front door hangs the symbol of the Hopi Indian sun god, representing the eternal cycle of fertility and growth. Constructed in 1911, the house features solid, 18-square-inch redwood beams, overhanging eaves, and rough board-and-batten exterior. The Sun House can be visited on the hour from noon to 3:00 P.M. Wednesday through Sunday.

Rather than sticking to the Redwood Highway, you may wish to get a taste of Northern California's famed ***Wine Country,*** hundreds of vineyards and wineries in a three-county piece of paradise. Fame has its price, however, and the entire Napa Valley and much of the Sonoma area are awash in wine-sipping visitors.

Trivia

For twenty-five days in 1846, Sonoma was capital of the independent Republic of California.

One of the nicest spots in Wine Country is ***Sonoma Plaza,*** a large park lined with historical sites, shops, and restaurants right in the middle of town. In fact, Sonoma City Hall, built with huge sandstone blocks, sits on the plaza. This area was in the thick of things during the Spanish-Mexican period, evident by the old mission (last in the original string), army barracks, and old adobe houses. A monument in the park honors those who proclaimed the

"California Republic" here by raising the Bear Flag in 1846. Several of these old structures form a state historic park.

More than the history, however, Sonoma's plaza has a wonderful mood about it, an unspoiled quality in the heart of so much tourism. Interesting shops are found in the Spanish-style El Paseo complex and on First Street, like Baksheesh, which offers handcrafted gifts from "the developing world." The Cheese Factory specializes in the local variety: Sonoma Jack. There are several good restaurants lining the square, including the Swiss Hotel, Plaza Bistro, and Cucina Viansa, which offer the best local wines along with the meal.

Jack London State Historic Park lies slightly off the beaten path, 8 miles north of Sonoma in the Valley of the Moon. You reach it by taking State Route 12 through a rural landscape of meadows and creeks to the pocket-size community of Glen Ellen. London Ranch Road leads to Jack London State Historic Park, located on part of the ranch the illustrious author carved out of "the most beautiful, primitive land to be found in California."

Trivia

Guenoc Estate, one of Lake County's finest wineries, was the home of famed actress Lillie Langtry.

Jack London fought his way up from the grimy factories and waterfront dives of Oakland to become one of the most popular and highest-paid writers in the land. He became widely known for his personal exploits and travels and was considered the rugged individualist incarnate (ironic, given his socialist beliefs).

Weary of roaming, at least for the time, London arrived here with royalties from the sale of *The Call of the Wild;* with the money he purchased 129 acres of land. For the next few years, he pursued a furious pace of living life to the fullest, including a daily writing stint, building and managing the ranch, riding his horse around the property, and entertaining a steady stream of guests—from fellow writers to passing tramps.

You can see the sad remains of one of London's most cherished projects—the grandiose ***Wolf House,*** a sprawling four-story home built with volcanic boulders, redwood logs, and Spanish tiles. Plans called for twenty-six rooms, including a dining room for fifty, nine fireplaces, and a fireproof manuscript vault. The author predicted that Wolf House would stand a thousand years, but soon after construction ended, word reached London and his wife that their dream home was on fire, probably at the hands of an arsonist. Except for the foundation and stone walls, the house was destroyed, and the stark skeletal ruins stand as a tragic reminder of the disaster.

Although London vowed to rebuild, he died just three years later, on November 22, 1916. He was forty years of age. The author's ashes lie beneath a reddish lava boulder on a weed-choked plot near the trail to the ruins.

The House of Happy Walls, built by his widow, Charmian, is steeped in London memorabilia. His study has been re-created with its big rolltop desk, Dictaphone, and other authentic pieces. The museum also contains some of the 600 rejection slips London received from publishers before success came and copies of stories filed during his stints as a war correspondent. Boxing gloves and fencing gear attest to London's combative spirit. And don't overlook the South Seas collection upstairs, which includes a photo of Jack wearing a costume made from human hair.

Jack London State Historic Park, 2400 London Ranch Road, is open daily from 9:30 A.M. to 7:00 P.M. for $3.00 per car. For information call (707) 938–5216.

Glen Ellen is a delightful little town to browse around in. Here, too, is an unusual place to do some "tasting"; not wine but local olive oil of exceptionally high quality. During the olive season (October through March) the press is in operation daily, churning out "extra virgin" oil of low acidity and distinctive taste. You can sample several varieties of oil with bread cubes amid the heady scent of crushed olives. The Olive Press tasting bar is located at 14301 Arnold Drive, Glen Ellen; (707) 939–8900.

From Glen Ellen, a delightful 11-mile drive via ***Oakville-Trinity Road*** snakes over the hills into Napa Valley. You pick it up just north of town and continue about 8 miles before getting your first view of the vineyards from atop a ridge, near a Carmelite monastery. The panorama here is so engaging that the monks must sometimes think they've died and gone to heaven! If you hate crowds, however, you will not stop to dawdle in the valley, but head northeast to visit an unusual town.

Just north of St. Helena, Deer Park Road heads east into the wooded foothills rising from Napa Valley. After a few miles you reach ***Angwin,*** a town inhabited largely by Seventh Day Adventists since the founding of Pacific Union College back in 1909. Here the students are different from those at, say, Berkeley, and tune into a campus radio station playing the "Inspirational Top Forty." Despite living amid the temptations of Wine Country, Adventists shun alcohol and likewise abstain from tobacco and meat. The local supermarket offers an astounding variety of vegetarian and alternative foods; only the pet food section contains meat products.

Down the road from Angwin lies ***Elmshaven,*** a stately Victorian home deemed a National Historic Landmark. Here Ellen G. White, who cofounded the Seventh Day Adventists, wrote numerous books inspired by hundreds of angelic "visions." Call (707) 963–9039 for information on scheduled tours. Both Angwin and Elmshaven evoke a special appeal, like remnants of another time and place slowly fading away.

Four twisting miles over the hill from Angwin along Howell Mountain Road lies arcadian ***Pope Valley,*** which looks like Napa or Sonoma must

Dipping in the Mud

I enter the room with some trepidation. This is my first mud bath, and I pause momentarily at the eerie scene: three seemingly disembodied heads floating in vats of bubbling black mud. In an instant my towel is removed by a no-nonsense attendant, and I'm politely but firmly ushered to a cement tub to wallow in the mire.

I roll over into the hot stuff and am immediately surprised—I don't sink. This is normal, because the mud—a mixture of scalding geyser water, volcanic ash, and peat moss—has the consistency of wet cement, dense and not slimy at all. The attendant scoops 100-degree black muck over me as I lie prone, and he warns me not to stand up because of the intense heat down below. Soon I'm immersed up to my Adam's apple and surprised by how heavy the mud feels as I lie motionless and seemingly weightless. My face is pouring sweat, and a cool cloth placed on my forehead feels wonderful. Soon my body seems to glow, and I feel deeply relaxed.

Situated at the north end of Napa Valley, Calistoga's medicinal water and mud baths, including my choice—Indian Springs on Lincoln Avenue—have attracted visitors for more than a century. At first people came to alleviate rheumatic ailments, but now it's stress, along with "exfoliation" of toxins. And, of course, there are the merely curious, like me. Most spas here sit atop a gigantic natural teakettle of boiling mineral water and offer comparable treatments for about $30.

After twenty minutes I roll out of the tub, and the attendant scrapes off most of the mud before I leap into a much-needed shower. Next I enter a claw-foot porcelain tub filled with steaming mineral water for a good scrub and more relaxation. With all the perspiring there's a danger of dehydration; however, I'm treated to an endless supply of chilled cucumber-lemon water and cool facial towels. Next comes a eucalyptus-scented sauna for more heat and steam, and on to a cooling-off room and towel wrap. I drink more water and slices of cucumber are placed on my eyes.

By now I feel as if I'm floating on a cloud of mist, almost tipsy, and a strange sort of euphoria has taken over my body and mind. I ponder my options—a massage or facial, perhaps, or a dip in the heated outdoor pool. I wonder if someone will have to cart me away in a wheelbarrow, but I don't really care. Right now worries seem to belong to another place, another lifetime.

have decades ago. Yet ironically the biggest attraction here is a bizarre monument to modern technology and one man's obsession: ***Litto's Hubcap Ranch.*** For thirty years Emanuele "Litto" Damonte amassed a personal collection of thousands of automobile hubcaps from every known make and model. These he carefully arranged—along with tractor tires, bottles, wooden ducks, and rose bushes—into clever and artistic configurations around his house.

Mr. Damonte passed away in 1985, but his family maintains the site, now a registered landmark proclaiming that "Litto, the Pope Valley Hubcap King, was here." Located 3 miles north of Pope Valley village, the site has no regular hours, nor is admission charged.

Returning to the Napa Valley, take the Silverado Trail north to ***Calistoga,*** a historic spa/resort deemed "California's Saratoga" by gold-rush entrepreneur Sam Brannan. Local geothermal activity created a sprouting geyser, a subterranean river, and huge pools of natural mineral water used in the town's numerous mud baths and hydrotherapy clinics, not to mention the well-known Calistoga bottled water.

Natural turmoil likewise created an interesting nearby attraction called ***The Petrified Forest,*** which has been attracting visitors since Robert Louis Stevenson wrote about it in 1883. Volcanic eruptions 3.4 million years ago covered the original redwood forest with lava and ash, and over millennia, water laden with silicates seeped into the tree fibers and transformed the wood into stone.

A shaded trail leads past the world's largest petrified trees, most with their original bark. Among them are "The Giant," a 60-foot-long tree already 3,000 years old when it was buried. A shop displays petrified worms, snails, clams, nuts, and coral, plus opalized wood and fossilized insects.

Located about 5 miles from Calistoga on Petrified Forest Road, it is open daily; admission charged. Call (707) 942–6667 for information.

Seven miles to the northeast ***Mount Saint Helena*** is the tallest of all "Bay Area" peaks at 4,339 feet. The view is almost as good as from Mount Diablo (see Bay Area chapter) but much less crowded because cars can't drive to the top. After a fairly rigorous 5-mile hike through chaparral and pine, you peer out on the entire Wine Country and beyond—to the emerald vineyards of Napa and Sonoma, the oak-studded hills of the Valley of the Moon, the vast Santa Rosa Plain, and redwood groves near the Russian River. On exceptionally clear days, you can see Mount Shasta, 192 miles away.

With a little imagination you can also conjure up much of the area's history. Among a Russian party that scaled the mountain in 1841 was Princess Helena, the beautiful wife of Alexander Rotchev, last commander at Fort Ross. Naturally, they named the peak after her patron saint. Later, mountain man George Yount—having been offered a land grant by General Vallejo—stood on the same summit and picked out his Napa Valley domain, present-day Yountville. He went on to plant the first vineyard here in the spicy volcanic soil that proved perfect for growing grapes.

In 1880 young Scottish writer Robert Louis Stevenson brought his bride, Fannie, to the mountain for their honeymoon, and they lived in an abandoned bunkhouse at the Silverado Mine. They spent much time exploring the area and sampling local wines, which Stevenson fondly called "bottled poetry."

At present rustic ***Robert Louis Stevenson State Park,*** along State Route 29 from Calistoga, takes in about 4,000 acres of the mountain. About a mile up the trail, a granite monument is inscribed with a quotation from the author, who "came and stayed and went, nor ever ceased to smile." (Remember, this is the man who spoke of bottled poetry.) The mountain still provides a wonderful getaway from the often frenetic activity of the valley below. The park is open daily from dawn till dusk. For information call (707) 942–4575.

A collection devoted to the author's life is located in the pretty little town of St. Helena in Napa Valley. The Robert Louis Stevenson Museum honors the author of *Treasure Island, Kidnapped,* and *Dr. Jekyll and Mr. Hyde* with displays of personal items such as a writing desk, a hammock, and an inkwell. Among the collection are rare first editions (including an autographed copy of *A Child's Garden of Verses*), original manuscripts, letters, photographs, and memorabilia. There's even a lock of the infant Stevenson's hair! The museum is open daily except Monday from noon to 4:00 P.M. Call (707) 963–3757 for further information.

Lake County lies to the north of the Napa Valley and is, aside from the highly visited Clear Lake area, largely overlooked. Yet it boasts a large number of vineyards and wineries and claims to have California's cleanest air. There's also a unique side trip that few know about. Continuing north on Highway 29 past Mount Saint Helena, you reach ***Middletown*** (about halfway between Calistoga and Clearlake) in the heart of the Mayacamas Mountains.

The big attraction here is a 30-square-mile area of geothermal energy called ***The Geysers.*** Twenty-one power plants produce clean energy, and a company called Calpine operates a ***Geothermal Visitor Center*** in Middletown. Here you can see a labyrinth of pipes and wires, turbines and flashing controls. This is a serious operation: Wells are drilled up to 2 miles deep to tap the steam and create electricity. Located at 15500 Central Park Road, the center is open Thursday through Monday from 9:00 A.M. to 4:00 P.M.; no admission charged. Call (866) 439–7377.

A very different use for this same thermal energy is found at ***Harbin Hot Springs,*** a "clothing optional" resort a few miles north of town. Its seven natural springs produce medicinal waters that visitors claim work miracles, and it just might be true. People have been coming here since before 1900. Today the place has taken on a "new age" flavor, with yoga, tantra, watsu, and a whole range of self-improvement seminars and workshops. For information about Harbin Hot Springs, write to P.O. Box 782, Middletown, CA 95461 or call (800) 622–2477.

PLACES TO STAY ON THE NORTH COAST

ALONG HIGHWAY 1 (MARIN–SONOMA–MENDOCINO)

Breakers Inn,
P.O. Box 389,
Gualala;
(707) 884–3200

Carriage House,
325 Mesa Road,
Point Reyes Station;
(415) 663–8627

Elk Cove Inn,
6300 South Highway 1,
Elk;
(800) 275–2967

Greenwood Pier Inn,
5928 Highway 1,
Elk;
(707) 877–9997

The Hotel Inverness,
P.O. Box 780,
Inverness;
(415) 669–7393

The Inn at Occidental,
3657 Church Street,
Occidental;
(707) 874–1047

The Inn at Schoolhouse Creek,
7051 North Highway 1,
Little River;
(707) 937–5525

John Dougherty House,
571 Ukiah Street,
Mendocino;
(707) 937–5266

Murphy's,
Coast Highway 1,
Jenner;
(707) 865–2377

Point Reyes Seashore Lodge,
10021 Highway 1,
Point Reyes;
(415) 663–9000

Thomas' White House Inn,
118 Kale Road,
Bolinas;
(415) 868–0279

LOST COAST/REDWOOD COUNTRY

Abigail's Elegant Victorian Mansion B&B,
Fourteenth and C Streets,
Eureka;
(707) 444–3144

Bayview Inn,
310 Highway 101 South,
Crescent City;
(800) 446–0583

Beachcomber Inn,
Shelter Cove Road,
Shelter Cove;
(707) 986–7733

Benbow Inn,
445 Lake Benbow Drive,
Garberville;
(800) 355–3301

Carter House Country Inn,
301 L Street,
Eureka;
(707) 445–1390

Curly Redwood Lodge,
701 Redwood Highway,
Crescent City;
(707) 464–2137

Eureka Inn,
518 Seventh Street,
Eureka;
(707) 442–6441

Ferndale Inn,
619 Main Street,
Ferndale;
(707) 786–4307

Lady Anne Inn,
902 Fourteenth Street,
Arcata;
(707) 822–2797

Shaw House Bed
& Breakfast,
703 Main Street,
Ferndale;
(800) 557–7429

Stonegate Villas,
65260 Drive–Thru
Tree Road,
Leggett;
(707) 925–6226

White Rose Mansion,
149 South Fred
Haight Drive,
Smith River;
(707) 487–9260

Along U.S. Highway 101 Corridor/Wine Country

Beltane Ranch,
11775 Sonoma Highway,
Glen Ellen;
(707) 996–6501

Best Western Sonoma
Valley Inn,
550 Second Street West,
Sonoma;
(707) 938–9200

Cavanagh Inn,
10 Keller Street,
Petaluma;
(888) 765–4658

Cottage Grove Inn,
1711 Lincoln Avenue,
Calistoga;
(800) 799–2284

Fetzer Vineyards
B&B at Valley Oaks,
13601 Eastside Road,
Hopland;
(800) 846–8637

Gaige House Inn,
13540 Arnold Drive,
Glen Ellen;
(800) 935–0237

Hotel La Rose,
308 Wilson Street,
Santa Rosa;
(707) 579–3200

Scott Courtyard,
1443 Second Street,
Calistoga;
(707) 942–0948

Sebastapol Inn,
6751 Sebastapol Avenue,
Sebastapol;
(707) 829–2500

Sunrise Inn,
650 South State Street,
Ukiah;
(707) 462–6601

Places to Eat on the North Coast

Along Highway 1

Bovine Bakery and Cafe
(American),
11315 Main Street,
Point Reyes Station;
(415) 663–9420

Cafe Beaujolais (French),
961 Ukiah,
Mendocino;
(707) 937–5614

Eggheads (American),
326 North Main Street,
Fort Bragg;
(707) 964–5005

Home Style Cafe
(American),
790 South Main Street,
Fort Bragg;
(707) 964–6106

MacCallum House
Restaurant (American),
Albion Street,
Mendocino;
(707) 937–5763

Olema Farm House
(American),
10005 Highway 1,
Olema;
(415) 663–1264

Rivers End (seafood),
Highway 1,
Jenner,
(707) 865–2377

St. Orres (French),
Highway 1,
Gualala;
(707) 884–3667

The Station House Cafe
(American),
11180 Highway 1,
Point Reyes Station;
(415) 663–1515

Wharf Seafood Restaurant
(seafood),
North Harbor Drive,
Fort Bragg;
(707) 964–4283

Lost Coast/Redwood Country

Cafe Marina Woodley's Bar
(seafood),
Woodley Island Marina,
Eureka;
(707) 443–2233

Curley's Grill (American),
460 Main Street,
Ferndale;
(707) 786–9696

Restaurant 301
(Continental),
301 L Street,
Eureka;
(707) 444–8062

Rolf's Park Cafe (German),
Highway 101
and Davidson,
Orick;
(707) 488–3841

Stanton's Restaurant,
Fifth and L Streets,
Eureka;
(707) 442–8141

Highway 101 Corridor/Wine Country

Cafe Andalusia (Spanish),
165 West Napa Street,
Sonoma;
(707) 996–5556

Chez Peyo (Continental),
2295 Gravenstein
Highway South,
Sebastopol;
(707) 823–1262

Della Santina's (Italian),
133 East Napa Street,
Sonoma;
(707) 935–0586

Garden Court Cafe
& Bakery (American),
13875 Sonoma Highway 12,
Glen Ellen;
(707) 935–1565

Hopland Brewery Tavern
and Restaurant
(American),
13351 South Highway 101,
Hopland;
(707) 744–1361

Madrona Manor
Restaurant (Californian),
1001 Westside Road,
Healdsburg;
(707) 433–4231

McNears Saloon & Dining
House (American),
23 Petaluma Boulevard,
Petaluma;
(707) 765–2121

Mistral (French),
1229 North Dutton Avenue,
Santa Rosa;
(707) 578–4511

Mount View Hotel Restaurant (Californian),
1457 Lincoln Avenue,
Calistoga;
(707) 942–6877

Powerhouse Brewing Co.
(American),
268 Petaluma Avenue,
Sebastopol;
(707) 829–9171

Helpful Web Sites for the North Coast

Blue Ox Millworks and Historic Park: www.blueoxmill.com

Crescent City–Del Norte Chamber of Commerce: www.northerncalifornia.net

Eureka–Humboldt County Convention & Visitors Bureau: www.redwoodvisitor.org

Ferndale: www.victorianferndale.org/chamber

Fort Bragg–Mendocino Coast Chamber of Commerce: www.mendocinocoast.com

Grace Hudson Museum: www.gracehudsonmuseum.org

Humboldt County Convention and Visitors Bureau: www.redwoodvisitor.org

Lake County Marketing Program: www.lakecounty.com

Marin County Convention & Visitors Bureau: www.visitmarin.org

Mendocino County Alliance: www.gomendo.com

Napa Valley Conference & Visitors Bureau: www.napavalley.com

Petaluma Visitors Program: www.petaluma.org

Point Reyes National Seashore: www.nps.gov/pore

Redwood Empire Association: www.redwoodempire.com

Russian River Area: www.russianriver.com

Sebastopol Chamber of Commerce: www.sebastopol.org

Sonoma County Tourism Program: www.sonomacounty.com

Sonoma Farm Trails: www.farmtrails.org

Worth Seeing/Doing on the North Coast

Clear Lake

Napa Valley Wineries

Old Faithful Geyser, Calistoga

Russian River

Scotia Lumber Mill

Skunk Train, Fort Bragg

Stinson Beach

Trees of Mystery, Klamath

The Central Valley

When mountain man Jedediah Smith first entered the Central Valley in 1828, he encountered great expanses of grassland, lakes that spread like pancakes in spring floods, vast herds of tule elk, and peaceful Indian tribes that had lived here for millennia. A century or so later, this same valley was the California first seen by dust-bowl families searching for a better life, drawn by the rich soil and bountiful farms.

Lying between the Sierra Nevada and the Coastal Range, the valley contains the world's most productive farmland, which yields an incredible one-quarter of America's table food. Some 450 miles long and 50 miles wide (larger than England), the Central Valley encompasses the two valleys of the Sacramento and San Joaquin Rivers, which flow into the California Delta southwest of Sacramento. This delightful capital city is an inland port with ocean access, as is workaday Stockton to the south.

The Central Valley is a part of California little known to visitors and ignored by most coastal residents, who tend to think of it as an alternately hot and foggy, painfully boring stretch crossed on the way to somewhere else. Driving the valley is sure to involve either the speedy, ramrod straight I–5 or Highway 99, which passes through most of the major towns and points of interest.

Lower Valley

Fresno and the rest of the sun-pummeled San Joaquin Valley may be short on visitor attractions, but one place is definitely worth a stop. ***Forestiere Underground Gardens*** began innocently enough in 1906, when a Sicilian immigrant named Baldasare Forestiere dug a shady cellar to escape the scorching summer heat. When he died forty years later, scores of rooms, patios, and passageways lay beneath a ten-acre plot north of Fresno.

Trivia

"Snowbirds": dark-eyed juncos spend summers in the Sierra Nevada, winters in the valley.

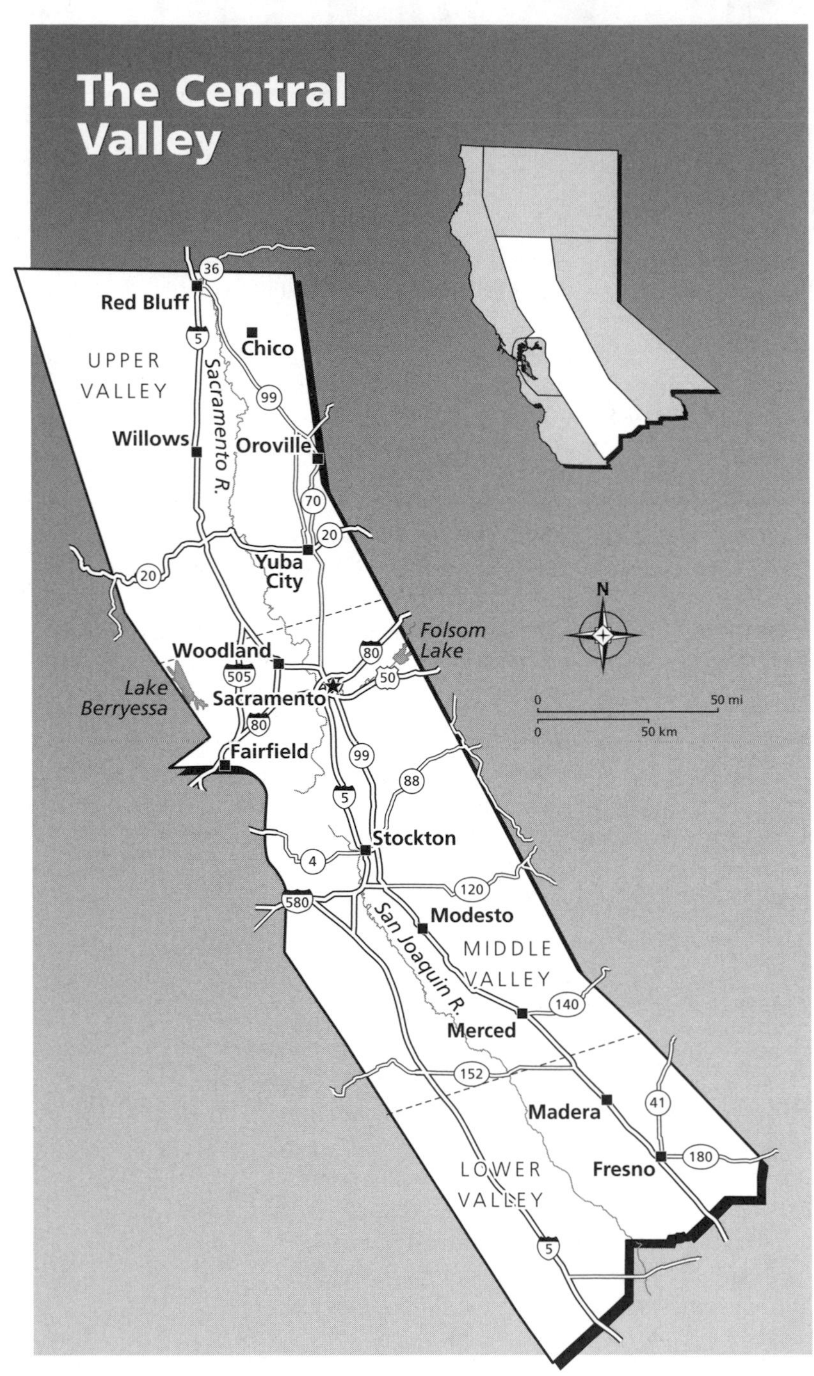
The Central Valley
Red Bluff
Chico
UPPER VALLEY
Sacramento R.
Willows
Oroville
Yuba City
Woodland
Folsom Lake
Lake Berryessa
Sacramento
Fairfield
Stockton
Modesto
MIDDLE VALLEY
San Joaquin R.
Merced
Madera
Fresno
LOWER VALLEY
N
0
50 mi
0
50 km
36
5
99
70
20
80
505
50
88
4
120
580
140
152
41
180

The Armenian Factor

Handwoven rugs to delight the eye, strange words to challenge the tongue, and delicious foods to tempt the palate are parts of the valley's rich Armenian heritage. Since the 1880s many thousands of immigrants have settled around the town of Fresno, where the culture of Armenia has taken root.

In markets and bakeries you can find lavash *(cracker bread), honeyed-nut baskets,* peda *(yeast bread), and* lahmejun, *an Armenian "pizza" topped with ground lamb. Antique Armenian wool carpets can be seen in specialty shops, and everyone's favorite writer is William Saroyan, Fresno-born son of Armenian immigrants.*

Using only hand tools and skills learned digging subways in the East, Forestiere tunneled into the hard soil with grand visions of his subterranean home. Today you can walk through the living room, two bedrooms, kitchen, and library and still see scars from his pickax and a unique ventilation system that ensures the flow of cool, fresh air. But his residence was only the beginning; later came cheese and wine rooms, a ballroom with a stage, an aquarium, a chapel, Roman-style stone walls and arches, gardens with fruit trees (one citrus bears seven varieties), and an 800-foot-long auto tunnel!

Yet despite the design and engineering complexities involved, Forestiere worked without a blueprint, and architects marvel at the sophisticated results. They are truly a monument to the spirit of one man with a shovel, a wheelbarrow, and a dream.

Forestiere Underground Gardens, 5021 West Shaw Avenue, is open in summer Wednesday through Sunday, and weekends only the rest of the year; call (559) 271–0734 for hours and information on group tours.

Trivia

California's first dude ranch, Wonder Valley Ranch Resort, is located in Sanger, east of Fresno in the Sierra foothills.

Middle Valley

Sitting smack in the middle of the Central Valley, Sacramento has been called the "quintessential California city." It boasts sunshine, palm trees, high-tech companies, and produce stands, and is surrounded by freeways and suburbs. But the state capital has its own distinct identity as well. Two major rivers, the Sacramento and American, traverse it, and most major auto routes pass through or near downtown.

Author's Top Ten in the Central Valley

Forestiere Underground Gardens

Historic Governor's Mansion

California State Capitol

B. F. Hastings Building, Old Sacramento

Delta River Road

Western Railway Museum

Hays Antique Truck Museum

Jedediah Smith Memorial Trail

Oroville Chinese Temple

Bidwell Mansion State Historic Park

To celebrate California's Sesquicentennial (150 years since the gold rush and statehood), more than one hundred buildings were renovated. Among them were the first theater built in California, an 1876 railway station, and a historic waterfront with warehouses and paddle wheelers depicting a nineteenth-century riverside scene.

Sacramento's most pleasing feature is the quarter of a million trees in parks and along streets lined with Victorian homes. Mostly Dutch elms, they arch overhead and create cool green tunnels. There are a dozen top sights, including a remarkably well-restored capitol building, a superb railroad museum in Old Sacramento, and Sutter's Fort. But the city teems with visitors (especially busloads of schoolkids), and avoiding them means seeking out some of the lesser-known attractions.

In a city with 150 grand Victorian homes, the ***Historic Governor's Mansion*** may just be the grandest of the bunch. After all, it served as the official residence for thirteen leaders of the Golden State and their families, from George Cooper Pardee to Ronald Reagan. But after just three months, Nancy Reagan spurned its soaring gables and cramped closets in favor of a ranch-style home. Among the illustrious tenants was Earl Warren, who called the place home for a decade before his appointment to the U.S. Supreme Court.

The mansion now sits in a quiet neighborhood amid impeccably tended gardens, replete with tree-size camellias. Built in 1877 for a wealthy hardware tycoon, the home features the finest craftsmanship of its day, especially in the hardware department, with handcrafted bronze hinges and doorknobs. The state bought it in 1903 for the paltry sum of $32,500 unfurnished, then poured in vast sums, making it fit for a king, or at least a California governor.

Trivia

The fastest Pony Express delivery on record, six days from Missouri to Sacramento, delivered the news of Abraham Lincoln's assassination.

Strolling through the sixteen rooms on an hour-long guided tour, you will see an Italian marble fireplace and French mirrors, handworked silver and gold-trimmed chinaware, thick Persian rugs and marble statues, not to mention a 100-foot mahogany banister that was a dream for children of the household—no matter what the governor said.

Your guide brings all these pieces to life with fascinating anecdotes about six decades of life at the mansion. It was the site of four weddings and one assassination attempt—an anarchist group called the Wobblies (Industrial Workers of the World) dynamited the kitchen in 1917 and inflicted minor damage. Look carefully at the bathroom off the master bedroom. Pat Brown's daughter Kathleen, who later ran for governor herself, painted the toenails of the claw-foot tub bright red. Even when memories of society balls and political infighting have faded, that playful stroke will endure.

The Historic Governor's Mansion, at Sixteenth and H Streets, is open daily with tours on the hour from 10:00 A.M. to 4:00 P.M. Admission charged. For information call (916) 323–3047.

The ***California State Capitol,*** modeled after the national counterpart in Washington, D.C., is of Roman-Corinthian design, with white columns and a 210-foot dome and cupola. Completed in 1874 and restored to its original splendor (1975–81) at a cost of $70 million, the interior has magnificent tiled mosaic floors, murals, a soaring rotunda, massive staircases, crystal chandeliers, and stately legislative chambers. Seven historic museum rooms are open daily to the public, with tours offered (open 9:00 A.M. to 4:00 P.M.). Outside, the grounds of Capitol Park cover forty acres (12 city blocks) and are planted with hundreds of trees and shrubs from around the world.

Sacramento's old cemetery is rich in early history: mossy gravestones and elaborate tombs crammed into twenty-eight acres of greenery, including the Historic Rose Garden. Thousands of early settlers lie entombed here, among them John Sutter Jr. and railroad baron Mark Hopkins, whose sarcophagus was made with 350 tons of red granite. There are special monuments to the Civil War

Top Annual Events in the Central Valley

Stockton Asparagus Festival *(late April)*

Gold Nugget Days, *Paradise (late April)*

Bidwell Bar Day Celebration, *Oroville (early May)*

Sacramento Jazz Jubilee *(Memorial Day weekend)*

Folsom Championship Rodeo *(July Fourth)*

California State Fair, *Sacramento (late August)*

Gold Rush Days, *Sacramento (Labor Day weekend)*

Lodi Grape Festival *(mid-September)*

California Prune Festival, *Yuba City (mid-September)*

Chico World Music Festival *(late September)*

Beckwourth Frontier Days, *Marysville (early October)*

The Big Fresno Fair *(mid-October)*

Trivia

Port Stockton on the San Joaquin River is California's largest inland seaport, 88 miles from the Golden Gate.

The Folsom Prison Museum at the famous penitentiary east of Sacramento contains artifacts and records dating back to the 1800s.

Capital Collections

Besides the dazzling California State Railroad Museum, largest of its kind in North America, Sacramento boasts a mind-boggling array of museums for every taste. Among the best:

- *California Military Museum contains more than 30,000 documents and memorabilia from the state's exciting history. Open daily except Monday from 10:00 A.M. to 5:00 P.M.; 1119 Second Street, Old Sacramento; (916) 442–2883. Admission charged.*

- *California State Capitol Museum features tours, films, museum rooms, and changing exhibits on the state's government and history. Open daily from 9:00 A.M. to 4:00 P.M.; Tenth and L Streets; (916) 324–0333. No admission charged.*

- *California State Indian Museum displays the rich and diverse cultures of its Native American people. Open daily from 10:00 A.M. to 5:00 P.M.; 2618 K Street; (916) 324–0971. Admission charged.*

- *California State Railroad Museum is the largest and most innovative of its kind in the country, with twenty-one restored locomotives. Open daily from 1:00 A.M. to 5:00 P.M.; Second and I Streets, Old Sacramento; (916) 445–6645.*

- *Crocker Art Museum features two centuries of California art, Old Master drawings, Asian art, and rotating exhibitions. Open daily except Monday from 10:00 A.M. to 5:00 P.M.; 216 O Street; (916) 264–5423. Admission charged.*

- *Discovery Museum houses more than $1 million in gold specimens and a working print shop. Open daily except Monday from 10:00 A.M. to 4:30 P.M.; 101 I Street, Old Sacramento; (916) 264–7057. Admission charged.*

- *Golden State Museum, at the California State Archives, explores the state's landscape, migrations, road to statehood, and entrepreneurial spirit. The museum's centerpiece is Constitution Wall, which spans six floors and towers over a courtyard. Situated at 1020 O Street; (916) 653–7524. Call for winter–summer schedules. Admission charged.*

- *McClellan Aviation Museum features thirty-three military aircraft dating through World War II. Open daily from 9:00 A.M. to 4:00 P.M. (Sunday from noon to 4:00 P.M.); McClellan Air Base, 3204 Palm Avenue, North Highlands (outside Sacramento); (916) 643–3192. No admission charged.*

- *Towe Auto Museum displays vintage cars and explains the history of the automobile in America. Open daily from 10:00 A.M. to 6:00 P.M.; 2200 Front Street; (916) 442–6802. Admission charged.*

- *Wells Fargo History Museum includes a restored Concord stagecoach, a gold scale, telegraph, and other exhibits related to the bank's pioneering role in California history. Open weekdays from 9:00 A.M. to 5:00 P.M.; 400 Capitol Mall; (916) 440–4161.*

dead and volunteer fire department (featuring a 1,900-pound bell). The cemetery, at 1000 Broadway Street, is open daily from 7:00 A.M. to dusk.

Trivia

The world's largest almond processing plant, doing twelve million pounds a day in high season, is Blue Diamond of Sacramento.

Old Sacramento, with its trove of shopping and sight-seeing treasures, is the city's most popular attraction. But most visitors overlook one low-profile site: the ***B. F. Hastings Building.*** While many old-town structures are reconstructions, this is the genuine article. It first housed Wells Fargo offices, then became the western terminus for the legendary Pony Express service from St. Joseph, Missouri, 1,966 miles away.

Riders had answered this want ad: "Skinny, wiry fellows not over 18. Must be expert riders, willing to risk death daily. Orphans preferred." A hundred joined up—among them fourteen-year-old Buffalo Bill Cody—for $25 a week and bragging rights. They transported half-ounce letters for $5.00 apiece in just ten days. But the service only lasted eighteen months, a victim of new technology called the telegraph.

Once again, the Hastings Building was in the thick of the action. The first coast-to-coast telegraph message was sent from here to Washington; in it members of the California Supreme Court assured President Lincoln that the state would remain loyal to the Union. Today you can sit down and click out a message to someone on the other side of the room, if you can manage to master the code. Ask to go upstairs, where the Supreme Court chambers appear just as they did when the first justices presided. The floor also contains a sitting room for "their honors" and the offices of Theodore Judah, the brilliant engineer who designed much of the transcontinental railroad.

The B. F. Hastings Building is at Second and J Streets; (916) 440–4263. It is open for free daily from 10:00 A.M. to 5:00 P.M.

Trivia

Tower Records began in a Sacramento drugstore with Clayton Solomon and his son selling records for 10 cents each.

Sacramento's climate lends itself to outdoor activities through most of the year. It's the kind of place to rent a raft or kayak for a day, take in a AAA baseball game of the Rivercats at Raley Stadium, or simply hop on a river taxi from Old Sacramento to the Garden Highway and enjoy an outdoor meal on a balmy summer evening. Old Sacramento marks the start of ***Jedediah Smith Memorial Trail*** for bicyclists and bird watchers, jogging or walking pedestrians, and even dogs (on a leash). Leaving downtown, the paved pathway follows the American River Parkway and rambles 23 tree-lined miles out to Folsom Lake in Placer County. About

Houseboats: Dawdling on the Delta

Huck Finn had the right idea: floating downriver and throwing a fishing line overboard; lying back in the warm sun and then jumping into the water to cool off. This lazy lifestyle can still be had on a houseboat with modern amenities—like wet bars and flush toilets—that Huck would never have imagined. Today you can truly "rough it" in luxury.

The California Delta has a thousand miles of navigable waterways and hundreds of islands, so there's lots of territory to explore. Several companies out of Stockton and Sacramento rent these 20- to 50-foot floating barges at modest rates (especially September through May). They say "no experience necessary," so even novices can handle the slow-moving boats after a couple of practice runs. Marinas are available for fuel, bait, beer, and groceries along the way.

The Delta is so big there's bound to be a surprise around every bend, whether a speedboat with water-skiers, a drawbridge, or an oceangoing vessel bound for one of the inland ports. (Beware of the wake!) The most popular area is called "The Meadows," with shady trees and wild blackberry bushes crowding the banks and a sandy beach revealed at low tide. You can find a cozy anchoring spot on a secluded slough and stay as long as you wish; swimming, trapping crawdads, picking berries, casting a fishing line, or doing nothing at all, Huck Finn style.

Contact the Delta Houseboat Rental Hotline for further information at (209) 477–1840 or www.californiadelta.org. Or write to Houseboats, 6333 Pacific Avenue, Suite 152, Stockton, CA 95207 for a free packet of brochures.

halfway out you can tour Nimbus Dam (on Lake Natoma) and watch salmon spawn at a fish hatchery.

For information about the state capital and surrounding area, contact the Sacramento Convention & Visitors Bureau at (800) 292–2334; 1303 J Street, Suite 600, Sacramento, CA 95814.

Movie director Sam Goldwyn once claimed the California Delta looked "more like the Mississippi than the real thing" and used it for filming *Huckleberry Finn.* Indeed, this dreamy farming and recreational area southwest of Sacramento, cut by two major rivers and several smaller streams, is quite unlike the rest of the state. More than a thousand miles of sleepy sloughs and quiet channels meander past rich farmland and small towns with landings for steamboats that will never come again. Some seventy bridges and five tiny ferries cross this intricate system of interlocking waterways, and you can drive through the heart of the Delta on the scenic ***River Road,*** starting just a few miles from the state capital.

Riverboat, Old Sacramento

During the gold rush the Sacramento and other rivers traversing the Delta served as a full-blown shipping highway, bringing picks, shovels, beans, and countless other necessities inland from San Francisco. Later, dejected miners tried their hand at farming and discovered California's "green gold" in asparagus, pears, grapes, alfalfa, corn, and other crops. The only problem was that spring often brought floods that washed shacks and chicken coops downriver, a situation unsolved until Chinese immigrants arrived to put up miles of levees.

Scows and schooners serviced the river towns, and paddle wheelers arrived to cheering throngs just like in the movies. But by the 1930s, river traffic had declined dramatically, and Delta towns became charming backwater anachronisms.

Today, the Delta has blossomed into an outstanding recreational paradise, where fishing and watersports abound. Houseboats set a pokey pace, and you can dally along for days without seeing the same channel twice, or tie up along a levee to fish Huck Finn style (a practice called "gunk holing"). Yet despite its popularity the Delta rarely seems crowded.

The River Road snakes from bank to bank along the Sacramento for about 35 miles between Freeport and Rio Vista, passing time-warp towns and old steamboat landings. The road sits atop the actual levee,

Trivia

Folsom Lake State Recreation Area welcomes more than 1.5 million people each year.

and you can look right down on the river and irrigated fields. (You pick it up by taking I–5 about 7 miles south from downtown Sacramento to State Route 160 at Freeport.)

First stop is ***Courtland,*** sitting in a sea of pear orchards and sumptuous mansions fringed with palm trees. Once a year, on the last Sunday in July, this somnolent settlement comes alive during the Pear Fair, with a parade and carnival, special pear foods and drinks like fritters and smoothies, and an award for the largest fruit. As you drive through, look for the ramshackle Wo Chong Co. "General Merchandise" Store and the defunct Bank of Courtland, standing proud as a Greek temple. One mile out of town, State Route 160 crosses the first bridge and continues toward Isleton. Be sure to stay on the River Road (E13); ***Locke*** lies 6 miles straight ahead.

Locke (population fifty-nine, elevation 13 feet) is a place so picturesque it seems like a movie set. It's the only town in the country built entirely by and for Chinese, back in 1912, and most of the residents can trace their ancestry to the first settlers, if they weren't actually there themselves! A handful of wizened old men sit in doorways reading Chinese newspapers or creak along the cramped streets of "Lockee," going no place in particular. One by one these old-timers are dying off, and no one (at least no one Chinese) is coming to take their place.

Savoring Crayfish

The Sacramento Valley is known worldwide for its tomatoes, rice, and other agricultural products, but in Sweden it's famous for its crayfish, known by some as crawfish or crawdads. In Europe consumers pay as much as $10 a pound for live California crayfish. It seems that signal crayfish found in the Sacramento River closely resemble the Swedish species wiped out during the 1960s, and most of those shipped to Sweden are eaten during a monthlong festival in August. Compared with Louisiana, the state's industry is small, but it's the California crustaceans that Europeans prefer. (About 90 percent of the local harvest is shipped abroad.)

Crayfish are caught in wire-mesh traps, marked by buoys, which are submerged in the river. These clever devices have one-way entrances so that the creatures can't escape once they've taken the bait, which can be anything from sardines to dog food. Crawdads look a lot like lobsters, but are much smaller (about ten to a pound) and live in freshwater. They are usually boiled and picked out of the shell but are hard to eat—one reason they haven't caught on with American consumers.

What you see is a ghost town in the making, a place of delightfully lopsided, woodframe buildings with cockeyed balconies and doorways, rickety staircases, and sidewalks that croak when you step on the planks. Things weren't always so; in fact, Locke was once a mecca for gambling and other illicit vices. It had a hotel (still barely standing), an "opera house" for traveling troupes, and three brothels.

The spirit of those long-gone days resurfaces at the ***Dai Loy Museum*** on Main Street, housed in a former gambling den that prospered from 1916 until a sheriff padlocked the doors in 1950. Games are laid out as if in progress: dominoes for *dow ngow* (battling bulls), tin cups and buttons for *fan tan*—and the table legs and crossbraces are worn smooth from years of nervous feet. The museum is open Friday through Sunday from 11:00 A.M. to 4:30 P.M.; call (916) 776–1661 for information.

Other points of interest include the Joe Shoong Chinese School and Al's Place, an areawide hangout with a rowdy bar and a larger-than-life reputation for steak dinners. (A better dining choice is Locke Garden Chinese restaurant.)

Trivia

Cache Creek Indian Bingo & Casino offers legal gaming in Brooks, near Woodland.

Sadly, Locke has become a tourist pit stop with cutesy gift shops, so if you find yourself jostled by a passing tour group, head down the road a mile to ***Walnut Grove.*** Straddling the river, it's larger than Locke but quieter, with an old quarter likewise going to seed and small businesses that probably seemed dated in 1950.

Founded in 1851, it once had both a Chinatown *and* a Japantown, an impressive theater, and the neoclassical Bank of Alex Brown, an early resident. But unlike Locke, today there's a new bank and a respectable number of residents.

You cross the river again here and rejoin Route 160 on Grand Island. At the tiny village of Ryde, the elegant Ryde Hotel has been impeccably restored to reflect the Delta's golden era. In the past it had a speakeasy and was owned by actor Lon Chaney Jr. You can still see a peephole in the door from Prohibition days. For reservations call (916) 776–1318.

Trivia

The largest gold nugget (at fifty-four-plus pounds) was unearthed near Paradise in Butte County.

A handful of sumptuous old homes dot the Delta, among them the ***Grand Island Mansion*** near Ryde. Standing stately amid rows of palm trees, this four-story, fifty-eight-room Italian villa was built for a fruit magnate in 1917. Once upon a time, wealthy and famous guests here must have danced on parquet floors and gazed into the gilt mirrors; today it's open for Sunday brunch March through December. Call (916) 775–1705 for reservations.

Final stop on your Delta tour should be ***Isleton,*** with its wonderfully obsolete Main Street lined with the decrepit remnants of a once-thriving Chinatown, among them Hop Fat and Co. Formerly the "Asparagus Capital of the West," Isleton still throws a humdinger of a crawdad festival every June, which draws crawdad connoisseurs from miles around. More than 20,000 pounds of crustaceans are devoured.

You should head west on Highway 12, crossing the Sacramento River one last time to reach the town of Rio Vista. Here is a place guaranteed to leave you shaking your head, either in admiration or disgust. ***Foster's Big Horn Saloon*** on Main Street (between Front and Second) houses one of the world's largest private collections of animal trophies, all shot by famed big-game hunter Bill Foster (now deceased).

Looking out over the long, narrow bar and adjacent dining room are stuffed heads from around the world: Alaska to South Africa to Australia. Bears, lions, gazelles, apes, moose, wolves, rhinos, tigers, and many more (a total of 250 animals) reside here. There are even the stuffed, lifeless heads of a giraffe (long neck and all) and an African bull elephant, thought to be the largest mounted mammal trophy in existence. Wall space not occupied by the trophies displays photos of the great white hunter himself.

Sixty years before BART (Bay Area Rapid Transit), the Sacramento Northern Railway ran between San Francisco and Chico via the state capital at speeds up to 70 miles per hour. Cars from this long-lamented line, together with dozens of other relics from the golden days of interurban train travel, crowd a railway yard at Rio Vista Junction. The ***Western Railway Museum*** sits about 10 miles west of Rio Vista off Highway 12, easily reached from the Delta.

Trivia

Sacramento was home to the first art museum in the West and the first theater in California.

During the 1950s, in an era when interurban trains were being phased out, members of the Bay Area Electric Railroad Association obtained their first car. The collection grew rapidly, and a permanent home at Rio Vista Junction, former flag stop on the Sacramento Northern, was selected in 1960. About one hundred pieces now occupy the twenty-five-acre site, including trolleys, streetcars, steam locomotives, and cable cars, the largest variety of

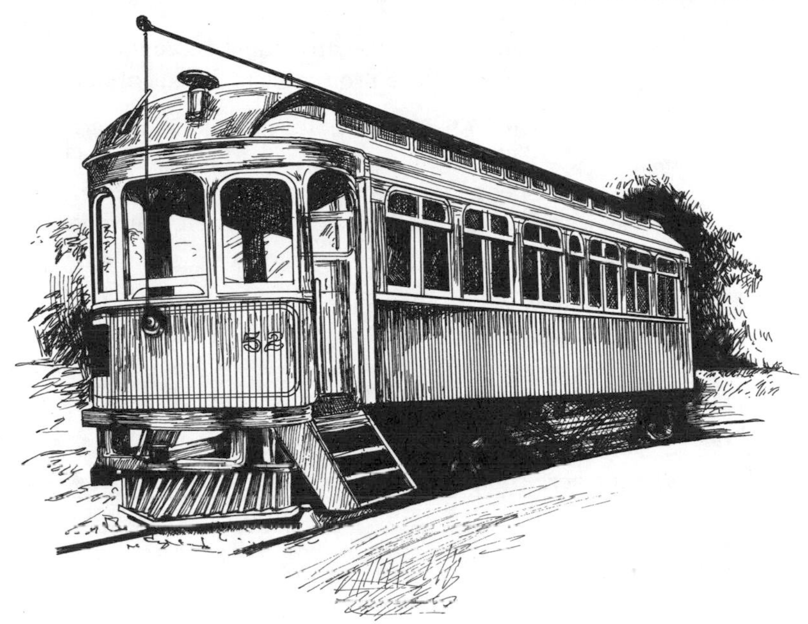

Western Railway Museum

operating engines and cars in the West. Among the notable examples are a New York City "El" train car, a Gay Nineties San Francisco streetcar, a wooden electric interurban car that hauled eggs and poultry as well as passengers, and a tram from Melbourne, Australia, vintage 1930.

The museum's goal is to present a real feel for this neglected heritage rather than an under-glass approach. Upon entering you will be greeted by volunteers spiffily dressed in the dark blue, gold-trimmed uniforms of conductors. All are electric train buffs, seemingly out of place in our trolleyless world. They will usher you onto one of the two train rides you can take. Streetcars leave every twenty minutes on rides around the museum grounds, and interurbans—bigger than streetcars—leave on the hour on leisurely 10-mile trips to Gum Grove station and back. As you hop aboard, bells clang, the air compressor thumps, and the motors growl.

A dozen different cars are kept in operating condition and interchanged for the tours. You might be aboard a Peninsular Railway car built in 1903 and used until 1932. The second ride might be on a 51,000-pound streetcar called "the iron monster," which ran along San Francisco's Market Street at a top speed of 25 miles per hour. All but two of these giants were scrapped in the late 1950s. You sit on comfortable wooden

Trivia

The Central Valley's most valuable agricultural product is dairy, followed by grapes and cotton.

benches that flip around and face the opposite direction when you come to the end of the line.

On the 1.5-mile route circling the property, you will pass more rolling stock, and two huge barns shelter more cars at various stages of restoration. If not for the dedicated volunteers here, a colorful era in transportation history would be lost forever.

The Western Railway Museum, 5848 State Route 12, is open from 10:30 A.M. to 5:00 P.M. weekends year-round and Wednesday through Sunday during June through August. Admission, including unlimited rides, is $7.00 for adults and $4.00 for children. For information call (707) 374–2978.

The ***Woodland Opera House,*** at the corner of Second Street and Dead Cat Alley, sits haughtily as a reigning star in the town of Woodland, northwest of Sacramento. (From Highway 12 drive north on Highway 113 through Davis.)

From 1896 to 1913 the Victorian-style opera house was the pride of Yolo County, and smart ladies and their gents came from as far away as the capital to see and be seen in the glow of gaslights. During those years only two "real" operas were staged (the term *opera house* was loosely defined at the time), but audiences were entertained with a steady stream of melodramas, minstrel shows, variety and magic acts, comedies, band concerts, and recitals. Among the many illustrious personages to appear were "Gentleman Jim" Corbett and John L. Sullivan, who starred in plays followed by sparring matches; John Philip Sousa and his rousing orchestra; and future Hollywood stars Sydney Greenstreet and Walter Huston.

Trivia

Knight's Ferry Covered Bridge near Oakdale, built in 1863, is the longest west of the Mississippi.

Then hard times hit, and the opera house closed for nearly six decades. A twenty-year restoration was finally completed in 1989, and regular tours now explore the old theater from top to bottom: the double entrance doors, the stage and balcony, dressing rooms, and the gaslight control panel where oxygen and gas were mixed. Much of the original building has survived, including the brick walls, cast-iron posts, wooden pewlike balcony seats, and trap doors from the dressing rooms to the stage above.

After the historical tour you just may want to attend a live performance in the 532-seat theater, usually classics like *Kiss Me Kate.* For information about tours and current productions, call (530) 666–9617.

Valley folk may have their cultural institutions, but for a real look at what life here is all about, you should visit the ***Hays Antique Truck Museum*** in Woodland. This outstanding collection of mechanical workhorses stretches from 1903 to the 1950s and includes more than one hundred trucks representing dozens of makes. Most are fully restored and on display inside two giant sheds.

The majority come from the 1910s and 1920s, when brass lamps, wooden spokes, open cabs, and solid rubber tires were the norm. There are gasoline, diesel, and electric models made by forgotten companies like Yellow Knight and Ruggles, as well as the more familiar Mack, GMC, and Fageol. Looking at some of the older models, you will come to realize the origin of the expression "built like a Mack truck." The museum also boasts the only Breeding Steam Truck in existence and a section of the Old Plank Road that ran across the desert from Yuma, Arizona, to California.

Mr. A. W. Hays bought his first vehicle, a Chevy, back in 1929 and just kept on collecting. Among the many noteworthy examples are a three-ton beast used by the army in World War I, a forest-green gasoline delivery truck, an old fire engine with wooden running boards, an antique paddy wagon with wooden bars, and a 1930 Dodge half-ton pickup painted pistachio-ice-cream green. They're all guaranteed to have you singing the country tune "I love my truck" as you leave.

The Hays Antique Truck Museum forms part of the Heidrick Ag History Center, 130,000 square feet of interactive exhibits highlighting agricultural equipment from the valley's bygone days. The center is located at 1962 Hays Lane, Woodland; open daily from 10:00 A.M. to 5:00 P.M., (530) 666–9700. Admission charged.

Upper Valley

If you are headed north, a pleasant alternative to I–5 is ***State Route 45,*** which runs along or near the Sacramento River past towns and scenery reminiscent of the Delta's River Road.

Whichever road you take north, you will undoubtedly spot the most unfamiliar familiar place in the Central Valley: ***Sutter Buttes.*** Rising a measly 2,000 feet, this pint-sized cluster of peaks is known as "the world's smallest mountain range." Yet because the surrounding terrain is so flat, Sutter Buttes thrust abruptly from the landscape like a stage set. Indeed, the Buttes form the only significant rise in the entire valley.

Trivia

Every January, millions of geese and other birds flock to Sacramento National Wildlife Refuge at Willows.

Owing their existence to volcanic activity in some distant era, the Buttes' twenty separate peaks form a rough circle about 10 miles in diameter, huddling together like a wagon train under attack. Native Americans called the place *ono lai tol* (the middle mountain), and it figures in their creation myths. Hot, dry summers and the dark volcanic soil and porous rocks mean semidesert conditions for the indigenous fauna and flora. Golden eagles nest on the craggy volcanic peaks, coyote and deer roam free, and cattle and sheep graze on the grass-covered lower slopes.

One reason the Sutter Buttes remain relatively unknown is that they lie entirely within private land, but you can visit with a little advance planning. All-day hikes with a guide range from gentle creekside rambles to strenuous climbs up to the Buttes' highest peaks. Other excursions concentrate on the local plant and animal life. In a state where everything seems to be on a grand scale, it's a refreshing change to learn that "small is beautiful" too! For information call the Middle Mountain Foundation at (530) 671–6116.

Trivia

Oroville Dam on the Feather River is the highest landfill embankment in the world.

The town of Oroville, about 70 miles northeast of Sacramento in Butte County, is a gateway to the Feather River Country of the northern Sierra Nevada. Bidwell Bar upstream was site of California's second major gold strike (the spot now lies at the bottom of Lake Oroville), and among the eager prospectors to arrive were a large number of Chinese. When their settlement burned to the ground in 1856, the Asian gold seekers moved downriver and built a tent town.

This temporary settlement soon grew to become the largest Chinatown in California, and in 1863 the Emperor T'ung Chich even helped residents build a place of worship, *Liet Sheng Kong,* the Temple of Assorted Deities for the three Chinese religions—Taoism, Confucianism, and Buddhism.

Today, the ***Oroville Chinese Temple*** sits in a quiet corner of town next to a river levee. Outside stands a two-ton bronze urn for burning incense presented by the royal family. Entrance to the original temple involves crossing a raised step and moving sharply to the right past the main door, obstacles designed to prevent "evil spirits" from entering. (Spirits supposedly travel only in a straight line.)

Inside are mirrors to further frighten the unwanted intruders with their own ugliness. You will receive a tour of the main room, where the carved figures on the large teakwood altar correspond to the three religions. All around lie the trappings of oriental mysticism: incense, candles, lanterns, fortune sticks, temple money for burning, and gongs for letting the gods know when an offering (in the form of smoke) is on the way.

Over the years buildings spread out from the main temple, and you are permitted to wander the grounds. The Council Room, for example, was reserved for business and social services, such as banking, settling feuds, and the reading and writing of correspondence by learned men for the often illiterate workers.

The Moon Temple upstairs became the place reserved for Buddhist worship. Here, you enter through a circular brick doorway symbolizing the circle of life or eternity. Inside are bamboo lantern holders, a pewter altar set, and a parasol presented by the Empress of China.

Across a tranquil courtyard lies Tapestry Hall, where the tradition and beauty of Chinese culture are highlighted. Here are ancient pillar rugs, tapestries with embroidered dragons and lions' heads, shadow puppets, bronze mirrors, and other objects, mostly from Canton province.

The Oroville Chinese Temple, 1500 Broderick Street, is open daily from 1:00 to 4:00 P.M.; admission is $2.00 for adults. For information call (530) 538–2496.

Oroville now is a quiet river town, but in times past it saw its share of gold-fever craziness. Around the turn of the twentieth century, one dredging company even offered to move the entire town lock, stock, and barrel in order to hunt for gold below. Citizens said no.

The source of all the wealth, the Feather River, was dammed in 1967 with the highest (770 feet) earth-fill dam in the country, creating ***Lake Oroville*** about 5 miles east of town. With its 167 miles of shoreline, the lake forms the centerpiece of a large state recreation area. From the visitor center a 47-foot tower overlooks the dam and reservoir and across a landscape of chaparral, oak, and pine. The center is open daily from 9:00 A.M. to 5:00 P.M.

Trivia

The town of Red Bluff hosts the largest three-day rodeo in the United States.

State Highway 70 follows the Feather River up into the Sierra, and 12 miles north of Oroville is a turnoff to the village of ***Cherokee.*** With only a dozen or so permanent residents, this former boomtown boasts an interesting collection of historic buildings.

Trivia

Bidwell Park in Chico is the largest municipal park (with 3,600 acres) west of the Mississippi.

Housed in a former boardinghouse, the Cherokee Museum displays a re-created miner's cabin, petrified mammoth bones, mineral specimens and local Indian relics, as well as a hand-carved diorama of the town in 1880 (open weekends only from 11:00 A.M. to 3:00 P.M.). The village pays its respects to famous visitor Rutherford B. Hayes with Hayes Hall, a ramshackle, barnlike building crammed with memorabilia from his one-day 1880 sojourn. President Hayes Day is observed every September 24th with special exhibits and a jug or two passed around. Other sights include Pioneer Cemetery and the ruins of the old assay office.

Blast-furnace heat is part of summer life in the valley, and it causes most visitors to run for shelter. If you find yourself in the vicinity, make a beeline to the town of ***Chico,*** nicknamed the "city of trees" and probably the valley's shadiest spot (shady as in *cool*). Chico presents a pleasant version of small-town America, with a homey downtown and a bandstand on a grassy, elm-shaded square.

It also boasts one of the nation's largest urban parks, which sets the town apart from most other valley hotspots. ***Bidwell Park*** starts near downtown and winds along both sides of Chico Creek for 10 miles into the foothills, 2,400 acres of the best land in town. In the lower area the creek tumbles into Sycamore Pool, an old-fashioned swimming hole, and there is a nature center offering interpretive walks and a native plant garden.

The upper stretches, on the other hand, are virtual wilderness reached by rigorous hikes up a steep canyon. You can then take a dip at one of three old-fashioned swimming holes. So arcadian is the park that old Hollywood filmmakers used it for parts of *The Great Waltz, The Adventures of Robin Hood,* and *Gone with the Wind.* And this delightful green oasis sprang from the gift of one woman, Mrs. Annie Bidwell.

The Bidwells were what today might be called "movers and shakers." John worked as a clerk for the famous Mr. Sutter in Sacramento, served in the Mexican-American War, then made his own gold strike on July 4, 1848. He later served on California's constitutional committee, was elected state senator and congressman, twice ran for governor, and owned one of the valley's largest farms.

In 1849 Bidwell purchased 26,000 acres and proceeded to "plant" a town: He laid out Chico and gave away plots to anyone who would build. A nature lover and gifted amateur horticulturist, he introduced hundreds of varieties of trees and plants to the barren landscape and is chiefly responsible for the leafy canopy the town enjoys today. In 1865 General Bidwell decided to build the finest house in the state, and three years later it became a wedding gift for his bride, Annie, the pretty, dark-haired daughter of a Washington politician.

Trivia

The towns of Gridley and Corning are, respectively, the kiwi and olive capitals of the United States.

At present you can join an entertaining tour of ***Bidwell Mansion State Historic Park,*** next to the campus of the state university at Chico (renowned as a "fun-loving" school). Here is a large rose garden with several rare varieties in which Annie took great pride. Surrounded by a neat lawn and towering ornamental trees, the three-story home was designed in the style of an Italian palazzo, and its brick walls are covered with pink plaster.

Inside are twenty-six graciously furnished rooms that in the past welcomed illustrious guests such as suffragist Susan B. Anthony, General William T. Sherman, naturalist John Muir, and President Rutherford B. Hayes. Mrs. Bidwell was an ardent feminist and conservationist, and she joined her husband in an almost fanatical support of the temperance movement. Indeed, in 1892 the old boy himself was nominated for president on the National Prohibition Party ticket.

Your guide will point out significant details, such as the fact that the home claimed the first indoor plumbing in California, including one of the original fixtures from England, manufactured by Thomas B. Crapper. Standing just 4 feet, 8 inches in height, Annie was what you might call petite, and you will see some of her doll-size shoes and undergarments, garters, and a bootjack with a protective panel so that no one could catch a glimpse of her ankles (considered provocative at the time) as she donned her shoes.

Bidwell Mansion, 525 The Esplanade, is open Wednesday through Sunday from noon to 5:00 P.M. with guided tours on the hour; for information call (530) 895–6144.

Many people cool off by floating down the Sacramento on inner tubes, and ***Scotty's Landing*** is a popular local hangout on the river (12609 River Road). It's an informal restaurant and bar with a patio and beach volleyball court. Still another way to stay cool is by visiting ***Sierra Nevada Brewery,*** 1075 East Twentieth Street, where guided tours and tastings of its famous pale ale and other varieties are conducted. For schedules and reservations call (530) 893–3520.

Even better, Chico is one gateway to ***Lassen Volcanic National Park,*** and Highway 32 takes you up through dense forests of conifers that provide welcome shade on the way to cooler altitudes high above the valley. (See the Shasta Cascade chapter for details on the park.)

PLACES TO STAY IN THE CENTRAL VALLEY

LOWER VALLEY

Best Western Village Inn,
3110 North Blackstone Avenue, Fresno;
(559) 226–2110

Comfort Inn,
5455 West Shaw,
Fresno;
(559) 275–2374

Merced-Yosemite Travelodge,
1260 Yosemite Parkway,
Merced;
(209) 722–6224

MIDDLE VALLEY

Amber House Bed & Breakfast Inn,
1315 Twenty-second Street,
Sacramento;
(800) 755–6526

Best Western Cordelia Inn,
4373 Central Place,
Fairfield;
(707) 864–2029

Best Western Sutter House,
1100 H Street,
Sacramento;
(800) 830–1314

Delta King Hotel,
1000 Front Street,
Sacramento;
(916) 444–5464

Holiday Inn Express,
728 Sixteenth Street,
Sacramento;
(916) 444–8000

Inn off Capitol Park,
Sixteenth & N Streets,
Sacramento;
(916) 447–8100

On the Bluffs B&B,
9735 Mira del Rio,
Sacramento;
(916) 363–9933

Savoyard B&B,
3322 H Street,
Sacramento;
(800) 772–8692

Valley Oaks Inn,
600 North East Street,
Woodland;
(530) 666–5511

Vizcaya B&B,
2019 Twenty-first Street,
Sacramento;
(916) 455–5243

UPPER VALLEY

Best Value Inn,
580 Oro Dam Boulevard,
Oroville;
(530) 533–7070

The Esplanade B&B,
620 Esplanade,
Chico;
(530) 345–8084

Holiday Inn Express,
894 West Onstott Road,
Yuba City;
(530) 674–1650

Johnson's Country Inn,
3936 Morehead Avenue,
Chico;
(530) 345–7829

Music Express Inn,
1091 El Monte Avenue,
Chico;
(530) 345–8376

Safari Garden Motel,
2352 Esplanade,
Chico;
(530) 343–3201

The Villa Court Inn,
1527 Feather River Boulevard,
Oroville;
(530) 533–3930

PLACES TO EAT IN THE CENTRAL VALLEY

LOWER VALLEY

The Branding Iron (American),
640 West Sixteenth Street,
Merced;
(209) 722–1822

George's Shish Kebab (Armenian),
2405 Capital Street,
Fresno;
(559) 264–9433

Giulia's Italian Restaurant,
3050 West Shaw Avenue,
Fresno;
(559) 277–7551

Knights Ferry Cafe (American),
17701 Main Street,
Knights Ferry;
(209) 881–3340

Manhattan Steakhouse (American),
1731 West Bullard,
Fresno;
(559) 276–3573

Pacific Seafood (American), 1055 East Herndon Street, Fresno; (559) 439–2778

Sir James (American), 1111 Motel Drive, Merced; (209) 723–5552

Middle Valley
Cafe Bernardo (American), Third and D Streets, Davis; (530) 750–5101

Cafe Lake Natoma (Californian), 702 Gold Lake Drive, Folsom; (916) 351–1500

Centro Cocina Mexicana (Mexican), Twenty-eighth and J Streets, Sacramento; (916) 442–2552

Delta King Pilot House Restaurant (Continental), 1000 Front Street, Sacramento; (916) 441–4440

Fat City Bar & Cafe (American), 1001 Front Street, Sacramento; (916) 446–6768

Il Fornaio (Italian), 400 Capitol Mall, Sacramento; (916) 446–4100

New Lu-Shan Chinese Buffet (Chinese), 403 J Street, Sacramento; (916) 444–2543

Paesano's Pizzeria (Italian), 1806 Capitol Avenue, Sacramento; (916) 447–8646

Rio City Cafe (Californian), 1110 Front Street, Sacramento; (916) 442–8226

Tower Cafe (Continental), Land Park Street & Broadway, Sacramento; (916) 441–0222

Upper Valley
The Albatross (American), 3312 Esplanade, Chico; (530) 345–6037

Black Crow Grill (American), 209 Salem Street, Chico; (530) 892–1391

The Depot (American), 2191 High Street, Oroville; (530) 534–9101

Nash's Restaurant (American), 1717 Esplanade, Chico; (530) 896–1147

Red Tavern (American), 1250 Esplanade, Chico; (530) 894–3463

The Refuge Restaurant & Lounge (American), 1501 Butte House Road, Yuba City; (530) 673–7620

Tong Fong Low (Chinese), 2051 Robinson Street, Oroville; (530) 533–1488

HELPFUL WEB SITES FOR THE CENTRAL VALLEY

California Delta Visitors Bureau: www.californiadelta.org

California State Parks: www.parks.ca.gov

Chico Chamber of Commerce: www.chicochamber.com

Fresno Convention & Visitors Bureau: www.fresno-online. com

Hays Truck Museum: www.aghistory.org

Merced Conference & Visitors Bureau: www.yosemite-gateway.org

Modesto Convention & Visitors Bureau: www.modestocvb.org

Old Sacramento: www.oldsacramento.com

Oroville Area Chamber of Commerce: www.oroville-city.com

Sacramento Convention & Visitors Bureau: www.sacramentocvb.org

State Capitol: www.assembly.ca.gov/museum

Sutter Buttes: www.middlemountain.org

Western Railway Museum: www.wrm.org

Woodland Opera House: www.wohtheatre.org

WORTH SEEING/DOING IN THE CENTRAL VALLEY

Anheuser-Busch Brewery Tour, Fairfield

Factory Stores, Vacaville

Knights Ferry Historic Village

Old Sacramento Historic District

Sacramento Zoo

Sutter's Fort State Historic Park, Sacramento

Waterworld USA, Sacramento

The Sierra Nevada

At 430 miles long by 80 miles wide, the Sierra Nevada range is a formidable natural barrier. The mountains rise gradually from the valley floor to more than 14,000 feet, then plunge sharply to the high desert country of eastern California, a thin strip sharing more in common with Nevada than the Golden State. Over millennia glacial sculpting left a landscape of jagged peaks and hundreds of lakes, such as stunning blue Tahoe, crown jewel of the Sierra. Glaciers also carved out alpine valleys, including world-famous Yosemite, a national park so beautiful that it's in danger of being "loved to death."

In 1827 mountain man Jedediah Smith became the first white person to cross the range, but just fourteen years later a wagon train loaded with settlers lumbered over the challenging terrain on its way to the promised land. Thousands more would join them. Then came the gold rush, when no barrier could hold back the floodwaters of immigration.

More than a hundred years later, the Sierra Nevada is traversed by several major roads, and crossing it by car is a snap except during winter storms. The mountains are a paradise for outdoor activities, and nature's challenges have become a part of the fun. It's quite a switch from pioneer days.

Although lying at an average of less than 2,000 feet, California's famous gold country unquestionably belongs to the Sierra Nevada. The mountains were, after all, the source of all the wealth. Gold had washed down streams over thousands of years, and prospectors first on the spot found dust, flakes, pebbles, and even fist-size nuggets, so much gold that it was harvested rather than mined.

In the beginning, it was said, you could stick your shovel into a river bottom and come up with more gold than gravel. One man unearthed a three-ounce nugget while digging a hole for a tent stake. Such stories lured gold seekers from around the world, and they flocked to a 300-mile strip along the western slope of the Sierra, where the climate was mild and the diggin's good. Some 500 mining towns, often just a scattering of tents or wooden huts, sprang up during the first decade. More than

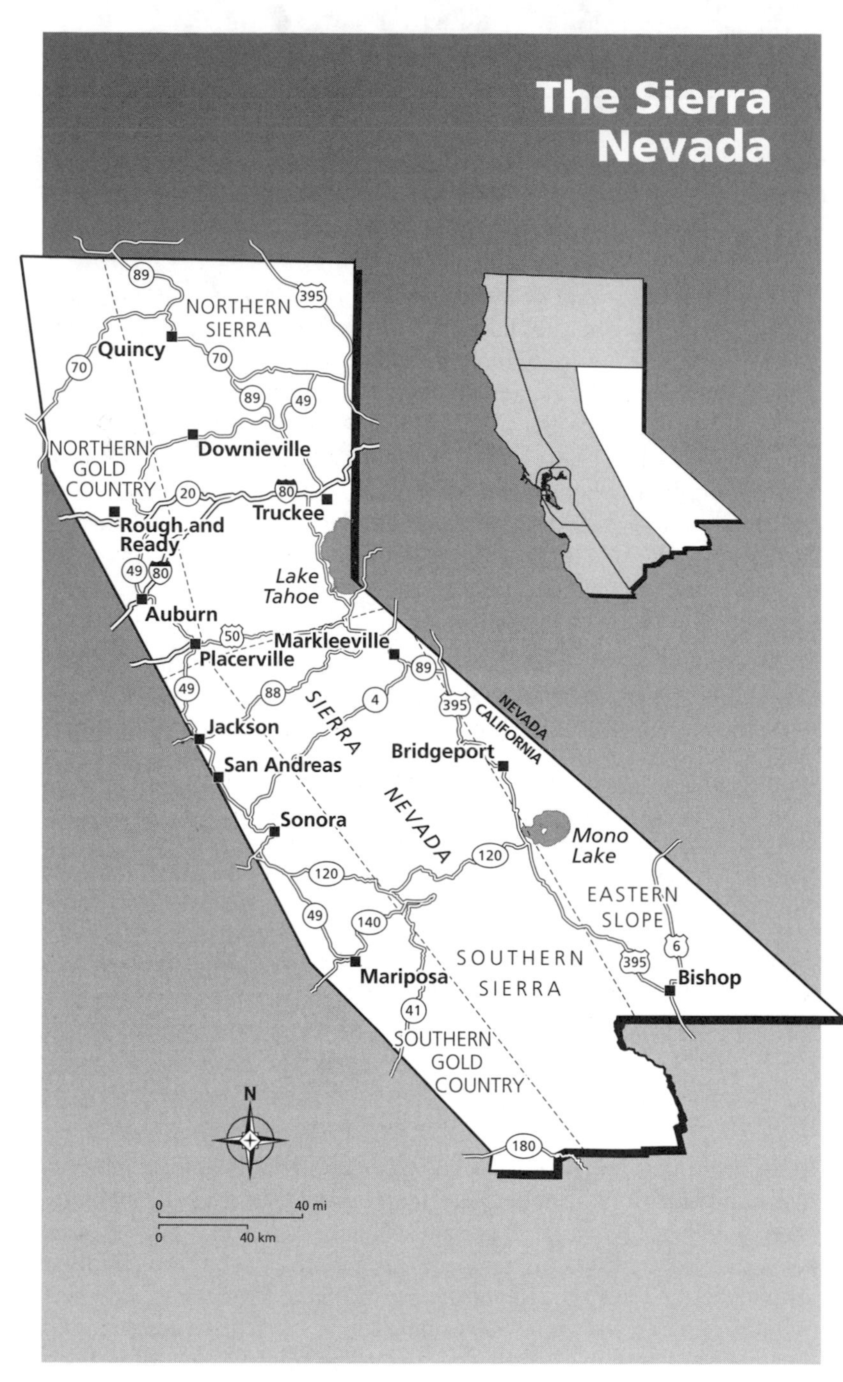

The Sierra Nevada
NORTHERN SIERRA
Quincy
Downieville
NORTHERN GOLD COUNTRY
Truckee
Rough and Ready
Lake Tahoe
Auburn
Markleeville
Placerville
SIERRA
NEVADA
NEVADA
CALIFORNIA
Jackson
Bridgeport
San Andreas
Sonora
Mono Lake
EASTERN SLOPE
Mariposa
SOUTHERN SIERRA
Bishop
SOUTHERN GOLD COUNTRY
N
0
40 mi
0
40 km

Author's Top Ten in the Sierra Nevada

Coulterville

Calaveras Big Trees State Park

Volcano

Vikingsholm

Markleeville

Bodie State Historic Park

Mono Lake

Downieville

Sardine Lake

Feather River Canyon

half have vanished, and many that remain are little more than colorful names on a map.

The spine of gold country is California Highway 49, named for the "forty-niners" of the wild-and-woolly year of 1849. It runs for 318 miles from Oakhurst in the south to Vinton near the Nevada border, passing through grassy hills dotted with oak and pine and scores of former gold rush towns. Often the road narrows to become the Main Street of these settlements, which means window-rattling traffic and pollution. The most heavily traveled stretch is the 100 miles or so between Sonora and Nevada City, which happens to parallel the richest part of a gold-laden vein of quartz called the Mother Lode. Discovering the real flavor of gold country means getting off this main track and scratching beneath the surface.

Southern Gold Country

Near the southern end of Highway 49, the town of ***Mariposa*** ("butterfly" in Spanish) sits in a pleasant, wooded valley surrounded by cattle and timber country. Although Mariposa features a fairly standard collection of historic and newer buildings, there are a couple of outstanding attractions here: the ***Mariposa County Museum and History Center*** and the California State Mining and Mineral Exhibit.

Your first stop, however, should be the old courthouse, scene of all official business within Mariposa County, which has no incorporated cities. Inside, maps show how Mariposa was at one time much larger, occupying one-fifth of the state when the original counties were laid out in 1850. The sprawling domain was later carved up to create six new counties and parts of five more. The courthouse, a sure sign that law and order had arrived to stay, has been in continuous use since 1854, making it the oldest in California. Located on Bullion Street at Ninth, it is open weekdays from 8:00 A.M. to 5:00 P.M. Tours are available by appointment; (888) 554–7081.

Enter the Museum and History Center and step into the wild and colorful era of the California Gold Rush. Among the clever re-creations here are the old Gagliardo General Store, its shelves lined with patent medicines, chewing tobacco, and hard-rock candy. An 1850s street scene features the original press and print shop of *The Mariposa Gazette*, a classroom from Bull Creek School, a tailor's shop, an assay office, a drugstore, and Rattlesnake Ike's Saloon, purveyor of rotgut whiskey. An early stagecoach on display, "The Cannon Ball," made the run to Yosemite Valley, which lies up the road from Mariposa and is the town's main claim to fame. You can also peer into a typical gold miner's one-room cabin, containing all his worldly possessions, however humble.

One of these crusty characters was Horace Snow, whose letters to his friend Charlie describing life in the mines are like a window on the past. There's also an exhibit on bandit Joaquin Murrieta, who supposedly turned to crime after his wife was murdered and who specialized in robbing Chinese, it was said. All this is so engagingly presented that the museum has won accolades from the Smithsonian Institution.

There is more outside: a stamp mill used for crushing gold-bearing quartz (each stamp weighs thousands of pounds); an authentic Indian village with bark houses and a sweat lodge; and a collection of mining equipment, including a mule-powered *arrastra* and steam pumps. The center is open daily year-round (except January) from 10:00 A.M. to 4:30 P.M. A $3.00 donation is requested. For information call (209) 966–2924.

When the World Rushed In

The California Gold Rush was the largest mass migration in American history. At least 22,500 forty-niners came in 1849 alone, traveling overland on a harsh, eight-month journey. Thousands more took the longer, more expensive sea voyage around Cape Horn or used a shortcut across central America. By 1852 there were several hundred thousand immigrants in California from dozens of countries, including about 25,000 Chinese.

The gold rush attracted a ready-made cast of characters for storytellers such as Mark Twain and Bret Harte. In a long line of desperadoes and scalawags, gentlemanly Black Bart (alias Charles E. Bolton) was the most infamous. He ambushed twenty-eight Wells Fargo stages, taking only the strongboxes and leaving his atrocious poetry behind.

Among the saucy ladies of the gold rush was dancer-actress Lola Montez, who once threatened to horsewhip a newspaperman who criticized her performance. This ex-mistress of mad King Ludwig I of Bavaria hit Grass Valley in 1853 and took the place by storm, keeping a bear on a chain in her front yard, among other stunts. Little redhead Lotta Crabtree, who lived up the street from Lola, learned how to entertain miners at raucous mining-town taverns. After finding fame and fortune in California, Lotta moved to New York and became one of the American theater's first millionaires, with a golden touch, it was said.

The outstanding ***California State Mining and Mineral Exhibit*** spent more than a hundred years in San Francisco before being moved here. It is fitting indeed that the collection should reside in a former gold rush town; after all, gold is the state mineral (serpentine is the state rock). Since 1988, the 20,000-piece collection has had a permanent home at the county fairgrounds.

On display is a head-spinning sampling of the stuff that all the fuss was about—ore, nuggets, and little vials of flakes locked inside a massive safe—plus a wide array of rocks and minerals from around the world: rare Dalfi diamonds, colossal quartz crystals, malachite, broccoli-green azurite, rhodochrosite from Argentina that looks like a scrumptious cream dessert, and oddities such as a petrified egg and a replica of a 242-ounce nugget found in 1932.

Also within the museum is a three-dimensional model of a mine's tunnels and shafts and a fully mechanized miniature stamp mill. A simulated mine tunnel leads you past muckers in flannel shirts and hard hats, a drifter machine for drilling horizontal holes, and other mining paraphernalia. The exhibit is open year-round; for information on hours and admission, call (209) 742–7625.

A fascinating side trip from Mariposa goes to one of the most unspoiled gold rush settlements, ***Hornitos,*** where you will see a ghost town in the making. In former times a rollicking community of 15,000, Hornitos (whose name means "little ovens") now has about fifty residents, occasionally seen drifting through the heat-hazed streets on their way to a Mexican-style plaza.

There the post office and other buildings survive in varying states of decay: Golden Stag Hall, Plaza Bar, and Roy's Cafe. One crumbling brick building nearby was where D. Ghirardelli, of San Francisco chocolate fame, got his start running a general store.

Hornitos was born when Mexican miners were forcibly evicted from Quartzburg. Ironically, a big strike was made near the new town, and it

Top Annual Events in the Sierra Nevada

Gold Discovery Day, *Coloma (January 24)*

Dandelion Days, *Jackson (mid-March)*

Calaveras County Fair & Jumping Frog Jubilee, *Angels Camp (mid-May)*

Mule Days Celebration, *Bishop (Memorial Day weekend)*

California Bluegrass Association Festival, *Grass Valley (mid-June)*

Tuolumne Lumber Jubilee *(late June)*

Secession Day Celebration, *Rough and Ready (late June)*

Miner's Day, *Downieville (early August)*

Feather River Railroad Days, *Portola (mid-August)*

Timberfest, *Loyalton (mid-August)*

Joaquin Murrieta Days, *Coulterville (mid-September)*

Historic Downtown Sonora Christmas Parade *(late November)*

Victorian Christmas, *Nevada City (December)*

became one of the richest and toughest of them all. Famous bad man Joaquin Murrieta, the "Robin Hood of the Mother Lode," used this as his hideout, specifically Rose Martinez's Fandango Hall and Saloon, where there was a secret escape tunnel.

If you like old buildings, stroll up to ***St. Catherine's Church*** (1862), a curious specimen combining wood walls and stone buttresses. Here is the town's boot hill, a mournful cemetery filled with crumbling tombstones and withered flowers. (Some say the name "Hornitos" came from the oven-shaped tombs here.) Surrounded by cacti, the old jail down the hill has 2-foot-thick granite walls and an iron door that would have made even Murrieta shudder.

You reach Hornitos via Mount Bullion, 6 miles north of Mariposa on Highway 49. Hornitos lies 13 miles away at 908 feet, one of the lowest-altitude mining towns. To return you can retrace this route or cut an 11-mile diagonal to Bear Valley.

From here, the town of ***Coulterville*** lies 16 miles away. Getting there means driving one of the least developed stretches of State Highway 49, through countryside almost unchanged since the days of the forty-niners. From rocky, scrub-covered hills, you make a tortuous descent into the Merced River Canyon, so steep and hot in summer that miners dubbed it Hell's Hollow.

After plunging to the bottom, you arrive at Lake McClure, then start another series of hairpin turns back up the other side, finally reaching Coulterville. This bucolic settlement is one of the less developed gold rush towns, its historic buildings still weathered and time-beaten, not yet prettied-up by developers, but surviving nonetheless.

Coulterville got its start in 1850, when Pennsylvania merchant George Coulter opened a supply business for miners. When the environs proved rich, the town grew to 10,000, including many Chinese, and life took on typically off-balance aspects. A slice of bread, for instance, cost a dollar ($2.00 if buttered). Coulterville burned to the ground three times before sturdier structures went up, and more than forty of them survive.

It's a town of covered boardwalks along ***Main Street,*** where twenty-five bars formerly stood. The renowned Jefferey Hotel (currently closed), which claimed Ralph Waldo Emerson and Teddy Roosevelt as guests, started as a Mexican cantina and fandango hall in the 1850s and has 30-inch-thick rock-and-adobe walls. Nearby are the local hanging tree, where Leon Ruiz was strung up for killing two Chinese miners, and the "Whistling Billy" locomotive, an eight-ton engine shipped around the

Horn and hauled here by mule train. Among other historical relics are an old trading post, the Gazzala Station saloon and dance hall; Bruschi Brothers warehouse; and a pint-size stone jail—small but effective. You can have lunch at Coulter Cafe and General Store, formerly a rooming house for prospectors.

The adobe Sun Sun Wo Store (and part-time opium den), on the outskirts of town, is a remarkably well-preserved reminder of Coulterville's Chinese heritage. Right next door sits Candy's Place, which for years did a thriving trade in assorted vices—until its owner ran off with a prominent citizen, never to return (it's now a private residence).

Fortunately for visitors Coulterville still retains much of its frontier spirit and atmosphere. For example, the town's big annual event is a Coyote Howl and Horseshoe tournament held every May.

Uncovering the most picturesque mining towns generally means getting off Highway 49, which bears the brunt of tourist traffic. ***Jamestown*** is one such place: Main Street is graced by a little park with a white gazebo and a row of brightly painted buildings with overhanging balconies. Most have been transformed into shops, hotels, and restaurants, so the place is hardly a throwback to the gold rush. Yet there's a certain aura of nostalgia hanging over the town that gives it a special appeal not found in other places. You can browse through piles of bric-a-brac at the Emporium, enjoy a fine meal across the street at the historic National Hotel, and then try your luck at prospecting. Look for a stuffed mannequin of a miner sitting outside Gold Prospecting Expeditions on Main Street. They promise to teach tinhorns how to use a sluice box and find the "pay streak" in a local stream. Of course, you get to keep any gold you find! Call (209) 984–4653 for information.

After the first local strike in 1848, the town mushroomed overnight in typical fashion and then served as gateway to the Mother Lode. Nicknamed "Jimtown," the area really boomed with the arrival of the railroad. The Sierra Railway ran between Oakdale and Jamestown and later all the way to Angels Camp. This story is re-created just outside town at ***Railtown 1897 State Park,*** which is the outdoor sister of Sacramento's famed railroad museum. Here are an old depot and fully working roundhouse and turntable, where you can watch old train engines being restored and maintained and stroll through a blacksmith shop and movie sets. (The park has been featured in more than 200 films and TV shows.) On weekends only an old train chuffs around the property on a 6-mile tour. The park is open daily from 9:30 A.M. to 4:30 P.M. with fees charged for tours and train rides. Call (916) 445–6645 for details.

Trivia

Geologists estimate that 70 percent of California's gold has yet to be discovered.

Moaning Cavern, 4 miles east of Angels Camp at Vallecito, takes its name from the strange sound said to emanate from the entrance. Indians believed the caves to be sacred, and 144 winding steps lead you down to a graveyard of prehistoric bones, the remains of about a hundred unfortunate souls who either fell or were thrown from above. In the 1850s, miners looking for gold lowered themselves into the cavern by rope, and today you can make the same descent on a challenging rappel tour, dropping 180 feet into the main chamber, which is large enough to hold the Statue of Liberty. For information call (209) 736–2708.

A century ago, well-to-do travelers made ***Calaveras Big Trees*** a must on their "grand tour" of California. These inspiring giant sequoia redwood giants along Highway 4 still receive a quarter of a million visitors annually. Most come in summer and flock to the popular North Grove Trail, with imposing specimens such as The Old Bachelor, with its massive, gnarled limbs, and a trio of elegant redwood monarchs called The Three Graces.

The grove became well known in 1852, and before long the hucksters had moved in. Entrepreneurs erected scaffolding and stripped the foot-thick bark off one tree in numbered sections, then shipped it to England for reassembly at an exhibition. (With this protective shield gone, the tree died; it's now just a fire-blackened hulk.) Another group held a contest to see how fast it could fell the largest tree. You can climb to the top of the 24-foot-wide stump they left as a legacy; it was used as a dance floor and for church services, among other things. The trunk itself served as a bowling alley. So much for John Muir's "monarchs of the forest."

If you arrive during the busy season, you can escape the crowds by visiting the less accessible ***South Grove,*** about 10 miles from park headquarters on the other side of the Stanislaus River. This is the largest stand of sequoias north of King's River, some 150 miles away, and contains the Louis Agassiz Tree, the park's largest single specimen, 250 feet high and 25 feet across. South Grove Trail winds along Big Trees Creek, passing about a thousand redwoods, many of them alive when the New Testament was being written half a world away. The path is remote and primitive, crowded with sugar pines (known for their 2-foot-long cones), azaleas, and dogwood.

For information on Calaveras Big Trees State Park, call (209) 795–3840. The North Grove Visitor Center is open weekends only in winter from

11:00 A.M. to 3:00 P.M., and daily in summer from 10:00 A.M. to 4:00 P.M.

Trivia

California's golden trout is found only in the icy streams of the High Sierra and is native to no other state.

Highway 4, the Ebbetts Pass Road, runs from Angels Camp into the high Sierra, joining Highway 89 about 5 miles south of Markleeville. East of Calaveras, the road climbs along a ridge above the Stanislaus River Canyon, flanked by granite outcrops and dense forests that are best seen from Liberty and Hells Kitchen vista points. The road continues to ***Bear Valley,*** a year-round recreation area where you can ski at Mount Reba in winter or see classical music concerts in summer. Next comes Lake Alpine at 7,320 feet, with superb mountain scenery and fishing. To the south is the 160,000-acre Carson-Iceberg Wilderness, which offers numerous soul-stirring hikes through pristine meadows and untouched lakes. From here the road climbs to Ebbetts Pass at 8,730 feet. (Note: Highway 4 past Bear Valley is closed from first snow until May.)

Amador County, with its seat at historic Jackson on Highway 49, lies in the heart of the gold country. But ***State Highway 88*** is another less traveled east-west route into the Sierra Nevada in the direction of Lake Tahoe.

Long before the frenzied cries of "Gold!" rang through these hills, Native Americans were living a simple, peaceful existence. When gold fever hit, the Miwoks were driven out of their traditional homes. Even so, each year they returned for ceremonies and celebrations, games and the gathering of acorns. One of these Miwok settlements is preserved at ***Chaw'Se Indian Grinding Rock State Historic Park,*** about a mile off Highway 88. It's a haven of tranquil meadows, a forest of manzanita and ponderosa pine, and the black oak trees that provided acorns, the staple food of the Miwok diet.

Trivia

The grizzly bear, which appears on the state flag and great seal, is now extinct in California.

As the park's name implies, the chief historic attraction consists of 1,185 holes ground into a granite outcropping with stone pestles and used for pulverizing acorns and other seeds. The resulting "flour" was made into a beverage, bread, or mush, and a typical family consumed about 2,000 pounds of the stuff each year. At first you see only a pockmarked rock, but closer inspection reveals the individual holes, or mortar cups, that were used until they became too deep.

The park's real attraction, however, is the pervasive atmosphere that hangs over the place like a cool mist. It's easy to imagine the primitive yet idyllic life before white people arrived to turn the Miwok's world upside down. A well-marked path takes you to the largest roundhouse (reconstructed) in California, with an entry door facing the rising sun. Inside, you can sometimes smell traces of smoke from recent ceremonies. If you listen carefully, you may think you hear chanting, and it's easy to imagine the native dancers attired in ceremonial garb.

The best time to convert these fantasies to reality is on American Indian Day, the fourth weekend in September, when there are songs, dances, arts and crafts, and Indian football. At this rambunctious spectacle, players are allowed to pick up and run with opponents who are carrying the ball, but only if they are female.

Chaw'Se Indian Grinding Rock State Historic Park, located on Pine Grove–Volcano Road, is open daily from sunrise to sunset. For information call (209) 296–7488.

Three miles off Highway 88, ***Volcano*** is a gold-country classic, a tiny town amid the pines that continues to bask in the memory of its days of glory. Is it a typical mining town? Not really; those were rough-and-raffish places bursting at the seams with energy. Volcano is about as sleepy as they come, with a few historic buildings and shops that open sporadically, depending on the weather and other variables.

Yet, there was a time when this must have seemed the center of Western civilization. As residents proclaim, Volcano had California's first library, first thespian and debating societies, first law school and astronomical observatory. The librarian, by the way, traveled the area by buggy, renting books at 10 cents a copy. Naturally, Volcano also had its requisite number of hotels, saloons, brothels, and bakeries, as well as a "court of quick justice."

Lying at the base of encircling hills, the town got its strange name from early miners, who thought the site resembled the caldera of a volcano. It grew to 10,000 residents, who scrapped and scraped for the gold stuff, and the valley once bragged of a 2.5-mile sluice box, surely one of the world's longest. The Chinese arrived late and literally cleaned up. By meticulously scouring all the old sluices and machinery with fine-haired brushes and scraping tools, they collected fortunes in gold dust.

Centerpiece of town is the wonderful old ***St. George Hotel*** (1862), in continual use for more than a century, not counting the three times it burned to the ground. The three-story, white-and-red-brick building is a gem of gold rush architecture, with suspiciously sloping balconies, pillars choked with climbing trumpet vine, and floors that creak even when you tiptoe.

The rooms range from elegant to sparse—iron-frame beds, old bureaus, wall hooks for your clothes—and bear names like "Poker Flat" and "Red Dog." The restaurant has been "serving food and grog since 1862." The Whiskey Flat Saloon remains Volcano's social center, its ceiling covered with dollar bills and business cards, and the walls dripping with odd pieces from just about everywhere, like the "rattlesnake" (actually a python skin) used to trick visiting tinhorns. Open Wednesday through Sunday; call (209) 296–4458 for reservations.

On a stroll around town look for the old assay office in a tin-roofed lean-to that really leans, now the visitor center; the Cobblestone Theatre, still going strong with regular plays; and the old country store, serving customers since 1852. In a ramshackle shed around the corner sits a Civil War–era cannon called "Old Abe," which helped the Volcano Blues put down a threatened Confederate "uprising." It's still hauled out on special occasions, such as the Fourth of July. Other historic buildings include the Bavarian Brewery (1856) and the Union Hotel (1880), which has been restored and is open for business, though some locals claim it's haunted.

The precious yellow metal may be gone, but each spring four acres near Volcano burst forth in floral gold, as well as white, pink, and a rainbow

Whiskey Flat Saloon, Volcano

of other colors. At ***Daffodil Hill*** more than 300,000 flowers (some 300 varieties) stand up and shout for a few weeks in March and April. (The exact blooming cycle varies from year to year.) It all started back in 1887, when members of the McLaughlin family began planting bulbs at the rate of about a thousand per year. Their descendants have carried on admirably with the planting, and they fling open the private ranch during blooming season only. Daffodil Hill, located 3 miles northeast of Volcano, is open daily at no charge.

Volcano seems suave and cosmopolitan after you've seen ***Fiddletown,*** just 10 miles to the north. There's no doubt where you are. A giant fiddle hangs above the community club, right next to the volunteer firehouse and a seedy cafe. If this drowsy village seems a bit on the scruffy side, it's probably because ruffians of one description or another have been drifting in and out for nearly 150 years.

According to local legend, Fiddletown was named after the original settlers from Missouri, who spent their leisure hours playing music and dancing. A snobbish local judge, embarrassed at having to tell people he was from a place called Fiddletown, actually changed the name to Oleta for some years, before local pride resurfaced to claim its heritage. Annual fiddling contests are held every September.

There was at one time an important Chinese community in Fiddletown, and the most important historical sight is the ***Chew Kee Store*** (Dr. Yee's Herbal Shop), recently restored and filled with shelves of potions and elixirs. Located on Main Street across from the old Chinese Gambling House, the historic store is open weekends from May through October from noon to 4:00 P.M.

Northward (east of Plymouth) lies the arcadian ***Shenandoah Valley,*** an area of rolling hills and vineyards, where you can get a whiff of traditional wine making. Today there are about twenty wineries in Amador County. Among the pioneers was D'Agostini Vineyards, the state's fourth oldest, founded by a Swiss immigrant in 1856. It has since been renamed Sobon Estate, and you can wander through a cellar of huge oak barrels and try some zinfandel, a local specialty. Open for tasting daily from 9:30 A.M. to 5:00 P.M. at 14430 Shenandoah Road; call (209) 245–6554 for information. Shenandoah Vineyards resides in noble stone buildings at the top of a gentle rise and offers an art galley, in addition to wine tasting. Open daily from 10:00 A.M. to 5:00 P.M. at 12300 Steiner Road in Plymouth; (209) 245–4455.

Southern Sierra

Returning to Highway 88 you climb steadily into the mountains through El Dorado National Forest, more than a half-million acres of get-away-from-it-all wilderness. (Take the Bear River turnoff.) The ascent to ***Kit Carson Pass*** (8,650 feet) skirts sparkling lakes and sawtooth peaks. Carson and John C. Fremont were the first to map a trail through these mountains, and it became a main avenue to the goldfields. Today it's the site of highly regarded Kirkwood Ski Resort. Just beyond the pass you can take Highway 89 north toward bustling Lake Tahoe.

Mark Twain wrote: "Three months of camp life on it would restore an Egyptian mummy to his pristine vigor and give him an appetite like an alligator." ***Lake Tahoe*** is a blue-green alpine jewel that encapsulates the best of the Sierra Nevada. Unfortunately, the lake's beauty and first-class recreational facilities bring legions of visitors summer and winter alike. Emerald Bay, at the southwestern tip, is the most famous scenic spot, a veritable *must* for anyone with a camera; however, most people miss a top-notch sight just a 1-mile hike away—a sprawling, thirty-eight-room mansion modeled on a Scandinavian castle.

Vikingsholm was the dream come true of millionaire heiress Lora Knight, who built her summer residence here in a style popular at the turn of the century—the eleventh century, that is. Swedish architect Lennart Palme and Mrs. Knight traveled extensively in Scandinavia, studying castles and homes for the final design, which was based on a medieval Norse fortress.

Trivia

Mark Twain lectured at the Nevada Theatre in Nevada City, the state's oldest continuously operating theater.

The trail to Vikingsholm starts near Eagle Falls. On the way down you will spot the little teahouse Mrs. Knight had built across a narrow strait on Fannette Island. Not until the trail's end, however, do you finally see the mansion. Rich folks really *do* like their privacy. The setting is superb, and because no trees were cut down during construction and only natural materials were used, the home blends harmoniously with the woods.

It is still amazing that Vikingsholm was built in only five months; one reason was that 200 workers lived on-site. Timber was barged across the lake, stone quarried nearby, and all metal pieces forged right on the job.

You enter the mansion, built around a circular courtyard, through a

Trivia

Portola's Railroad Museum boasts a 120-plus vintage-train collection.

heavy wooden door and pass into a living room of antique furniture and carved beams, then on to the dining room. During its heyday, the castle had a staff of sixteen maids, chauffeurs, and cooks, and in summer, park rangers set out the same elegant china used by Mrs. Knight. Upstairs, heavy Scandinavian rugs cover the floor of the bedroom, where Mrs. Knight slept in a replica of a queen's bed found on a 1,200-year-old Viking ship.

Vikingsholm is open from 10:00 A.M. to 4:00 P.M. weekends only starting Memorial Day, and daily from July 4 to Labor Day. For information call (530) 525–7277.

Rather than fighting the crowds at Lake Tahoe, you could turn south on Highway 89 (at the junction with Highway 88) and drive about 20 miles along a highly scenic route of pine forest and granite outcrops. ***Markleeville*** is a picturesque hamlet and the seat of Alpine County, the state's smallest, with fewer than a thousand full-time residents spread over 727 square miles. The county boasts only one traffic light, a flashing yellow signal, which makes Markleeville (population 165) a veritable urban center.

Tucked between mountain folds at about 5,500 feet, the town was named after founder Jacob Marklee, an ornery fellow who built a toll bridge across a local creek in 1861. Apparently this led to a heated argument in which Marklee was killed (the other man got off by pleading self-

At the Rim of the World

The Tahoe Rim Trail (TRT), opened in 2001, is a 165-mile path that traverses the ridgeline of Lake Tahoe's crown of peaks. It offers soul-stirring views and inspiring scenery and is available for both casual day hikers and backpackers from mid-June through October.

The TRT winds its way through valleys, along ridges, and up the granite peaks of the Carson Range, joining at some points the rugged Pacific Crest Trail. The flora changes according to season, from spring wildflowers to fall foliage. Among the many scenic highlights are Freel Saddle at 10,000 feet and Lake Aloha's islands of granite boulders. The best views can be found at Christopher's Loop, South Camp Peak, Twin Peaks, and Rose Knob Peak. Though much of the terrain is challenging, there's an easy 1.3-mile interpretive trail at Tahoe Meadows (8,740 feet) that's even wheelchair accessible. For more information contact the Tahoe Rim Trail Association at (775) 588–0686.

defense). This story is recounted at a small historical museum (open sporadically) devoted to silver mining.

The Markleeville general store has been serving customers the basics since 1865. Across the road (on Highway 89 at Montgomery Street) sits the Creekside Lodge from the same period; it has a good restaurant heated by an old Franklin stove. Next door is the ***Cutthroat Saloon,*** a rowdy bar whose walls sport a collection of mounted deer heads.

During summer, visitors come to Markleeville for trout fishing, rafting, and hiking, and for cross-country skiing and fireside relaxing in winter. Four miles from town ***Grover Hot Springs State Park*** sits in the shadow of 10,000-foot Hawkins Peak. It offers two outdoor pools, one fed by 104-degree water from six natural mineral springs and the other for cooling off. The park is a perfect place to relax after a long day of hiking or skiing local trails, and at night you're sure to have that appetite Mark Twain wrote about!

Grover Hot Springs State Park is open year-round; call (530) 694–2249 for further information.

The Eastern Slope

From Markleeville Highway 89 continues south and east to Monitor Pass (8,314 feet), then quickly descends the Sierra Nevada's east side to ***U.S. Highway 395*** in California's high desert. Here tourists are few and the sights spectacular.

Trivia

The state's motto, Eureka!, *is a Greek word meaning "I have found it." It originated with the discovery of gold in 1848.*

A drive along Highway 395 during winter or spring is the best way to see the jagged peaks and glaciers of the range in all their majesty. It's a region of extraordinary contrasts, with perennial snowfields at 13,000 feet overlooking sagebrush-dotted desert. For geologists the eastern Sierra provides a textbook example of fault-block mountains, created when a huge chunk of the earth's crust was detached and uplifted.

Lest you think that all mining towns sprang up on the Sierra's western slope, take a side trip to the bad old town of ***Bodie,*** which some people claim was the "baddest" of them all. Lying high (8,375 feet) in the steep hills southeast of Bridgeport, 13 miles off Highway 395, it can certainly lay claim to being the West's most authentic ghost town.

The state parks service, while not doing restoration, keeps about a hundred original pine buildings in a condition of "arrested decay," a kind of suspended animation so realistic it looks as if townsfolk just up and left one day. Naturally there's lots of dust, and things have begun to decay, but all the furniture is original, and the bedbugs in the sagging mattresses may still bite. You can peek into the old saloon and see a roulette wheel, poker chips and decks of cards, and bottles of rotgut whisky. There's also a Methodist church with wooden pews and a pipe organ, proving that at least some folks here were not scoundrels.

Bodie got its name from an early prospector, William S. Body, who froze to death in a storm. After gold was discovered, a camp went up nearby, and legend has it that a sign painter simply misspelled the name. Gold seekers and assorted parasites swarmed in, a ragtag collection of men who unearthed fortunes by day and squandered them by night.

Bodie was wild and wicked, with rotten whisky and mean men, opium dens, and ladies of easy virtue. Fistfights, stabbings, and robberies were commonplace, and during one violent period there was a killing a day. Even the weather was nasty, with bitterly cold winters and

A Mustang Sally

Incredibly, about 50,000 horses still live free on unfenced lands in the West. It's possible to see some of these wild mustangs in their natural habitat along California's Eastern Slope, where the snow-dusted Sierra Nevada looks like a giant stage setting. Outfitters based in Bishop offer horseback treks through Inyo National Forest near the Nevada state line, where thousands of the animals live in remote canyons and on the open range. Both experienced riders and novices are welcome to join the small groups, which are led by seasoned wranglers along old stagecoach roads and high desert country pocked with chaparral and sagebrush.

The small and wiry mustangs are descendants of the original barbs brought here by Spanish conquistadors and later mixed with other breeds. They run in groups of up to fifty animals, defiant in their freedom and very wary of people. But the tour groups usually get close enough for photos and to see and hear the wild horses cavorting as nature intended—truly a magnificent sight.

Mustang-viewing trips are offered by Rock Creek Pack Station in spring and early summer; call (760) 872–8331 or 935–4493 for details. In addition, about fifteen outfitters offering various kinds of horse and mule trips belong to the Eastern High Sierra Packers Association. For information write to them at 690 North Main Street, Bishop, CA 93514, or call (760) 873–8405.

scorching summers. The town claimed sixty-five saloons and a flourishing red-light district along Maiden Lane and Virgin Alley. There's a story that one small child, upon learning that his family planned to move there, knelt down and prayed, "Goodbye, God, we're going to Bodie!"

Trivia

The ancient bristlecone pines of Inyo National Forest are the oldest living trees on earth, dating back to at least 2,000 years before the birth of Christ.

The town's heyday ended about 1890, when the mine petered out. There were several fires, and in 1932 a boy playing with matches behind the saloon started a blaze that ripped through the old wooden buildings. Soon after, Bodie was abandoned. What you see now are only about 5 percent of the original buildings, slouching and leaning like aging derelicts. But there's still a lot to see: a well-stocked general store, the old hotel, a jail and iron bank vault, and wooden coffins stacked next to a funeral carriage. You can walk the dusty streets and plank sidewalks and be thankful you won't be leaving town in a pine box.

Bodie State Historic Park is open daily from 8:00 A.M. to 5:00 P.M. (until 7:00 P.M. in summer), but the road is closed in winter due to harsh weather. Admission is $2.00 per person (kids fifteen and under are free). For information call (760) 647–6445.

A few miles south of Bodie lies iridescent-blue ***Mono Lake,*** shimmering like a mirage as you approach. Here the only sounds are the cries of birds and the crunch of the salt-encrusted mud as you walk a shoreline ringed with spirelike mineral formations. This eery landscape seems to belong to another time or another planet. Indeed, Mark Twain called Mono Lake "the loneliest spot on earth."

Born half a million years ago, Mono Lake is a remnant of a once-vast body of water, one of a handful of lakes remaining in the Great Basin after the last Ice Age. Until recently scientists feared that time was running out for Mono Lake. In 1941 the thirsty city of Los Angeles (which had already sucked dry Owens Lake to the south) began diverting water from streams that emptied here. The lake's water level dropped about 40 feet, transforming islands into peninsulas, and the water became more saline as salt and other minerals were concentrated. Mono became two and a half times saltier than the Pacific Ocean, and the high alkalinity made it impossible for fish to survive. The lake seemed to be dying.

Then, in 1994, the State Water Board resolved the long controversy by allowing the diverted streams to again flow into the lake. Since then, it has risen 8 feet, a clear sign that Mono Lake has been saved.

Yet despite man's intrusions, nature somehow adapts and endures, and life goes on at the once "dying" lake. In winter, blooming algae turn the lake pea-soup green, providing a feast for brine flies and brine shrimp in summer, when they reproduce in the billions. These creatures, in turn, provide food for astonishing numbers of seasonal birds: eared grebes, snowy plovers, California gulls (90 percent of the state's total gull population are born here), and about eighty other species that gorge on the abundant food. (Each bird eats thousands of shrimp and flies a day.)

Visitors who decide to take a swim will find themselves floating on the highly saline water, which is slippery to the touch. The high alkaline content makes it very cleansing, and old-timers claim that a soak in the lake will cure almost anything.

The unusual mineral formations along the shoreline, called *tufa,* are created when calcium from freshwater, welling up from underground springs, combines with carbonates in the lake. The brittle calcite builds up around the mouths of the springs, forming towers up to 30 feet tall and other strange and spectacular shapes. The best place to see tufa formations is the lake's south shore.

Another top sight is nearby ***Mono Craters,*** the youngest mountains on the continent. (Some were formed as recently as five hundred years ago.) Rising more than 2,000 feet, the twenty-one craters are set in a valley of soft lava pumice atop a huge magma chamber, some 6 miles deep. But be forewarned: Geologists say that future eruptions here are certain. For a close look take Route 120 to Panum Crater, where a trail leads to the rim of a still-active volcano.

The Mono Lake Visitor Center, housed in a spectacular building, is located just north of the town of Lee Vining. It features imaginative exhibits on the area, art and photography exhibits, and also an award-winning film. The $3.00 entrance fee is also good at Bodie State Park. For information about free guided tours, call (760) 647–3044.

Northern Gold Country

Back on the western slope of the Sierra Nevada, Gold Country becomes mobbed along the stretch of Highway 49 from Jackson north to Nevada City (in California). That's hardly true about the sleepy burg of ***Rough and Ready,*** 4 miles west of Grass Valley, except maybe on Secession Day each June (on the last Sunday), when local patriots and lots of visitors commemorate the town's brief independence back in 1850.

Founded by a miner who had fought under General Zachary "Old Rough and Ready" Taylor during the Mexican War, the town boasted rich diggings nearby. So when the government declared a tax on mining claims, residents officially seceded from the Union for three months, elected their own president, and drafted a constitution. But come July 4 they got sentimental and recanted without bloodshed. There are a couple of sights from those wild days, such as the original blacksmith's shop.

The Tragedy of the Donner Party

Even before the gold rush, California beckoned. In April 1846 two Illinois brothers, George and Jacob Donner, gathered their families and possessions and headed west in six covered wagons. They joined others at Independence, Missouri, where George was elected wagon master of a group of eighty-nine men, women, and children.

Delayed along the trail, the exhausted and demoralized Donner party reached the eastern approach to the Sierra Nevada by late October. After a week of hesitation, they decided to press on over the pass toward Sutter's Fort (Sacramento). But winter came early that year, and one of the worst storms in history pummeled the hapless pioneers. Snowbound, they hunkered down around a lake that would come to bear their name. And food quickly ran out.

In December, one group tried to escape and was hit by a Christmas storm. Half of that group died huddled under their blankets. Famished and despairing, the survivors resorted to cannibalism. When rescuers finally arrived in late February, they were shocked to find the evidence; but when another big storm hit, they too partook of all that was available at a place later named Starved Camp.

In winter Donner Summit is still brutally cold and the snowfall can be enormous, up to 400 inches. The lake is beautiful and seldom crowded, as motorists whiz by on I–80 between the Central Valley and Reno. A monument erected at Donner Memorial State Park near Truckee marks the snow depth of that horrific winter of 1846–47 at about 22 feet.

The Emigrant Trail Museum here has a map of the 2,000-mile California Trail and numerous railroad and ski exhibits. The real draw is the Donner story. There's a list of those who survived—forty-seven of the original eighty-nine—and those who perished: their names, ages, and identification (eleven people from the rescue groups were also eaten). Near the museum a short trail leads to cabin sites where some of the Donners dined and died.

The museum at Donner Memorial State Park is open daily from 10:00 A.M. to 5:00 P.M. For camping and picnic sites, reservations are necessary in summer; call (800) 444–7275.

Since 1959 most visitors have come to make a union of a different sort at the ***Wayside Wedding Chapel,*** a one-room country church with stained glass and six white pews—ideal for romantic wedding or renewal of vows. Unlike the quickies at nearby Reno, weddings here need to be planned, but *everything* can be arranged for a price (starting at $250), from the minister (all faiths) to witnesses. For further information call (530) 273–6678.

Gold prospectors were a wild-and-woolly breed, hell-bent on extracting the shiny stuff whatever the cost. When they became more desperate as placer deposits dwindled in the 1860s, a practice called hydraulic mining was particularly disastrous for the environment. The process is clearly

Riding the Rails

You can ride through Donner Pass and the massive Sierra Nevada in a style pioneers would have happily enjoyed aboard Amtrak's Super Liner, the California Zephyr. *This double-deck train runs year-round between Chicago and Oakland along a route considered one of America's most beautiful, and many people from the Bay Area travel the stunning stretch to Reno for a bit of weekend action. (They say the eastbound trains are always more festive than the westbound.)*

Pulling out of Emeryville (near Oakland) in the morning, the Zephyr *skirts San Pablo Bay and the Carquinez Strait, then heads into the valley with a stop at Sacramento. The splendid scenery begins after Roseville as the tracks start to climb toward Colfax in the high Gold Country, taking on what railroaders call "The Hill." The Sierra is soon revealed in all its glory, and from glass-encased observation cars travelers see awe-inspiring real estate, such as the American River Canyon, not visible from the road.*

When the train finally reaches Truckee and Donner Summit, it's around lunchtime. In addition to the dining car, there's a lounge car serving snacks that doubles as the train's social center. Many people bring their own food and drink. The trip over the Sierra Nevada to Reno takes about six hours, and the service is top-notch, including an onboard sight-seeing guide.

Though the amenities may be modern, the route is hardly new—trains have traveled these rails for more than a century. Amtrak's California Zephyr *follows the route of the first transcontinental railroad built by the Central Pacific. This incredibly rugged stretch was finished in just five years as 10,000 men, mostly Chinese laborers, raced east from Sacramento and up 7,000 feet into the Sierra, then down the other side to Nevada, where they met workers from the Union Pacific coming from the opposite direction.*

For further information on this thrilling trip, contact Amtrak at (800) USA–RAIL or see its Web site: www.amtrak.com.

seen at ***Malakoff Diggins State Historic Park,*** located 29 miles northeast of Nevada City on a remote and little-visited site.

Here the miners literally blasted gold from the hillsides with high-pressure water hoses shooting liquid at more than two million gallons an hour. The water then flowed through a series of sluices to extract the ore, and this process turned mountains into molehills and sent thousands of tons of mud downstream, so much that the runoff created havoc with valley farmers and even caused major floods like the one at Marysville in 1875. Finally, hydraulic mining was banned after eighteen years of devastation.

You enter the park through a huge man-made ravine with fluted cliffs and contorted rocks that are strangely beautiful in their starkness, reminiscent of the Dakota Badlands or deserts of Utah. Here up to 50,000 tons of earth were washed away each day, leaving a pit more than a mile long and 600 feet deep. You can take a 6.5-mile trail around its rim and floor and see what a few gold-maddened men with water cannons accomplished.

The diggings are a short walk from the old mining town of ***North Bloomfield,*** with about thirty dilapidated buildings and a dozen reclusive residents. A fistful of historic exhibits includes an old livery stable, a church, and a general store (with miners' clothing, oil lamps, and so forth) as well as a small museum that chronicles the destruction wrought here over two decades. It also houses a few curious displays, such as 12-foot-long skis and a portable undertaker's table.

To reach the park take Highway 49 north from Nevada City for 12 miles, turn east on Tyler-Foote Road, and proceed 17 miles along a winding mountain road. It's open from 10:00 A.M. to 5:00 P.M. during summer, but call other times of the year for schedules and fees; (530) 265–2740.

Of all the old gold rush towns, ***Downieville*** is the one that should not be missed. It was originally called The Forks because of its site at the confluence of two rivers, but Major William Downie bribed enough residents into renaming the settlement in his honor. Rich placer deposits were discovered nearby, producing the kind of stories that set people's blood racing. One woman, for example, found $500 worth of gold while sweeping the earthen floor of her kitchen.

The typical boomtown growth hit, and by 1851 about 5,000 gold seekers had arrived. But Downieville had nowhere to grow; it's hemmed in by steep hillsides, and old homes cling to the slopes above town like terrified mountaineers. Although the present population hovers at only about 400, the town is the seat of Sierra County.

Trivia

Used just once, in 1888, Downieville Gallows is preserved as a state historic monument.

A trip to Downieville is twice as nice because the road getting there, ***Highway 49*** out of Nevada City, is among the state's most scenic, especially the stretch beyond Camptonville along the Yuba River. The landscape gradually becomes higher, cooler, and less crowded as you follow a narrow canyon and rock-strewn river basin. At last the picture-perfect town of tin-roofed houses, cradled in a canyon where the Yuba and Downie Rivers meet, leaps out just ahead.

Downieville is a place of narrow streets lined with weathered wood-frame buildings and covered sidewalks, where you can ponder the scene in the shade of an overhang or dine on a terrace fronting a rushing stream. Notable historical relics include the salmon-colored Craycroft Building (formerly a courthouse, saloon, and dance hall) and the Mackerman Building, home to the *Mountain Messenger,* the first newspaper (1853) in these parts and still going strong as California's oldest weekly. It has 3-foot-thick walls and fireproof iron doors for the inevitable fires that ravaged all mining towns. At a bar next door called St. Charles Place, a sign reads: CHECK ALL GUNS AND LONG KNIVES.

Downieville can claim the only authentic gallows left in California, conveniently built next to the old courthouse, which was destroyed some years ago. This grim wooden landmark is protected by a group called Friends of the Gallows. And speaking of hangings, a plaque on Main Street recalls a rare event, even in this wild country—the execution of a woman. The unfortunate Juanita, who stabbed Jack Cannon to death after a quarrel, swung from a Downieville bridge in 1851, a few years before the gallows were built.

The ***Sierra County Museum*** on Main Street, with gold nuggets and the usual collection of mining artifacts, sits in an attractive brick building that in the past housed a Chinese gambling den. You see more mining history at Lions Memorial Park near the fork of the two rivers. It's filled with discarded hardware, including a steam boiler, and a rusting iron car filled with hefty chunks of quartz, the kind that used to bring a gleam to the eye of any hard-rock miner.

A good deal of gold prospecting still takes place in this area, and a few lucky miners strike it rich in traditional fashion, clutching gold nuggets while crying out "Eureka!" For example, in 1993 two men near Alleghany unearthed a 141-ounce crystalline gold nugget valued at $250,000.

Another pleasant drive awaits on the 12-mile stretch from Downieville to ***Sierra City,*** hardly a city at all with just 200 residents, but a pretty little hamlet at 4,000 feet. Miners arrived about 1850 and started building in a narrow canyon overlooked by the Sierra Buttes. The settlement was leveled three times by avalanches sweeping down the canyon, but the diggings were so rich that even this could not make miners abandon their little piece of ground.

Just east of town the ***Kentucky Mine Museum*** resides at a former mining site drilled into solid granite. The tour here gives a good idea of the entire process of hard-rock mining, including "jaw crushers" that broke chunks into smaller rocks and a stamp mill that ground them into powder. Later, mercury was used to extract the precious gold flakes for further refining. Call (530) 862–1310 for admission and tour schedules.

Northern Sierra

Highway 49, "The Golden Chain," continues to Yuba Pass in the high Sierra. An alternate route 5 miles east of Sierra City, ***Gold Lakes Road,*** leads to a spectacular alpine region with several beautiful lakes. Among them is exceptionally picturesque ***Sardine Lake,*** whose waters mirror the ragged spires of the Sierra Buttes, lording over the landscape at 8,587 feet. When there's snow on the peaks, you may just think you're in the Swiss Alps. The 2-mile hike to Upper Sardine Lake, along a wide trail accessible to four-wheel-drive vehicles, offers a good workout and spectacular scenery; bring water and a picnic lunch. Another nearby spot in nearly pristine condition is ***Packer Lake,*** which has a lodge and a few rustic cabins for families and trout fishermen. About a mile away is the trailhead for a great hike to the top of Sierra Buttes.

From here, it's a short hop to Plumas County and Feather River Country, the final piece in the Sierra Nevada puzzle. This region is not easy to define, especially since there's no single Feather River until the various branches link up at Oroville on the fringes of the Central Valley. The area is roughly bordered by Highways 49 and 70 and includes portions of five counties (primarily Plumas) and two national forests. Elevations range from 1,000 feet in the west to the summit of Mount Ingalls (8,377 feet). This northernmost part of the Sierra Nevada is much less crowded than the Lake Tahoe region, but it offers great scenery and plenty of outdoor activities on more than 1,000 miles of rivers and a hundred lakes.

Heading north from gold country, you reach the former lumber town of ***Graeagle,*** now a neatly planned little community with a lake, golf courses, and a wooden Indian named Chief Graeagle to welcome visitors.

A few miles west, in the Mohawk Valley, is the Eureka Mining complex, centerpiece of ***Plumas-Eureka State Park.*** Park headquarters and visitor center occupy the former bunkhouse of a once-thriving gold mine, right down the road from scenic Johnsville.

During 1851, miners exploring near Jamison Creek came across an exposed ledge of quartz and gold some 400 feet long and 20 feet wide, sitting 4 feet above the granite base. Needless to say, many claims were filed over the next few years. A tent city grew into freewheeling Jamison City, and three tramways were built to bring ore down to the central mill near Johnsville. (One of these was said to have served as the world's first ski lift, used by the fun-starved miners.) Mining went on until 1943, resulting in 63 miles of shafts and tunnels.

From just outside the visitor center, the ***Mining Trail*** leads past a smattering of mining equipment—"chill wheels" used to crush quartz, a waterwheel to power the stamp mill, an air compressor, and other remnants from the days when hundreds of men toiled here. The old Mohawk Mill has been partially reconstructed with new timbers. At one point the mill had sixty stamps, each weighing 600 to 950 pounds, which crushed

Getting High in the Sierra

Standing dizzy and fear-frozen on a meshed grate, desperately clutching the metal railing, I look straight down a 1,000-foot vertical drop and wonder. Am I mad? I actually busted a gut to get here. But as the nausea and nervousness subside, I feel a certain euphoria at having reached this beautiful place all by myself.

The two-hour climb to the top of Sierra Buttes is one of the best hikes anywhere. This walk-of-a-lifetime starts at the Packer Saddle Trailhead near the Packer Lake Lodge (a good place for coffee before and a brew after). The trail climbs about 1,700 feet over 2.5 miles, but there are numerous switchbacks to make things easier. The first half or so rises gradually, and there's time for a rest at a mountain terrace; then the real climb begins. Finally the trail emerges above the forest at the craggy spires, and you soon see the soaring forest-service lookout station—the final challenge.

Crowning the 8,587-foot summit of the buttes, it is an engineering wonder to behold, reached by climbing a series of metal stairs jutting out miraculously over the abyss. It's downright scary to reach this lofty pinnacle, but you'll never regret it for a minute. The views of Gold Lakes Basin and far beyond are truly inspiring.

For more information about this and other hikes in Tahoe National Forest, contact the North Yuba Ranger District, 15924 Highway 49, Camptonville, CA 95922; (530) 288–3231.

small pieces of ore into sand. With each stamp dropping up to eighty times a minute, the slamming could be heard for many miles around.

The museum has a fully operational model of a stamp mill (ask to see it turned on) and various displays on mining and skiing history. For example, you learn that the first organized ski races in America were held at nearby Onion Valley in 1861. You can also see a pair of oak skis used by Snowshoe Thompson, the famous Sierra character who for two years ferried up to eighty pounds of mail on his back between Placerville, California, and Genoa, Nevada, a distance of 90 miles! The museum is open daily from 8:00 A.M. to 4:30 P.M. in summer and variable hours the rest of the year. Call (530) 836–2380 for information.

Trivia

Feather Falls is the country's sixth-highest waterfall.

A ten-ton waterpowered wheel, supposedly the world's largest, is found at the North Star Powerhouse Mining Museum in Grass Valley.

If heading north from here, you can turn off into the spectacular ***Feather River Canyon*** (along State Route 70) or continue on Highway 89 to Lake Almanor at the far northern edge of the Sierra Nevada range. Created by damming the North Fork, Almanor is a large, virtually undeveloped lake framed by pines, with majestic Lassen Peak looming to the north. The lake offers excellent fishing (trout, bass, king salmon) and warm summer water temperatures for swimming and other sports.

State Route 70 takes you along the steep, rock-strewn Feather River Canyon of the North Fork, a highly scenic route that traverses three tunnels and nine bridges. Railroad tracks run parallel to the road, and en route you will probably spot a train or two passing through the canyon. There is camping in Plumas National Forest and a few small resorts at towns such as Belden and Quincy.

The Feather Falls Scenic Area shelters granite domes and sheer ravines northeast of Lake Oroville. The main attraction of the 15,000-acre preserve is the waterfall, which Native Americans attributed to an angry and noisy monster living in a chasm. A 4-mile-long trail to the falls winds in and out of canyons, along streams, through a forest of firs and ferns, and finally along a steep ridge to a dramatic overlook. Here hikers can watch the Fall River cascading from a high cliff onto scattered boulders in a box canyon below. At 640 feet, Feather Falls ranks as California's highest waterfall outside Yosemite Valley.

Another attraction is South Branch Falls, a series of seven beautiful cascades on the Feather River that range from 30 to 150 feet in height. The best time to visit the Feather Falls Scenic Area is spring, when the snowmelt has swollen the river and wildflowers are flaunting their colors.

The heart of the preserve is located about 30 miles from Oroville via State Route 162, but it can also be reached from La Porte on the east side. For a map with detailed directions, call (530) 534–6500.

For further information, contact the Plumas County Visitors Bureau, (800) 326–2247.

Places to Stay in the Sierra Nevada

Southern Gold Country and Sierra

El Campo Casa Resort Motel,
12548 Kennedy Flat Road,
Jackson;
(209) 223–0100

Eureka Street Inn,
55 Eureka Street,
Sutter Creek;
(209) 267–5500

Fallon Hotel,
11175 Washington Street,
Columbia;
(209) 532–1470

Hotel Leger,
8304 Main Street,
Mokelumne Hill;
(209) 286–1401

Kit Carson Lodge,
Kit Carson Road,
Kit Karson;
(209) 258–8500

Mariposa Hotel-Inn,
5029 Highway 140,
Mariposa;
(209) 966–4676

Meadow Creek Ranch,
2669 Triangle Road,
Mariposa;
(209) 966–3843

Murphys Historic Hotel,
457 Main Street,
Murphys;
(209) 728–3444

National Hotel,
77 Main Street,
Jamestown;
(209) 894–3446

Woodford's Inn,
20960 Highway 89,
Markleeville;
(530) 694–2410

Yosemite Gold Country Motel,
10407 Highway 49,
Coulterville;
(800) 247–9884

Eastern Slope

Best Western Lake View Lodge,
30 Main Street,
Lee Vining;
(760) 647–6543

The Cain House,
340 Main Street,
Bridgeport;
(760) 932–7040

Chalfant House B&B,
213 Academy Street,
Bishop;
(760) 872–1790

Joseph House Inn,
376 West Yanley Street,
Bishop;
(760) 872–3389

Murphey's Motel,
51493 Highway 395,
Lee Vining;
(760) 647–6316

Northern Gold Country and Sierra

Deer Creek Inn,
116 Nevada Street,
Nevada City;
(530) 265–0363

Downieville River Inn & Resort,
121 River Street,
Downieville;
(800) 696–3308

Feather River Inn,
P. O. Box 67,
Graeagle;
(888) 324–6400

The Featherbed B&B,
542 Jackson Street,
Quincy;
(530) 283–0102

Graeagle Meadows,
Feather River Highway,
Graeagle;
(530) 836–1100

Gray Eagle Lodge,
5000 Gold Lake Road,
Graeagle;
(800) 635–8778

Herrington's Sierra Pines,
100 Main Street,
Sierra City;
(530) 862–1151

Pullman House B&B Inn,
256 Commercial Street,
Portola;
(530) 832–0107

Richardson House
B&B Inn,
10154 High Street,
Truckee;
(530) 587–5388

Riverside Inn,
206 Commercial Street,
Downieville;
(530) 289–1000

Sardine Lake Resort,
P.O. Box 216,
Sierra City;
(530) 862–1196

Sierra Shangri-La,
P.O. Box 285,
Downieville;
(530) 289–3455

Yuba River Inn,
P.O. Box 236,
Sierra City;
(530) 862–1122

Places to Eat in The Sierra Nevada

Southern Gold Country and Sierra

Murphys Hotel Restaurant
(American),
457 Main Street,
Murphys;
(209) 728–3444

National Hotel Restaurant
(American),
18183 Main Street,
Jamestown;
(209) 984–3446

The Palace Restaurant &
Saloon (Continental),
76 Main Street,
Sutter Creek;
(209) 267–1300

St. George Hotel
(American),
16104 Main Street,
Volcano;
(209) 296–4458

Sierra House Restaurant
(American),
20153 Highway 88,
Pine Grove;
(209) 296–4894

Upstairs Restaurant
(American),
164 Main Street,
Jackson;
(209) 223–3342

Wolf Creek Restaurant
(American),
14830 Highway 89,
Markleeville;
(530) 694–2244

Eastern Slope

Firehouse Grill
(American),
635 North Main Street,
Bishop;
(760) 873–4888

Mono Inn Restaurant
(American),
55620 Highway 395,
Lee Vining;
(760) 647–6581

Restaurant 1881
(Continental),
362 Main Street,
Bridgeport;
(760) 932–1918

Whiskey Creek Restaurant
(American),
524 North Main Street,
Bishop;
(760) 873–7174

Northern Gold Country and the Sierra

Buckhorn Lodge
(American),
Highway 49,
Sierra City;
(530) 862–1170

Downieville Diner
(American),
8 Main Street, Downieville;
(800) 289–3616

Grizzly Grill (American),
250 Boneta Street,
Blairsden;
(530) 836–1300

Iron Door (American),
Main Street,
Johnsville,
(530) 836–2376

Paulette's Country Kitchen
(American),
11875 Sutton Way,
Grass Valley;
(530) 273–4008

Riverview Pizza
(Italian-American),
Highway 49,
Downieville;
(530) 289–3540

Sardine Lake Lodge
(Continental),
Sardine Lake Road,
Sierra City;
(530) 862–1196

Scheidel's Old European
Restaurant (German),
10100 Alta Sierra Drive,
Grass Valley;
(530) 273–5553

Sweet Lorraine's
(American),
384 Main Street,
Quincy;
(530) 283–5300

Trolley Junction
(American),
400 Railroad Avenue,
Nevada City;
(530) 265–5259

HELPFUL WEB SITES ON THE SIERRA NEVADA

Alpine County Chamber of Commerce:
www.alpinecounty.com

Bishop Visitor Bureau:
bishopvisitor.com

California Campgrounds:
www.california campgrounds.org

California Caverns:
www.caverntours.com

California State Parks:
www.parks.ca.gov/

Gold Country Visitors' Association:
www.calgold.org

Mariposa County Visitors Bureau:
www.mariposa.org

Mono Lake/Inyo National Forest:
www.r5.fs.fed.us/inyo

Plumas County Visitors Bureau:
www.plumas.ca.us

Sacramento Visitors Bureau:
www.discovergold.org

South Lake Tahoe Visitors Authority:
www.virtualtahoe.com

Tahoe Rim Trail Association:
www.tahoerimtrail.org

Yosemite Area Traveler Information:
www.yosemite.com

WORTH SEEING IN THE SIERRA NEVADA

Columbia State Historic Park

Empire Mine State Historic Park, Grass Valley

Lake Tahoe, North Shore

Marshall Gold Discovery State Historic Park

Placerville's Hangtown

Yosemite National Park

Shasta Cascade

COME TO ANOTHER CALIFORNIA, the signs and bumper stickers proclaim. If this sounds like advertising hype, the message is not. This often forgotten corner of the state is truly a world apart.

Most Californians are only vaguely aware of the Shasta Cascade region, and if they visit, it's along fast, impersonal I–5. Stretching from the eastern slopes of the Coast Range to Nevada and from the Oregon border to the southern fringes of the Cascades, it is sparsely populated and largely untouched.

This unspoiled chunk of the Golden State offers tremendous diversity: volcanoes (including the biggest plug dome on earth); many of California's largest lakes; the world's second-highest man-made waterfall; and a peculiar version of the Abominable Snowman, called Bigfoot. Spotted from time to time (usually during snowstorms), these hairy creatures are said to stand up to 12 feet tall and weigh 800 pounds. If visitors manage to steer clear of these beasts, they can find nearly unlimited outdoor opportunities in Shasta Cascade—whether angling for salmon and steelhead or snowshoeing beside bubbling lava pits.

Getting there is easy: I–5 forms the north-south backbone, and Highway 299 is the main east-west route. The two cross at Redding, unofficial capital of Shasta Cascade, with about 80,000 residents. It's considered the hub of the region, and it can be used as a base for exploring. For a mountain of information (including a sixty-four-page visitor guide), write the Shasta Cascade Wonderland Association, 1699 Highway 273, Anderson, CA 96007; (530) 365–7500 or (800) 474–2782. The group also operates an official California Welcome Center based here.

Klamath–Trinity Wilderness

Trinity County is larger than the state of Delaware but has only about 13,000 residents. A full 97 percent of the land is forested and includes such primitive terrain as the Shasta–Trinity National Forest, the second-largest slice of virgin land in California. Nearly one-

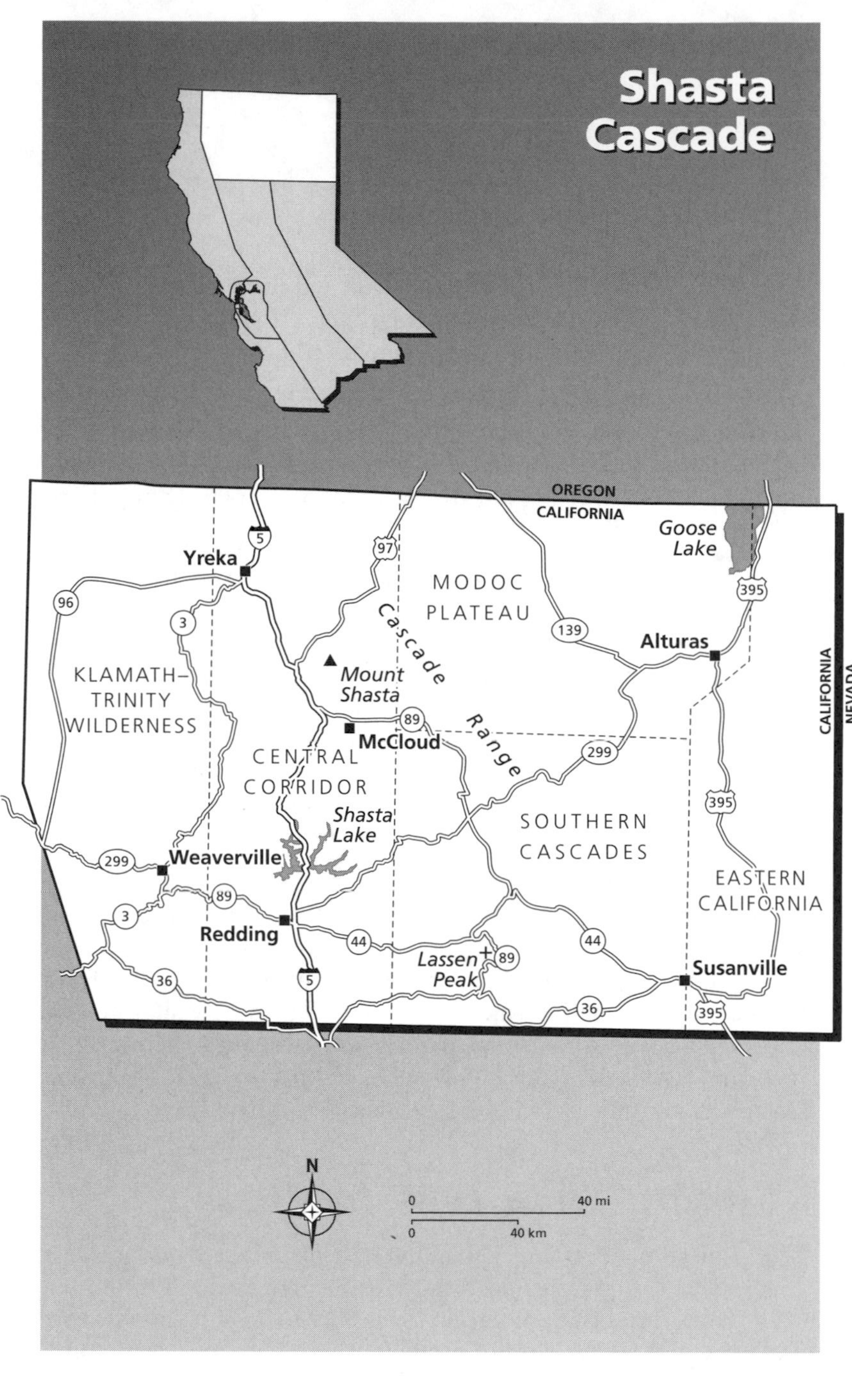

Shasta Cascade
OREGON
CALIFORNIA
Goose Lake
Yreka
MODOC PLATEAU
Cascade Range
Alturas
Mount Shasta
KLAMATH-TRINITY WILDERNESS
McCloud
CENTRAL CORRIDOR
Shasta Lake
SOUTHERN CASCADES
Weaverville
EASTERN CALIFORNIA
Redding
Lassen Peak
Susanville
CALIFORNIA
NEVADA
5
97
96
3
139
395
89
299
44
36
N
0
40 mi
0
40 km

third of the county's inhabitants live in ***Weaverville,*** one of the state's oldest towns, about 45 miles west of Redding on Highway 299.

Author's Top Ten in the Shasta Cascade

Weaverville
Trinity-Alps Wilderness
Castle Crags State Park
Mount Shasta
McCloud
Lassen Volcanic National Park
Burney Falls
Lava Beds National Monument
Cedarville
Fort Bidwell

In July 1848 Major Pierson B. Reading found gold on a sandbar in the Trinity River, which launched the familiar stampede. After three prospectors built the first cabin here, they drew straws to decide the name of the new settlement—and John Weaver won. Like so many other mining towns, Weaverville grew willy-nilly and was soon big enough to support two theaters and attract Lotta Crabtree, a highly touted performer, in 1855. Later, nearby LaGrange Mine became the world's largest hydraulic gold-mining operation.

Its streets still lined with woodframed houses, picket fences, and honey locust trees, Weaverville has changed little over the years, except for the relentless traffic thundering down Main Street. You can pick up a walking tour map at the History Center and stroll under covered walkways past several notable buildings, painted rust red with white trim. Among them is the Court House, with iron shutters and thick walls for fireproofing. Erected in 1856, it served as a hotel, saloon, and store before changing roles in 1865, after the original courthouse became infested with bedbugs.

Trivia

The Weaverville Drugstore was filling prescriptions nine years before Abraham Lincoln took the oath of office, and it continues to do so today in the same Main Street location.

Weaverville is known for its spiral staircases, hand forged by a blacksmith from Bavaria. They were designed to sidestep the problem of different ownership of upper and lower stories and to preserve valuable Main Street frontage that might otherwise go to building staircases. The ***Weaverville Drugstore*** (oldest in California) has been serving customers at the same location since 1852. On display are patent medicines, a "suppository machine," and bottles of whiskey used for "medicinal purposes." Spirits are also sold across the street at ***The Diggins Tavern,*** complete with swinging doors and customers dressed in buckskin.

Trivia

Weaverville's Joss House is the country's oldest continuously used Chinese temple.

Many Chinese came to the "land of the golden mountains," and a town within a town developed here, with its own shops, opera house, and gambling parlors. The Temple of the Clouds and Forests was constructed in 1853, burned down twenty years later, then rebuilt in 1874. The ***Weaverville Joss House*** (*Joss* being Chinese pidgin English, from the Portuguese word for God, *deos*) is the oldest surviving Chinese temple in America. It sits amid gardens and a stream crossed by an arched stone bridge and looks north toward the Trinity Alps.

The temple was designed exactly as in China except that wood was used instead of stone and tile, and the facade was painted white and blue to resemble masonry. Intricate carvings of fish and dragons on the roof were meant to ward off evil spirits, especially needed, it was believed, because funeral processions for whites passed right in front of the temple.

Just beyond the main entrance are two tall wooden doors, "spirit screens," to keep out evil spirits. Inside, a state ranger reels off a brief history of the place, pointing out pictures of "immortals" painted on glass,

Historic building on Main Street, Weaverville

a lion-dance headdress, an abacus, opium pipes, and other curiosities. Worshipers prayed before the three altars, but they were forbidden to ask specifically for riches. "Joss money" was burned in offering to the gods, and to gain their attention a drum and bell sounded during the ceremony.

All around the room are grinning, frowning deities and signs written by immigrants in Chinese. Among them is this simple request: "I want to make my fortune and go home again." Estimates are that about one-third of the immigrants *did* return; the rest stayed on, hoping to realize their golden dreams someday. Call (530) 623– 5284 for information.

There were less peaceful sides to Chinese life. The ***J. J. Jackson Memorial Museum*** exhibits trident-like spears and other weapons used in the infamous Weaverville Tong War of 1854. For reasons long forgotten two rival factions found themselves in a feud and began battle preparations. They placed orders for weapons (spears, shields, swords, tin hats) with local blacksmiths and drilled for a month, while townspeople wagered on the upcoming encounter. Finally, in a spot east of town called Five Cent Gulch, a two-minute melee took place before throngs of cheering spectators. When the dust cleared, seven Chinese were dead and twenty wounded.

Top Annual Events in the Shasta Cascade

Red Bluff Round-Up Rodeo, *(mid-April)*

Kool April Nights Car Show, *Redding (mid-April)*

Shasta Art Fair, *Old Shasta (Mother's Day weekend)*

Old Lewiston Peddlers Faire, *(early June)*

July 4th Celebration, *Weaverville (July 4)*

Paul Bunyan Mountain Festival, *Westwood (early July)*

Fandango Days Celebration, *Alturas (early July)*

Microbrewery Festival, *Mount Shasta (late August)*

Montague Rotary Balloon Faire, *(late September)*

Western Open Fiddle Championships, *Red Bluff (late October)*

The museum also houses a good collection of mining and Indian artifacts, antique firearms, an aspirator used to remove body fluids, and authentic jail cells, complete with graffiti, moved over from the courthouse. Call (530) 623–5211 for more information.

Trivia

Shasta Dam has the highest overflow spillway in the world.

Weaverville is home to one of two ranger stations for the ***Trinity Alps Wilderness,*** until recently known only to dedicated outdoor adventurers. These mountains thrust upward in sharp, snow-capped ridges, with glacial canyons and alpine lakes sprinkled amid thick forests of fir and ponderosa pine. Because the range can't be seen clearly from the east, most people are surprised to learn how high and rugged it is. The landscape of granite peaks, standing at 7,000 to 9,000 feet (Mountain Thompson is the highest), resembles the Sierra Nevada but is much more compact. The timberline is lower here, too, and the area is wetter and greener because of its proximity to the coast.

The Trinity Alps are laced with hundreds of miles of trails throughout a 500,000-acre wilderness area. They are perfect for solitary adventures, unless you happen to encounter a wolverine, pine marten, mountain lion, or black bear. Trinity Forest claims the highest concentration of bears in California, about one per square mile. And who knows? It's said that Bigfoot stalks these mountains as well.

One popular trek goes to the exceptionally beautiful Caribou Lakes Basin, with four lakes cradled in a spectacular granite setting. Another leaves from Hobo Gulch, northwest of Weaverville, and takes in lakes, waterfalls,

Bigfoot: Legend or Fact?

Native Americans talk about "Sasquatch" and Tibetans have their "Abominable Snowman." Here in northwestern California, powerful creatures of similar stature rule the wild Siskiyou and Klamath Mountains between Willow Creek and Happy Camp. According to a scattering of unconfirmed reports, the "Bigfoot" creatures stand about 8 feet tall and weigh 500 pounds or more, with a light covering of body hair that easily distinguishes them from the furry brown bears common in the area. Those who claim to have spotted a Bigfoot, usually peeking through the trees or around rocks near a campsite, describe their high-pitched voices and wide, flaring nostrils.

Stories of "giants" roaming the earth go back to the Bible, in the confused era before the great flood, and most ancient civilizations had their Titans and other superhuman creatures. Much later, Spanish conquistadors wrote about extremely tall, blond men running wild around the Andes. Two were supposedly captured but died en route to Spain. Today, some believe that humanoids similar to Bigfoot roamed much of the earth before the end of the last ice age, about 12,000 years ago, and that a handful survived in isolation.

Historical references to California's Bigfoot trace back to the 1880s, and over the years numerous reports surfaced from miners, loggers, and campers, more than forty separate incidents in all. Plaster casts were made of footprints and even a few photos and a home movie taken of one creature running away, whose authenticity have been vigorously challenged. In fact, most scholars and authorities think the whole legend is utter nonsense. But those who claim to have seen a Bigfoot in the flesh swear they are real.

Statue of Bigfoot

and an abandoned gold mine. Many trailheads into the wilderness start near the west shore of Trinity (Clair Engle) Lake.

For more information on the area, contact Shasta–Trinity National Forest, P.O. Box 1190, Weaverville, CA 96093; (530) 623–2121.

Heading west from Weaverville, this stretch of Highway 299 has been dubbed the ***Trinity River Scenic Byway.*** The churning river cuts through some impressive mountain scenery dotted with campgrounds and cottages and is very popular with fishermen and river rafters. Along the way are a few points of interest: the La Grange mining operation, Simon Legree's Bar (at Ironside), and China Slide, where some Chinese prospectors were buried under 200 feet of mud. But for the best views, you need to pull over and peer right down into the narrow river canyon.

The town of ***Willow Creek*** (in Humboldt County), sitting amid a vast forest of Douglas fir

Trivia

Shasta Lake is called the "Houseboat Capital of the World," with more than 400 commercial vehicles for rent.

trees, is known as the gateway to "Bigfoot Country," with its 9-foot wooden sculpture greeting visitors and a museum dedicated to the hairy beasts (open summer only). From here Highway 96 pushes north along the little-traveled ***Bigfoot Scenic Byway,*** following the North Fork of the Trinity and Klamath Rivers, both renowned for trophy-size fish and white-water rafting. The route passes right through the Hoopa reservation, whose main settlement offers a well-stocked tribal museum of history and crafts and the bustling Lucky Bear Casino. The village of Weitchpec, perched beside a bridge overlooking the Klamath, lies in the heart of Bigfoot country, rugged mountains that have yielded lots of speculation and a few grainy photos and plaster casts

Will the North Rise Again?

They say the folks around Yreka have an ornery streak that surfaces from time to time. Back in 1941 this little blue-collar town north of Mount Shasta led a brief movement to secede from California and create (along with southern Oregon) a new state named Jefferson. Even today a spirit of self-determination lingers in this distinct region of loggers, prospectors, and other rugged individualists.

At the time, locals were having trouble getting their copper to market (due to World War II, the price had rocketed), and in November of 1941 disgruntled miners met at Yreka. Here they formed an alliance with miners from southern Oregon suffering from similar problems, and what began as a protest against bad roads quickly snowballed into the so-called Jefferson Rebellion. Grizzled men armed with hunting rifles set up roadblocks and handed out proclamations of independence from California to bewildered motorists.

Siskiyou, Modoc, and Del Norte Counties joined forces with Curry County in Oregon, and they elected a governor and provisional government. They even chose a state seal: a double cross on a gold pan to "symbolize" how both California and Oregon had treated them. Secession had succeeded, and reporters from around the country arrived to see what state officials in Sacramento would do next.

But fate stepped in—just three days after the new governor's inauguration, the Japanese bombed Pearl Harbor, and the Jefferson snowball quickly melted as the nation's attention turned elsewhere. Some people claim the movement pushed the government to improve the roads, and sure enough I–5 makes a puzzling jog west to skirt the town of Yreka, which boasts three *highway exits.*

T-shirts and bumper stickers sold here proclaim "Jefferson, a state of mind" and similar sentiments showing that the dream lives on. Said one local sage, "You can't tell what folks up here will do when they get a notion."

of oversized footprints (see Bigfoot: Legend or Fact sidebar).

Trivia

The famous Alcan Highway (U.S. 97) to Fairbanks, Alaska, starts not in Canada or even Washington but in the town of Weed near Mount Shasta.

At the old logging town of Happy Camp (82 miles from Willow Creek), there's another Bigfoot sculpture outside the post office and a handful of mining-era buildings. This is the heart of the would-be State of Jefferson (see Will the North Rise Again? sidebar). Here Highway 96 turns east and follows the Klamath River through forested hills alive with songbirds and wildflowers, passing an evocative old cemetery (1869) filled with mossy tombstones at Fort Goff. Farther on, the route enters an entirely different landscape, treeless and volcanic, near I–5. A scenic shortcut through Shasta River Valley (Highway 263) heads south to Yreka, Siskiyou County seat.

People drive I–5 if they are in a hurry. A slower but much more scenic alternate for north-south travel is ***State Route 3*** between Weaverville and Yreka, the old California-Oregon wagon road. The southern portion runs parallel to Trinity (Clair Engle) Lake and the Trinity Alps, although you have to leave the main road to get a good look at the lake.

Trivia

California's largest Indian reservation lies in Hoopa Valley, nestled in the mountains of northern Humboldt County.

Trinity Lake was created in 1961 behind a 538-foot earth-fill dam, and at full capacity it's 20 miles long with 145 miles of shoreline sheltering many secluded coves. A part of the Whiskeytown–Shasta–Trinity National Recreational Area, the lake is known for its trout, salmon, and bass fishing, and most facilities are located on the west side in the shadow of the Trinity Alps. Completely equipped houseboats are available for rental, and, unlike busy Shasta Lake, you may find yourself alone with the fish.

Highway 3, dubbed the ***Trinity Heritage Scenic Byway,*** continues north past pine-draped slopes and craggy cliffs but seldom another car. Finally, at Scott Summit (5,401 feet) the road straightens out and descends into idyllic ***Scott Valley,*** a little patch of rural paradise first settled by beaver trappers. Among the small towns here is Callahan, at the headwaters of the Scott River (John Scott was an early gold miner). This former stage stop and trading center is slowly succumbing to time, its famous Emporium, once called "the biggest little store in the world," now padlocked shut.

The town of ***Etna*** (12 miles north) is quiet—you have to leave the main road to find it—but merits a quick drive around. Originally called

Trivia

The Shasta Cascade region is about the size of Ohio and boasts seven national forests and eight national or state parks.

Rough and Ready, the town supplied local miners. Today you can visit Etna's historic cemetery and the Native Daughters of the Golden West Museum, above the library on Main Street. Etna Hardware has been around for 120 years. The Etna Brewing Company, at 131 Callahan Street, produces a variety of "all natural" beers, including root beer, and offers tours and tastings. For details call (530) 467–5277.

Fort Jones was established in 1852 to protect the area from attacks by the bellicose Rogue River Indians. Ulysses S. Grant was ordered here and declared AWOL when he failed to take command (he later showed up with a good excuse). Now it's a quiet town with stores such as Fort Jones Frontier Hardware, selling "sporting goods and tourist supplies," and Charley Bob's Bar with cocktails "off sale" (for takeout only). The Indian Rain Rock and burial rock are among the displays at the Fort Jones Museum on Main Street; (530) 468–5568.

From here another beautiful stretch leads to Forest Mountain Summit, at 4,097 feet, for a panoramic view of Scott Valley. State 3 ends at ***Yreka*** (at the junction with I–5). Few people know about this town's very respectable collection of Victorian homes, about seventy-five of them, including many listed in the National Register of Historic Places.

They are found chiefly on Miner Street, the old commercial hub, and nearby residential streets such as James Place. Other stops of interest are the Native American Heritage Park, with a full-size replica of a traditional sweat lodge, and a gold display at the Siskiyou County Courthouse, 311 Fourth Street. Among the eye-catching pieces, carefully watched by two sherriffs, are a crucifix made from a single nugget and a solid gold watch. Yreka is also home to the Blue Goose excursion steam train, which runs Wednesday through Sunday in summer to the town of Montague.

For a color brochure describing all the scenic byways of the Shasta Cascade area, "Gateway to a Getaway," call (800) 474–2782. Another publication, "An Adventure Around Every Corner," features more challenging trips for off-road vehicles.

Central Corridor

If traveling north from Redding and Shasta Lake along I–5, don't miss ***Castle Crags State Park,*** about 6 miles south of Dunsmuir at Castella. Called *Castillo del Diablo* (Devil's Castle) by Spaniards, the glacier-scoured granite peaks rising from the forest are truly spectacular.

Unrelated geologically to its more famous neighbor, Mount Shasta, Castle Crags was formed millions of years ago when hot granitic material below the surface was forced upward like a rising air balloon. Much later the forces of erosion—ice, water, and wind—sculpted and polished the gray-white rock into stark shapes thrusting up 4,000 feet from the valley of the Upper Sacramento River.

At a scenic overlook called Vista Point, reached via a 1-mile corkscrew road, the landscape spreads out like a textbook on geology of the last 300 million years. The river and I–5 run along a fault zone between the Cascade and Klamath mountain ranges, to the east and west respectively. Castle Crags belongs to the Klamaths, which were formed

Visiting Shasta Abbey

Standing in the snow outside an iron gate, I'm greeted cordially by a man dressed in a fur cap to cover his shaved head and a brown robe made of coarse cloth. I've requested a visit to Shasta Abbey, a Buddhist monastery tucked beneath Black Butte on the fringes of Mount Shasta City. The "reverend" and I begin our stroll around the spacious grounds.

Shasta Abbey was founded more than thirty years ago by an English woman who remains as head abbess. The order of Buddhist contemplatives here practice the tradition known as Soto Zen. In this area of astounding spiritual diversity, where dozens of religious groups are based, Shasta Abbey is a fully recognized seminary for the Buddhist priesthood.

The American reverend accompanying me on this tour swears that the mountain's famed mystical powers have nothing to do with the abbey's location. He has spent the past two decades here and, like most of the three dozen monks in residence (including some females), has no intention of ever leaving. Indeed, they all seem content, smiling and bowing to each other as they pass in the corridor or perform chores.

The abbey has its own vegetable gardens and is largely self-contained, and we walk along covered walkways lined with firewood past solid stone buildings. We stop at an odd exhibit of old toys and discarded objects called "Quon Yin's Garden," which is supposed to represent the universe's many spiritual realms. Next we look into a large hall reserved for morning services, adorned with lanterns and several Buddhas carved in gold. A typical day here begins at 6:00 A.M. with prayers and meditation, followed by a meal, and chores, more meditation, another meal, and so on until the evening service.

The abbey opens to outsiders for weekend retreats and seminars teaching Buddhist precepts and meditation techniques, and there's even a Sunday school for local kids. Shasta Abbey is located at 3612 Summit Drive, Mount Shasta; for further information call (530) 926–4208.

Trivia

Mount Shasta, at 14,162 feet, is the highest volcano in California and the second tallest in the U.S.

when the sea floor was crumpled and thrust upward by the collision of two tectonic plates. Just across the valley sits Girard Ridge, the western edge of the Cascades, and, beyond that, snow-shrouded Mount Shasta.

Ambitious hikers can take the 2.7-mile Crags/Indian Springs Trail from Vista Point, which is a bit strenuous as it rises 2,250 feet to the base of Castle Dome, thrusting skyward like a clenched fist. Serious rock climbers say Castle Crags is far less crowded than Mount Shasta in summer and provides equally great challenges, such as a nearly vertical outcrop of Castle Dome nicknamed "The Cosmic Wall."

Quicksilver rather than gold was mined here, and the area is still a favorite of rock hounds and amateur archaeologists, who have found an abundance of Native American rock art. In 1855 a violent encounter between Modoc Indians and white settlers took place nearby, the so-called Battle of the Crags. (Battle Rock is state historical landmark number 116.) The Modocs fought from a towering stronghold using only bows and arrows and were soundly routed, but not before California poet Joaquin Miller was seriously injured by an arrowhead.

Castle Crags State Park is open daily year-round, sunrise to sunset, for $4.00 per vehicle. Campsites are available, but reservations are required in summer; call (530) 235–2684 for information.

For a really different experience, try the ***Railroad Park Resort*** within sight of Castle Crags. You can sleep in an antique caboose or deluxe box car, among many others, and each is furnished in period style with antiques and special touches like claw-foot tubs. A restaurant and lounge occupy other retired railroad cars, each embellished with hand tools, lamps, steam gauges, and other memorabilia. Call (530) 235–4440 for reservations.

Trivia

About 300 wild horses roam free in Modoc County, protected by the Wild Horse and Burro Act of 1971.

Dunsmuir was formerly an important stop on the regular Southern Pacific line between San Francisco and Portland, and the historic downtown retains a feel of those bygone times. It's a dyed-in-the-wool railroad town, and locals relive the past every June during Railroad Days. You can wander down from Dunsmuir Avenue for a whiff of the old ways, then take in the Upper Sac River Exchange Center, a hands-on museum and information center for fishing, hiking, and ecology located at 5819 Sacramento Avenue; (530) 235–2012. Other nearby attractions are the botanical gardens and Hedge Creek Falls.

"Lonely as God and white as a winter's moon" was the way poet Joaquin Miller described ***Mount Shasta,*** and famous naturalist John Muir claimed his "blood turned to wine" when he first saw it. Clearly, this is no ordinary mountain. Soaring to 14,162 feet, the snow-clad, dormant volcano dominates the landscape for hundreds of miles in all directions. Unlike higher peaks such as Mount Whitney, lost among a cluster of summits, Shasta stands alone, rising majestically about 10,000 feet from the surrounding terrain.

Shasta has a permanent cap of ice and snow, and runoff from its five glaciers feeds dozens of streams, most importantly the McCloud, Shasta, and Sacramento Rivers. Although no eruptions have occurred during the past 200 years, hot sulphur springs near the summit show that the volcano, like many other Cascade peaks, is far from extinct.

Shasta is probably an Indian word, but others claim it derives from the French *chaste* (pure) or even the Russian *tshastal* (white or pure). But

Skiing Mount Shasta

Long in the shadow of Lake Tahoe ski resorts, Shasta Cascade offers some excellent downhill and cross-country skiing right on the slopes of the famous mountain. Opened after an avalanche demolished the old station, Mount Shasta Ski Park on the mountain's south side is a family-oriented resort with mostly intermediate skiing: twenty-five trails spread over 425 acres with 1,400 feet of vertical drop. Views from on high are superb: across the Sacramento River Canyon to Lake Siskiyou, Castle Crags, and the Trinity Alps.

This idyllic winter area is located just 12 miles off I–5, about halfway between Mount Shasta City and McCloud, so it's very convenient from points north and south. In addition, many hotels offer stay-and-ski packages. Though elite skiers might eschew these slopes, the snow conditions are good from November through April, a 150-day season, and the station features northern California's largest night-ski facility.

There's also on-site Nordic or cross-country skiing with miles of groomed trails through peaceful forest (none of those pesky snowboarders!) and the ungroomed "Wild Side" trail, where you can even bring Rover along! For information on the ski park, call (530) 926–8686 or the Mount Shasta Visitors Bureau at (800) 926–4865.

More cross-country skiing is available along Everitt Memorial Highway (the road to the old Ski Bowl) leading up the mountain's west side from downtown Mount Shasta. There are marked trails at Sand Flat and Red Fir Flat at about 6,000 feet and limited parking. For more information contact the Mount Shasta Ranger Station at (530) 926–4511.

Trivia

McCloud Golf Club, built in 1926, is the oldest public golf course in Northern California.

whatever it's called, this extraordinary white mountain inspires awe. Local Indians believed that the Great Spirit created it by dropping ice and snow through an opening in the sky. He then converted the mountain into his tepee and built a fire in the center; this helped explain the smoke that appears during volcanic activity. Out of respect to the Great Spirit, the Native Americans would not step foot above the timberline.

But this was only the beginning of the mountain's mystical drawing powers. At present several metaphysical groups flourish in the nearby town of Mount Shasta. Some believe that inside the mountain are secret cities inhabited by ***Lemurians,*** descendants of an ancient race that fled the continent of Mu when it sank into the Pacific. The most famous of this race is Phylos, who supposedly appears in a flowing white robe and invites climbers into a golden temple to listen to soft music.

Other mountaineers claim that kindly dwarfs have shown them caves of gold, or that they have spotted strange lights and fogs and heard booming bells. According to some believers one group called the Yaktayvians of the Secret Commonwealth has bells tuned so precisely that they can create giant landslides whenever outsiders come too close. Naturally, UFO sightings are common in the area.

Riding into the Sunset

For the perfect blend of mountain scenery, old-fashioned railway travel, and gourmet dining, hop aboard the Shasta Sunset Dinner Train. The elegant service runs most of the year round-trip between McCloud and Mount Shasta City (with an alternate route east to McIntosh Vista), taking diners for a three-hour sight-seeing trip capped with a four-course feast. (The trains poke along at just 10 to 22 mph.)

The McCloud Railway Company uses both steam and diesel engines to pull its collection of four vintage railway cars, olive green with gold-leaf lettering outside and brass fittings and mahogany paneling inside. Dinner, served on white linen set with fine china and cutlery, includes a choice of entrees such as Beef Wellington or fresh salmon and desserts (try the Decadent Turtle Cheesecake). Each meal ends with a complimentary glass of port to sip while pulling into McCloud Station (and back to reality) at around 9:00 P.M.

For rates and schedules contact the Shasta Sunset Dinner Train at (800) 733–2141.

A 15-mile paved spur road winds up Shasta's southwest flank to just above the timberline at about 6,800 feet. From here a 2-mile uphill hike along Bunny Flat Trail leads to ***Horse Camp,*** site of a Sierra Club lodge and beginning of one of the West's great hiking adventures: the ascent of Mount Shasta. The 6,000-foot-plus climb over volcanic rubble, ice, and snow can be punishing, but it is accessible to anyone in good physical condition with basic climbing gear. (Mountaineering equipment is not required.)

Every summer several thousand climbers attempt the summit; about half succeed. But success takes planning, conditioning, and luck. The mountain makes its own weather and is often hit by violent, fast-moving storms. For an information packet on the climb, contact the Forest Service at (530) 926–4511.

Another first-rate hike is Black Butte Trail to the summit of a steep, nearly treeless cone of andesite on the west flank of Shasta. This pile of dark volcanic slag was formed by four successive eruptions about 10,000 years ago, practically yesterday in geological time. Northbound I–5 aims straight for it, only to veer away at the last minute. The steep, rocky trail is about 2.5 miles from the trailhead to the summit at 6,325 feet (vertical climb is 1,845 feet). It can get very hot in summer, so carry water; and beware of rattlesnakes napping on sunny rocks. Finally, you must traverse a narrow ledge to the remains of an old lookout, where it can get very windy. The views are worth it.

The town of ***Mount Shasta*** boasts an eclectic blend of residents, from regular outdoor types to New Agers and followers of numerous spiritual traditions. Among the many local shops with a metaphysical flavor, mostly along Mount Shasta Boulevard, are Golden Bough Books, Middle Earth Crystal Room, and several art galleries such as Wingbeat and Visions. Healing centers abound, including the Circle of Life Wellness Center for Conscious Living, Archangel Michael's Soul Therapy Center, and Light Touch Therapy. For a complete list of local businesses, look in the monthly *Mount Shasta Magazine.*

Highly recommended is a trip to the town's city park for a look at the headwaters of the Sacramento River. From a lava tube deep within the mountain, icy clear water gushes forth into Cold Creek amid an arcadian scene of ferns and moss-covered rocks. To reach the park, follow Mount Shasta Boulevard north about 1 mile from the business center. Open daily from dawn to dusk.

On the east side of the mountain lies the postcard-perfect community of ***McCloud,*** queen of the old lumber towns. First there is the setting, a magnificent backdrop of Mount Shasta pasted against the sky; then you notice the architecture, a charming collection of simple cabins and woodframed houses laid out neatly, as if someone planned the whole thing. They did.

For most of its days, McCloud was a company town for mill workers, who paid with scrip at the company store and lived in houses built with lumber they had milled. (The first settlement dates from 1827, when Alexander McLeod led trappers to the area in search of beaver.)

Main Street McCloud is a delight to walk, starting with the Mercantile Building, a log structure housing stores and a cafe. Nearby stands the McCloud Railway Company, which offers regular service during most of the year. The historic yellow-and-white McCloud Hotel (1916) has been restored and remodeled for discerning travelers who enjoy special touches like afternoon tea and scones. A stroll away is the Stoney Brook Inn, popular with "New Agers" for its soul-stirring views of the mystical mountain.

Another overnight option is the McCloud Guest House, which served as home of the lumber company's president and later welcomed visiting VIPs. Among them were Herbert Hoover, Jean Harlow, and various members of the Hearst family, who own a fair amount of property near McCloud. (William Randolph Hearst built a huge castle called Wyntoon on the McCloud River.) They came for the mountain and for spectacular McCloud Falls, just as visitors do today.

Southern Cascades

Lassen Peak was the Mount Saint Helens of its day. On May 30, 1914, after centuries of slumber, the volcano blasted out rock and smoke at a foreboding rate. Over the next year, about 150 small eruptions kept locals on edge. Then, suddenly and ferociously, Lassen blew its top in a tremendous explosion that created a huge crater. Twenty-ton boulders were tossed around like pebbles, and ash spewed 30,000 feet in the air, covering the streets of Reno hundreds of miles away. Later, an 18-mile-long mud flow, triggered when scalding lava poured onto the ash-laden snowfields, killed vegetation for miles around.

Smaller eruptions continued over the next seven years, leaving the landscape littered with debris. All this makes ***Lassen Volcanic National Park*** a living laboratory for the study of volcanoes. With about 80,000 acres of wilderness, this park looks more like Montana or Wyoming than what you expect to find in California. Parts are dry and lava encrusted, looking like a battlefield or moonscape, while other sections are heavily wooded with conifers or splashed with wildflowers. There are fifty cobalt-blue lakes, six of them accessible by car, and countless hot springs, geysers, and boiling mud pots. In addition, 150 miles of trails (including 17 miles of the Pacific Crest Trail) weave through a landscape alternately luxuriant and devastated.

Standing at 10,457 feet, Lassen Peak is considered young by geological standards. It's also a mole hill compared to an ancient volcano called Tehama, which once covered the entire area before collapsing like a deflated balloon. At ***Sulphur Works*** thermal area, you can see a diagram of Tehama's 11,500-foot profile and spot your position some 4,700 feet below its former peak.

This was the location of Mount Tehama's central vent, and the volcano still whispers. Fumaroles hiss; hot springs bubble; mud pots boil, splatter, and sputter; and from deep below, immense cauldrons of red-hot magma belch evil-smelling fumes. Water seeping down into the earth is heated by this magma and rushes upward in the form of searing steam, reaching 195 degrees Fahrenheit (the boiling point of water at this altitude). A short walk from Lassen Park Road, Sulphur Works is the most accessible place to view volcanic activity, with easy trails on elevated walkways. Not far away, a trail leads to Bumpass Hell, the world's hottest hot springs at upward of 200 degrees Fahrenheit. The odd name comes from Kendall Bumpass, who discovered the spot in 1865 and lost a leg after plunging through the shallow crust into a sulphur pool.

Bizz Johnson Was Here

Imagine walking alone through the forest along a gently sloping path or gliding silently on skis through fresh virgin snow. The only sounds you hear are wildlife and the rushing water of restless Susan River. That's the scene on the Bizz Johnson National Recreation Trail near Susanville, which follows the old Fernley-Lassen railway line for 25 miles along rugged Susan River Canyon. It's become a local favorite with hikers, horseback riders, mountain bikers, and cross-country skiers. Fishermen and kayakers also use the cliff-flanked trail to access the river, but it is little known outside this area. Named in honor of a former U.S. congressman, the wide and relatively easy trek starts at historic Susanville Depot and heads west to Mason Station near Westwood. The latter settlement became a lumber company town after the area was developed around 1890 by Minnesota loggers. The railway was built to haul out lumber, but abandoned during the 1950s. Along the trail stand a few remnants of that bygone era, slowly crumbling away. For further information and a trail map, contact the Susanville Bizz Johnson National Recreation Area, (530) 257–0456.

A 30-mile road wraps around the mountain, climbing to 8,500 feet, where a 2.5-mile trail zigzags to the summit. (It takes about two hours to climb the 2,000 feet.) From here a staggering view takes in the mile-wide caldera. Other sights reached via the park road are the Devastated Area, about 3 square miles of scorched terrain, and ***Manzanita Lake*** (near the northwestern entrance). The Cinder Cone nature trail (4 miles round-trip) winds past stark, black chunks of lava, vast cinder and ash fields, and heat-scorched trees, on the way up to a 700-foot cinder cone.

The park's biggest drawback is the closure of the main road due to snow from October through mid-June. The rest of the year visitors can only enter at the fringes for a peek. (The best place to do so is the southwest entrance, 10 miles from park headquarters at Mineral.) Excellent cross-country skiing and snowshoe trails partially compensate for this inconvenience.

Lassen National Park has information centers at Manzanita Lake and park headquarters. For further details contact Lassen Volcanic National Park, Highway 36, Mineral, CA 96063; call (530) 595–4444.

The town of ***Susanville,*** about 60 miles east on Route 36, witnessed the Sagebrush War of 1862. This four-hour gun battle, followed by a beer-drinking session, determined that nearby Honey Lake Valley belonged to California, not Nevada. At present Susanville is the eastern gateway to Lassen Volcanic National Park and to a full menu of attractions in the southern Cascades and northern Sierra Nevada, the Bizz Johnson Trail (see sidebar) and Lake Almanor among them.

Trivia

California has three active volcanoes: Mt. Lassen and Mt. Shasta in the Cascade range, and Mt. Mammoth in the Sierra Nevada range.

Most intriguing of the bunch is ***Eagle Lake,*** about 16 miles north of Susanville. It's the state's second-largest natural lake, with more than 100 miles of shoreline, and sits in a basin fringed with sagebrush and juniper to the north, pine and fir to the south. What makes Eagle Lake special is that it's so undeveloped—no motels, no shops, no fast-food franchises. The public recreation complex at the south end (including a marina, store, campground, and swimming beach) is positively lilliputian by California standards—perfect for anyone trying to get away from it all.

Eagle Lake is really a misnomer: The man who named it, a Lieutenant Beckwith, actually saw ospreys along its shoreline, not eagles. In any case the lake is a favorite with scientists. Its highly alkaline water supports an astonishing variety of animal life, including jumbo trout (up to 20 inches long) that can survive nowhere else and seventy-five species of birds. Antelope, porcupines, and other animals come to drink at its shores.

Trivia

The Fall River Valley produces 25 percent of the wild rice marketed in the entire world.

Moreover, the lake abounds with creatures that were thought to be extinct until they were rediscovered here. Among them are prehistoric snails and ice crickets. Ordinary garter snakes are weirdly colored here, unlike anything found in textbooks, and two types of rattlers have combined to create a species of snake found nowhere else!

American Indians called waterfalls "laughing waters"; today we see them mostly in Tarzan movies and beer commercials. Specifically, Coors chose ***Burney Falls*** as the watery backdrop for an ad a few years back, even though the beer is made in Colorado. That's how beautiful these falls are.

Burney Creek splits just before reaching a spectacular 129-foot drop, and the two silver threads are joined by hundreds of secondary cascades that form a lacy curtain of water seeping from the mossy rock. The final aesthetic touch comes on sunlit mornings when a rainbow appears in the mist below. It's not surprising that Teddy Roosevelt supposedly called the falls "the eighth wonder of the world."

McArthur–Burney Falls State Park lies halfway between Mount Shasta and Susanville, about 60 miles east of Redding (6 miles from the junction of Highways 89 and 299). A 1-mile nature trail glides past the falls and through a landscape of sharp lava rock, ponderosa pines, and Douglas firs. From an observation platform near the parking lot, you slowly descend into a gorge, gaining new perspectives on the falls with each bend in the trail. A cool spray of water clings to your face, and the constant roar soothes your senses.

Even on the hottest days, nature's air conditioning keeps the ambient temperature at about 65 degrees Fahrenheit. (The water itself is a cool 42°–48°F.) Depending on the time of year and other variables, each day between 100 and 200 million gallons of water rumble over the falls into a deep emerald pool filled with trout. Behind the shimmering sheet of water live hundreds of black swifts, nesting in lichen-covered cavities from March through October and easy to spot because of their erratic, batlike flight.

The trail continues alongside a slope covered with black basalt chunks, at one time part of a horizontal layer on which the creek flowed. The canyon is littered with basaltic debris left behind as the falls moved

Trivia

Klamath Basin National Wildlife Refuge has the largest winter population of bald eagles in the U.S.

upstream, relentlessly eroding the sediment below. It's an ongoing process; in fact, the falls reached their current location only a few thousand years ago and will continue to move as the rock is worn away.

The trail crosses the creek and weaves up along the other side, passing the spot where the water plummets over the edge. Burney Creek comes from a subterranean source, and in dry summer weather it actually emerges from the porous lava about a half mile upstream of the falls. The creek bed above that point can be completely dry, but the underground aquifer miraculously surfaces just in time to make the downward plunge. The exact size and origin of the underground reservoir that makes all this possible remain a mystery.

McArthur–Burney Falls State Park is open daily from sunrise to sunset for $4.00 per car admission. For further information write to 24895 Highway 89, Burney, CA 96013 or call (530) 335–2777.

Modoc Plateau

The country north and east of the falls along Highway 299 is dry and rough, dotted with scrub grass and scrawny trees. From the tiny settlement of Fall River Mills to the Nevada border, the road slashes across the Modoc Plateau, following the gaping canyon of the Pit River much of the way. This slab of rocky volcanic residue, covering some 13,000 square miles, could be called California's "Empty Quarter." There are just a handful of settlements, and mile after mile with nothing but a barn or a fence to mark the horizon. This is probably the farthest you can wander from the "beaten path" in all California, yet each mile seems to take you even farther away from somewhere.

A case in point is ***Lava Beds National Monument*** near the Oregon border; even on its busiest days it looks deserted. Over a period of thousands of years, rivers of liquid rock from Medicine Lake Shield Volcano spread over the land. Upon cooling, it formed a fantasyland of lava tubes, yawning chasms, ice caves, towering cinder cones, and vast fudgelike lava flows punctuated by an occasional tree or bush. Lava Beds forms an essential part of any geologic tour of the region.

Trivia

Siskiyou County boasts the largest mule and black-tailed deer herds in California.

The area also witnessed California's only major Indian conflict. During the Modoc War (1872– 1873), a handful of braves held off the U.S. Army for six months. The Indians called this "the land of burnt out fires" and thought no one would want it. But they were wrong.

For an overview of both natural and Native American history, drive to the visitor center, 16 miles from Highway 139. The easiest landmark to explore is ***Mushpot Cave,*** right outside the center, with lights and interpretive signs explaining the geological story. This is a perfect example of a lava tube, created when rivers of liquid basalt hardened on the surface (which cooled faster), but continued flowing below, forming narrow, elongated tunnels.

Indeed, it gets quite cramped in places, and you have to crouch to pass low ceilings dripping with "lavacicles." This cave, along with many others, was formed about 30,000 years ago by flows from Mammoth Crater on the monument's southern boundary.

About 400 of these cylindrical tubes honeycomb 72-square-mile Lava Beds; the largest is some 75 feet in diameter, and the smallest is too cramped to crawl through. They lie near the surface, and about twenty of them are "developed," that is, accessible with flashlight and "bump-hat," most of them along Cave Loop Road.

Among the unique caves at the monument is Merrill Ice Cave, with its "frozen" river and waterfall, formed when rain collects inside and freezes. Because lava is such a good insulator, the ice remains year-round, even if it's 100 degrees outside. Big Painted Cave and Symbol Bridge have a number of Indian paintings on the walls, and Fossil Cave has yielded the bones of a mastodon and a camel, long extinct in these parts.

The best time to explore the terrain topside is during early morning or late afternoon, when warm light softens the harsh contours. (Winter is particularly dramatic.) Among the many natural landmarks is Fleener Chimneys, where volcanic gasses propelled plasticlike globs of lava into the air, which were plastered onto three spatter cones as they fell. These cones straddle a large fault block, which provided a natural conduit for magma boiling up from deep below. The broad Devil's Homestead Lava Flow originated here.

Gillem's Bluff, a high wall of lava rock splashed with green vegetation, rears up just west of the flow. Nearby ***Schonchin Butte,*** at 5,200 feet one of the larger cinder cones, provides an exceptional view over the entire monument, a barren world covered with scrawny grasses and clumps of sagebrush all the way to Medicine Lake Volcano and Mount Shasta.

Mankind's role in this rugged landscape has been nearly as violent as nature's. Located not far from Gillem's Bluff was the main camp of the

U.S. Army during its frustrating efforts to flush out the Modoc Indians from their stronghold. War broke out in 1872, when the government tried to force the Modocs onto a reservation shared with the Klamaths, their traditional enemies.

Finally, a charismatic leader named Kientpoos, Captain Jack as he came to be known, led 160 men, women, and children into hiding. You need to visit ***Captain Jack's Stronghold*** to understand how just sixty fighting men could hold an army at bay for months, inflicting heavy casualties while suffering few themselves. The Modocs brilliantly used the narrow, trenchlike corridors between thick lava walls, formed by fissures in the crust. The harsh terrain proved ideal for defense, the Modocs sniping from behind rocks while the army advanced in a straight line, as in Civil War battles. One officer reported that he lost several men one day without ever seeing a single Indian.

Trivia

The Sacramento River, California's longest, begins at Mount Shasta and flows into San Francisco Bay.

Canby's Cross marks the site of a bloody massacre. Goaded on by those who shunned compromise, Captain Jack pulled out a pistol during peace talks and murdered General Canby. An Indian agent named Meacham was partially scalped during the fracas, but recovered to tell many a tale. The Indians could not hold out forever, and this was Jack's last desperate effort to make the army give up. Instead, the attackers toughened and finally wore down the Modocs. Jack was hanged with two others, and his people were rounded up and herded off to Oklahoma, a sad ending to a long, tragic story. Fortunately, the Modocs survived as a living people.

Lava Beds National Monument is open continuously, and the visitor center stays open from 8:00 A.M. to 5:00 P.M. Admission is $5.00 per car; for further information call (530) 667–2284. The monument is reached via State 139 from State 299 or from Weed on Highways 97, 161, and 139.

Not far from Captain Jack's Stronghold, the West Wildlife Lookout offers a good panorama of Tule Lake, which was eight times larger when the Modocs made their last stand. You can drive to the lake directly from Lava Beds on a dirt road, or return to Highway 139 and proceed to the north entrance.

Northeast of the national monument proper, lying on a flat, dry plain that was formerly part of the lake bed, is the Petroglyph Section, where an abundance of prehistoric art has been found. Petroglyph Point is a stony mound about 1,200 feet long and 100 feet high. According to archaeologists a stratum of soft volcanic tuff from ground level up to 15 feet high was incised with hundreds of symbols, including serpents and other figures, concentric circles, and drawings resembling floor plans of large buildings. Not typical of local Indian art, these strange petroglyphs have been attributed by some to stranded Lemurians!

Tule Lake National Wildlife Refuge boasts one of the world's most impressive displays of bird life. Named for the bulrush that flourishes in marshy areas, Tule Lake shares the Klamath Basin (at about 4,000 feet) with the Lower Klamath Refuge, hugging the Oregon border. Every year approximately two million ducks and one million geese from as far away as Siberia stop here to feed and rest, and when a large flock arrives or departs together, the sky is literally darkened by the sheer numbers.

The migration starts in early September with pintails and white-fronted geese, and by late October other waterfowl have joined them in the largest concentration on the continent. Endless flocks of ducks and geese stream by both day and night, filling the sky in masses that seem to block the sun. With Mount Shasta looming in the distance, many birds land and take up temporary residence here, feeding and chattering incessantly. Come November, thousands of hunters flock here as well.

Trivia

Dorris, in Modoc County, is home to the world's tallest flagpole.

Although the big show is seasonal, any time of the year is good for bird-watching. From December through February, 1,000 bald eagles from Alaska prey on the wintering waterfowl and local rodents while nesting in cliffs overlooking the lake. In spring hundreds of species stop to rest and feed on the way to Canadian breeding grounds, and from May through August tens of thousands of ducks, geese, and marsh birds are born and raised here. Mid-summer is a good time to see pelicans, egrets, herons, gulls, terns, and other marsh birds, which usually stay until October.

The refuge is open daily during daylight hours for $3.00 per vehicle. For more information write the Klamath Basin National Wildlife Refuge, 4009 Hill Road, Tulelake, CA 96134; (530) 667–2231. Located west of the town of Tulelake, it provides maps and tour information; open daily from 8:00 A.M. to 4:30 P.M.

Between the village of Canby (at the junction with Highway 139) and Alturas, Highway 299 weaves across 20 miles of a rocky plateau known as "The Devil's Garden." The town of ***Alturas*** is the best place to go for accommodations while visiting the Modoc Plateau. The surrounding countryside is a blend of dry scrubland and good farmland spotted with grazing cattle and sheep, irrigated fields, lava rock, and a smattering of pine forest. This kind of land was a magnet for Basque sheepherders and farmers all across the West, so it's no surprise they settled here, too.

One of the town's more popular restaurants, The Brass Rail, specializes in Basque cuisine. Another, the Historical Niles Hotel & Restaurant, features a plank ceiling and floor and one of those big oil paintings of frolicking youths found only in pretentious Wild West hotels and saloons. Outside, on a second-story balcony, a hand-lettered sign reads NILES HOTEL AND SALOON; it's been a cowboy watering hole since 1908.

The ***Modoc County Museum's*** fine local collection emphasizes the taming of this wild country. There are crude Indian arrowheads and tomahawks, stones and fossils, a rattlesnake skin and mounted animals, a Swiss bow gun, and branding irons. Firearms steal the show. Guns and bullets of all calibers are laid out for inspection, from a pint-size thirty-caliber "gartergun" to a homemade shotgun with four ten-gauge barrels that could bring down one hundred geese with a single blast. The museum, at 600 South Main Street, is open for free May to November from 10:00 A.M. to 4:00 P.M. Tuesday through Saturday. Call (530) 233–6328.

Eastern California

Alturas is gateway to the ***Warner Mountains,*** which form a natural boundary between the Modoc Plateau and the arid Great Basin sweeping eastward across Nevada and Utah in a sea of desert sagebrush. This isolated range, a remote spur of the Cascades, offers few trails and fewer signposts, but it does provide rugged scenery and solitude, even in summer. If the Warners were near a city, they would probably be famous and crowded; instead, they are filled with wildflowers in spring and wildlife all year-round.

The highest and most scenic part is the ***South Warner Wilderness,*** sprawling over almost 70,000 acres. The 24-mile Summit Trail here skirts the three tallest peaks and looks out on Nevada and much of the Shasta Cascade region. It starts at the Patterson Ranger Station, 42 miles from Alturas, and ends at Pepperdine's Camp. Trout fishing is superb at Patterson Lake, and you can see mule deer in abundance. Horseback trips into the South Warner Wilderness are based in Alturas.

The only paved road across the Warners is Highway 299 through Cedar Pass (elevation 6,305), where there is a small ski area and campground, part of Modoc National Forest. From here, the road drops quickly through a wild canyon to the sleepy hamlet of ***Cedarville*** in the Surprise Valley, 23 miles from Alturas. Main Street here looks like an old snapshot, with false-fronted buildings and wooden sidewalks, a handsome redbrick grocery, and a drugstore with a soda fountain. Yet there are few people about, and one might expect a tumbleweed to come rolling down the street at any moment.

The nicest spot in town is a little park crossed by a creek, site of the ***Kressler and Bonner Trading Post,*** Cedarville's first building (1865), which supplied wagon trains bound for Oregon. The rough-hewn log structure with shingled roof is surrounded by a split-rail fence; to one side a historical marker states that the original settlement, called Deep Creek, was established by James Townsend, who was killed by Indians. In 1886 Kressler and Bonner purchased the post, and it served in that capacity for another decade.

To visit the most remote spot in the entire state, closer to Boise than San Francisco, drive north from Cedarville along the Surprise Valley National Backcountry Byway, passing ranch land and parched desert where the spirit of the American West lives on. Just a century ago this valley was deemed "The Bloody Ground" for its history of mind-numbing violence, first between settlers and Indians and later feuds among farmers, sheepherders, and cattlemen.

About 25 miles to the north, a white church steeple poking through the trees marks the approach of ***Fort Bidwell,*** a former army post established in 1868 at the foot of the Warner Mountains. Main Street boasts a couple of lopsided historical buildings, their windows smashed and paint peeling, and a redbrick schoolhouse stands forlornly on a hill. The Fort Bidwell General Store on Water Street (1874) was built of stone with a sod roof, and terrified residents used to hide inside its fireproof walls during Indian raids when the troops were on patrol.

The town's historic cemetery sits on a sage-dotted slope overlooking the Great Basin, with dozens of weathered tombstones of cavalrymen and their families. They stand as testimonials to the harsh frontier life where hostile attacks and disease, drought, and winter storms always threatened.

The real attraction here is being so far *off the beaten path*. The ribbon of road heading east is just a gravel track along the old Emigrant Trail. Like a mirage, it peters out in the desert somewhere near the Nevada state line, as far as you can travel and still be in California. Visitors to Fort Bidwell finally come to understand what it really means to be "in the middle of nowhere."

Places to Stay in Shasta Cascade

Redding and Weaverville Area

Best Western Hilltop Inn,
2300 Hilltop Drive,
Redding;
(530) 221–6100

Bradley's Alderbrook Manor,
836 Main Street, Etna;
(530) 467–3917

Brigadoon Castle,
P.O. Box 324,
Igo;
(530) 396–2785

Coffee Creek Ranch,
HC2 Box 4940,
Trinity Center;
(530) 266–3343

Motel Etna,
317 Collier Way, Etna;
(530) 467–5330

Pit River Lodge,
P. O. Box 920,
Fall River Mills;
(530) 336–5005

Red Hill Motel,
P. O. Box 234,
Weaverville;
(530) 623–4331

Trinity Alps Resort,
1750 Trinity Alps Road,
Trinity Center;
(530) 286–2205

Trinity Canyon Lodge,
27025 Highway 299,
Junction City;
(530) 623–6318

Central Corridor

Castle Stone Cottage Inn,
Castle Loop Road,
Castella;
(530) 235–0012

Cave Springs Resort,
4727 Dunsmuir Avenue,
Dunsmuir;
(530) 235–2721

Drakesbad Guest Ranch,
Warner Valley Road,
Chester (Lassen Volcanic National Park);
(530) 529–9820

McCloud Hotel,
407 Main Street,
McCloud;
(530) 964–2822

McCloud River Inn B&B,
325 Lawndale Court,
McCloud;
(530) 964–2130

Mount Shasta Ranch B&B,
1008 Barr Road,
Mount Shasta;
(530) 926–3870

Mount Shasta Resort,
1000 Siskiyou
Lake Boulevard,
Mount Shasta;
(800) 958–3363

Mount Shasta Wilderness Cabins,
P. O. Box 100
Castella;
(530) 235–4466

Mountain Air Lodge,
1121 South Mount Shasta Boulevard,
Mount Shasta;
(530) 926–3411

Nutglade Station,
5827 Sacramento Avenue,
Dunsmuir;
(530) 235–0532

Stoney Brook Inn B&B,
309 West Colombero Drive,
McCloud;
(800) 369–6118

Southern Cascades

Best Western Trailside Inn,
2785 Main Street,
Susanville;
(530) 257–4123

High Country Inn,
3015 East Riverside Drive,
Susanville;
(530) 257–3450

Lava Creek Lodge,
Glenburn Star Route,
Fall River Mills;
(530) 336–6288

Rippling Waters Resort,
16241 Highway 89,
Hat Creek;
(530) 335–7400

Shasta Pines Motel,
37386 Main Street,
Burney;
(530) 335–2201

St. Francis Historic Hotel,
830 Main Street,
Susanville;
(530) 257–4820

Modoc Plateau and Eastern California

Best Western Trailside Inn,
343 North Main Street,
Alturas;
(530) 233–4111

Dorris House B&B,
P.O. Box 1575,
Alturas;
(530) 233–3786

Ellis Motel,
2238 Highway 139,
Tulelake;
(530) 667–5242

JK Metzker House,
520 Main Street,
Cedarville;
(530) 279–2650

Niles Hotel Country Inn,
304 North Main Street,
Alturas;
(530) 233–3261

Sunrise Motel,
54889 Highway 299,
Cedarville;
(530) 279–2161

Surprise Valley Hot Springs,
Highway 299,
Cedarville;
(530) 279–2040

PLACES TO EAT IN SHASTA CASCADE

REDDING AND WEAVERVILLE AREA

C. R. Gibbs American Grille (American),
2300 Hilltop Drive,
Redding;
(530) 221–2335

Corina's (Italian),
1630 Hilltop Drive,
Redding;
(530) 221–6422

DeMercurio's Restaurant (Continental),
1647 Hartnell Avenue,
Redding;
(530) 222–1307

Hatch Cover (American),
202 Hemsted Drive,
Redding;
(530) 223–5606

La Grange Cafe (Continental),
226 Main Street,
Weaverville;
(530) 623–5325

Trinidele (American),
201 Highway 3,
Weaverville;
(530) 623–5856

CENTRAL CORRIDOR

Cafe Maddalena (Italian),
5801 Sacramento Avenue,
Dunsmuir;
(530) 235–2725

Casa Ramos Restaurant (Mexican),
1136 South Mount Shasta Boulevard,
Mount Shasta;
(530) 926–0250

Highland House Restaurant (American),
1000 Siskiyou Boulevard,
Mount Shasta;
(530) 926–3030

Lilly's (American),
1013 South Mount Shasta Boulevard,
Mount Shasta;
(530) 926–3372

McCloud Hotel Dining Room (American),
407 Main Street,
McCloud;
(530) 964–2822

Old Boston Shaft Restaurant (Continental),
1801 Fort Jones Road,
Yreka;
(530) 842–5768

River Inn Expresso (American),
325 Lawndale, McCloud;
(530) 964–2130

Salt H_2O Restaurant (Seafood),
5740 Dunsmuir Avenue,
Dunsmuir;
(530) 235–4422

Serge's Restaurant (French),
531 Chestnut Street,
Mount Shasta;
(530) 926–1276

SOUTHERN CASCADES

Alpine Drive In (American),
1412 Main Street, Burney;
(530) 335–2211

Chinese Kitchen (Chinese),
2455 Main Street,
Susanville;
(530) 257–6228

Fall River Hotel (Continental),
34860 Main Street,
Fall River Mills;
(530) 336–5550

Josephina's (Mexican),
1960 Main Street,
Susanville;
(530) 257–9262

The Outpost (American),
Highways 89 and 299,
Burney;
(530) 335–2835

Walker's (American),
1600 Main Street,
Susanville;
(530) 257–3212

Modoc Plateau and Eastern California

Country Hearth (American), Main Street, Cedarville; (530) 279–2280

Historic Niles Hotel & Restaurant (American), 304 North Main Street, Alturas; (530) 233–3261

Mi Casa (Mexican), 304 South Main Street, Alturas; (530) 233–3261

Mike and Wanda's Restaurant (American), 429 Modoc Street, Tulelake; (530) 667–3226

Helpful Web Sites in Shasta Cascade

Dunsmuir Chamber of Commerce: www.dunsmuir.com

Klamath Basin Visitors Center: www.klamathnwr.org

Lassen County Chamber of Commerce: www.lassencountychamber.org

Mount Shasta Chamber of Commerce: www.mtshastachamber.com

Mount Shasta Ski Park: www.skipark.com

Scenic Byways: www.volcaniclegacybyway.com

Shasta Cascade Wonderland Association: www.shastacascade.com

Shasta Mountain Guides: www.shastaguides.com

Trinity County Chamber of Commerce: www.trinitycounty.com

Worth Seeing/Doing in Shasta Cascade

Lake Shasta Caverns, O'Brien

Lake Siskiyou, Mount Shasta

Shasta Lake

Shasta State Historic Park, Old Shasta

Sisson Museum, Mount Shasta

Turtle Bay Exploration Park and Museum, Redding

Whiskeytown Lake

General Index

D

E

F

T

Museums

National and State Parks

About the Author

Mark Williams is a freelance writer whose travel articles have appeared in many publications, including the *International Herald Tribune, Washington Post, Los Angeles Times, San Francisco Chronicle, Travel/Holiday,* and *Westways.* He has been senior writer for *Lookout Magazine* (Spain) and chief editor of Chevron *USA/Odyssey.* His other books include *The Story of Spain* and *In Search of Lemuria.*

Mr. Williams has also worked as a roustabout in Alaska and a teacher at international schools in Europe. He has an M.A. in history from the University of California, Santa Barbara. He is a native of the Golden State and lives near San Francisco with his wife and dog.